1989

W9-ABR-427

Joint Ventures between Hospitals and Physicians
A Competitive Strategy for the Healthcare Marketplace

Joint Ventures between Hospitals and Physicians

A Competitive Strategy for the Healthcare Marketplace

Linda A. Burns, M.H.A.
Douglas M. Mancino, J.D.

DOW JONES-IRWIN
Homewood, Illinois   60430

© Dow Jones-Irwin, 1987

ISBN 0-87094-710-9

Library of Congress Catalog Card No. 86-71813

Printed in the United States of America

1 2 3 4 5 6 7 8 9 0 K 4 3 2 1 0 9 8 7

This book is dedicated to
Carol Mancino
and
W. Raymond C. Ford

Foreword

The successful healthcare organizations of the future will be those that successfully integrate the interests and talents of physicians, hospitals, and payers. The
next generation of the healthcare industry is evolving in the late 1980s as a
result of the turbulent environmental change of the previous five to seven years.
The industry will be defined by:

- Financing the move to managed care systems
- Hospital consolidations and alliances
- The changing physician marketplace
- Specialized and niche services

At the center of these major components of change, and bringing them
together, will be a new health corporation: the key organization of the future
integrating hospitals, physicians, financing, and specialty care.

The more farsighted and aggressive physician groups and hospitals are taking a first step toward this integration through joint ventures. As with any new
development, joint ventures are taking many different forms, with different
motivations, and are achieving different degrees of success and failure. A great
deal of experimentation and learning is being achieved in this process. Hope-
fully, this is the first stage in the development of integrated provider systems
which will then link with financing mechanisms to achieve the integrated new
health corporation.

The authors have created a comprehensive presentation of the issues that
need to be addressed when a joint venture approach is used, particularly as a
means of diversification by hospitals and physicians. Both authors have a significant body of experience and background and make a very real contribution
to the "state of the art" through this book.

Even though viewed by some as only a stage in this development of an
integrated health system, joint ventures must be viewed as long-term relationships that, if successful, will build a base of confidence, working relationship,
professional incentive, and financial interdependence which will serve as a positive base for future developments. One of the dangers many of us have observed in reviewing numbers of joint ventures and through our own experience
in creating joint ventures is the attitude that the joint venture is a transitory or

short-term proposition. This book speaks clearly about the need for a long-term view and structure for hospital-physician joint ventures. I would certainly endorse that concept and attitude.

As the authors suggest, managers at all levels of the organization, as well as boards of directors, must become significantly more knowledgeable about joint venture opportunities and must develop additional skills in order to evaluate and manage joint ventures. All too often these important activities are viewed as ancillary to the main business of the enterprise. In fact, they are at the very heart of the business of health care. To think otherwise and plan otherwise will surely spell trouble for the prospective joint venturer.

Not all of our integration activities between physicians and hospitals will be successful. As healthcare providers enter an era of unprecedented risk taking, joint venturers will see their share of failures as well as successes. We must be prepared to deal with those failures, to learn from them, and yet be prepared to venture again. Successfully carrying out the strategy of the full integration of hospitals, physicians, and payers will require many attempts.

This book makes a real contribution by helping the reader think through many of the critical success factors of a joint venture. One of its contributions is to point out that joint ventures are not going to be a strategy for every institution or every group of physicians. This book underscores the importance of using the joint venture approach toward business development as only one of many tools that deal with some specific needs in the marketplace.

It seems clear that joint ventures will be a part of many organizations' successful strategy integration for the future. This book makes a real contribution toward that strategy.

Donald C. Wegmiller
President
Health Central Corporation
Minneapolis, Minnesota

The central issue facing healthcare leaders and the medical profession in the United States in the mid-1980s is the imperative to operate the delivery system significantly more efficiently than it has ever been operated in the past. The requirements for efficiency are driven by declining input of resources on the part of those who purchase healthcare services, including government, industry, and individuals who pay for their health care directly. As a consequence, the financial incentives that affect both physicians and healthcare organizations are being remorselessly and compellingly reordered.

To accomplish the delivery of more effective health care, healthcare organizations and the physicians who constitute their professional staffs are using many different approaches, all of which are classified under the term *managed health care*. The painful reality of managed health care is the fact that it means exactly what it says: management of health care. Management means planning what needs to be done; organizing to carry out the plan; carefully staffing to meet the requirements of the plan; precisely controlling the use of all resources as the plan is put into operation; obtaining constant feedback about the quality, cost, and effectiveness of operations; and constantly replanning and fine-tuning as needed to assure flexibility and adaptation to an ever-changing environment. It works in recognition of the fact that health care is now a zero sum game in which winning (and in some cases, surviving) requires taking market share away from others. It is a highly rigorous system. The traditional organization of health care, consisting of many independent hospitals and hundreds of thousands of individual physicians all operating in relative independence, is not functional. The most successful organizations now are those which can maximize the effectiveness of their human and financial resources, including those of their professional staffs. Those organizations are resolving the fundamental and historic conflict of interest between physicians and the healthcare organization. They are resolving the power struggle that characteristically exists between the management of healthcare organizations and the professional prerogatives of the medical profession which is responsible for the patient and for the quality of healthcare services delivered.

The resolution of conflicting values in healthcare organizations is possible through a variety of different approaches. Under any approach, the financial incentives impacting the organization and the medical profession must be dealt with equitably and in responsible partnership. The joint venture organization between physicians and hospitals, which works to resolve organizational conflict by creating financial equity for these constituencies, has now emerged as a favorite strategy of hospitals and segments of the medical profession. It recognizes the imperative of efficiency and it works toward creation of common goals, especially financial goals.

Despite the bold competitive course that American society has taken in health care in the early 1980s, it remains an area of deep concern to Americans and involves fundamental values that Americans hold as a nation. The verdict on the effectiveness of the procompetition model in health care is not in, and many thoughtful observers have raised an alarm about its impact on the health of the economically underprivileged and its effect on medical education and healthcare research. But there is no indication that policy can turn back to the "golden age of medicine" when resources were unlimited. There are many problems that must be solved, and it is improbable that Americans will fail to educate the future healthcare providers of this country or that she will allow people to die in the street for lack of care. The delivery process will be reordered. There will be winners and there will be losers within that process in the healthcare business. Some will organize and some will prevail to maintain and increase their market share. This can best be done by managing the delivery of effective healthcare services which are of a quality that will please and attract the interest of healthcare consumers.

The problem that is before the healthcare industry, and especially the medical profession, is how to fit into managed healthcare systems with the implied organizational imperative they bring with them. The commonality of interests of all healthcare organizations and all physicians is dramatically addressed in many joint ventures now emerging throughout the country. Both physicians and hospitals need to plan these joint ventures very carefully and to execute them with great sensitivity for the needs and concerns of their joint venture partners. This book takes a significant step forward in documenting techniques that must be mastered to that end. Both Ms. Burns and Mr. Mancino are to be commended for their contribution in this important area.

David J. Ottensmeyer, M.D.
President
Lovelace Clinic
Albuquerque, New Mexico

Preface

The economic interdependence of hospitals and physicians has never been greater than it is today. Yet competitive pressures and technological advances exerted on both hospitals and physicians are straining their traditional business relationship and are eliciting from them new financial arrangements and ways of organizing healthcare services. Joint ventures between hospitals and physicians are emerging as a premier management strategy of this decade. Structuring and implementing successful joint ventures, however, requires hospitals and physicians to address a set of complex issues.

This book grew out of discussions of the strategic, economic, legal, and ethical questions raised during the course of our work in structuring and implementing joint ventures. Much of the information presented in the book is based on our experiences working with hospital executives, board members, and physicians in launching and managing joint ventures for ambulatory care services and facilities, health maintenance organizations, preferred provider organizations, and diversified health services.

This book provides a comprehensive discussion and analysis of the issues that need to be addressed when a joint venture approach is used to capitalize on the most promising diversification opportunities in the healthcare industry today. We have attempted to give executives, physicians, and trustees an understanding of the reasons for developing joint ventures, a method for classifying joint venture opportunities and structures, and a step-by-step process of developing and implementing joint ventures. We have included a chapter on ethical considerations because we feel that in the haste to achieve an advantage in the marketplace, hospital leaders and physicians should not overlook these important considerations. We also have included information on the numerous legal issues, financing alternatives, and marketing aspects of developing successful joint ventures. Besides the technical areas, we have also included reflections on physicians' participation in joint ventures and the role and responsibilities of the hospital's chief executive officer and board members. Finally, we have included three case studies which reveal the results and consequences of joint venture initiatives.

We expect that joint ventured programs, facilities, and activities will increase. We hope this book provides a practical guide to those who wish to consider this strategy.

Linda A. Burns
Chicago

Douglas M. Mancino
Los Angeles

Contributors

AUTHORS AND EDITORS

Linda A. Burns, M.H.A.
Manager
Amherst Associates Inc.
Chicago, Illinois

Douglas M. Mancino, J.D.
Partner
McDermott, Will, and Emery
Los Angeles, California

CONTRIBUTING AUTHORS

Cary M. Adams, J.D.
Partner
Memel & Ellsworth
Sacramento, California

Arthur D. Aston
Chairman of the Board and CEO
Health Dynamics, Inc.
Van Nuys, California

Richard A. Baehr, M.A., M.S.
Chairman of the Board
Amherst Associates Inc.
Chicago, Illinois

Ronald B. Barkley, M.S., J.D.
President
Program Development Associates
Pacific Palisades, California

Enzo V. DiGiacomo, M.D.
Vice President of Medical Affairs
Mercy Hospital
Springfield, Massachusetts

Norman C. Fost, M.D., M.P.H.
Professor, Vice Chairman of
  Pediatrics and Director of
  Program in Medical Ethics
University of Wisconsin
Madison, Wisconsin

Douglas D. Gregory, Ph.D.
Vice President for
  Corporate Development
Main Line Health, Inc.
Villanova, Pennsylvania

Douglas D. Hawthorne, M.D.
President
Presbyterian Medical Center
Dallas, Texas

Michael L. McCullough, M.D.
President
Baylor Physicians, P.A.
Dallas, Texas

Gary Meller, M.D., M.B.A.
Director of Practice Development
Humana, Inc.
Louisville, Kentucky

John K. Springer, M.H.A.
President and CEO
Hartford Hospital
Hartford, Connecticut

Wesley B. Thompson, M.B.A.
Vice President of
  Ambulatory Surgery
IHC Professional Services, Inc.
Salt Lake City, Utah

Contents

1 Joint Venture Defined, *Linda A. Burns and Douglas M. Mancino*   **1**

Section I Marketplace Dynamics   **5**

2 Changing Hospital-Physician Relationships: Joint Ventures as Strategic Alliances, *Linda A. Burns and Douglas M. Mancino*   **7**
Introduction. The Uneasy Partnership. Changes Affecting Hospitals. Changes Affecting Physicians. Growth of Health Maintenance Organizations. Growing Power of Group Purchasers. Technological Change. The Changing Role of the Consumer. The Effects of Change on Hospitals and Physicians. Emergence of New Strategic Relationships.

3 Why Engage in Joint Ventures?
Linda A. Burns and Douglas M. Mancino   **15**
Introduction. Sources of Capital. Acquire Professional Skills or Technical Expertise. Increase Utilization and Obtain Referrals. Retain Market Share. Increase Market Share. Expediency. Conclusion.

4 Identifying and Classifying Joint Venture Opportunities, *Linda A. Burns*   **21**
Introduction. Health-Related versus Nonhealth-Related Ventures. Degree of Integration and Shared Control among Ventures. Capital Intensity. Expected Return on Investment. Who Will Be Involved? Existing Services versus New Services. Conclusion.

**5 Step-by-Step Approach for Developing and
    Implementing a Joint Venture,** *Linda A. Burns*   **29**
Introduction. Organizing for Joint Venture Development.
Screening New Ventures. Step-by-Step Process for
Developing Joint Ventures: *Step 1   Determine Services
and Scope of Program to Be Joint Ventured. Step 2   Is
the Proposed Business of the Joint Venture Program
Consistent with the Strategic Plan? Step 3   Perform
Market Assessment. Step 4   Prepare Functional and
Space Program and Staffing and Equipment Requirements
for the Program. Step 5   Determine Organizational and
Ownership Structure. Step 6   Determine Capital Budget,
Pro Forma Financial Statements, and Financial Feasibility
for the Joint Venture. Step 7   Present Joint Venture
Proposal and Decide Whether or Not to Proceed with
Implementation. Step 8   Develop Business Plan. Step
9   Prepare Legal Documents, Offering Documents,
Securities Registration, and Other Documents. Step
10   Present Joint Venture Proposal to Prospective
Physician Investors. Step 11   Implement Preogram. Step
12   Evaluate Performance Program/Joint Venture.* Joint
Venture/Business Development Team.

Section II   Ethical Considerations   **41**

**6 Ethical Considerations of Hospital-Physician Joint
    Ventures,** *Norman C. Fost*   **43**
Introduction. Physician Self-Interest is Not New. Profit and
Nonprofit Distinctions May be Overdrawn. Ethical
Differences between Medicine and Other Businesses/
Professions: *Provision of Essential Services, Regardless of
Ability to Pay. Supplying Competitors with the Latest
Information. Enticement of Needless Consumption.
Discouragement and Exclusion of Unprofitable Customers.
Willingness to Lie.* Is a Business Orientation Bad For
Patients? Possible Benefits of a More Businesslike Trend:
*Improved Efficiency Reduced Costs. Consumer
Orientation. New Sources of Capital. New Sources of
Taxes.* Possible Hazards of a Business Orientation:
*Reduced Access by the Poor. Loss of Academic Influence.
Compromises in Quality of Care. Reduction in
Unprofitable Services. Loss of Trust.* Practical Implications
and Recommendations: *Prohibit "Kickbacks". Require
Full Disclosure of Physician Conflicts of Interest. Establish*

Vigorous and Regular Outside Review. Seek Consumer Input. Maintain a Commitment to the Indigent. When Appropriate, Establish Guidelines for the Preservation of Academic Values. Conclusion.

Section III Legal Considerations 57

7 **Legal and Regulatory Issues Affecting Joint Ventures,** *Douglas M. Mancino* 59
Introduction. Put It in Writing: *The Business and Business Opportunities. Capital Requirements. Profits and Losses. Management. Distributions. Books and Records. Withdrawals and Transfers. Termination.* The Formation Stage of a Joint Venture: *Authority to Enter into Joint Ventures. Selection of a Legal Structure. Contractual Issues Affecting Hospitals. Contractual Issues Affecting Physicians. Control and Related Issues. Franchising. Certificate of Need and Section 1122 of the Social Security Act. Regulation of Securities. Ethical Considerations. Special Problems of Public Hospitals.* The Operational Phase of a Joint Venture: *Licensure Requirements. Payment for Services. Quality Assurance and Peer Review. Corporate Practice of Medicine and Division of Fees. Accreditation. Professional and Other Liability Concerns. Ownership Limitations and Disclosure Requirements.* The Dissolution Stage of a Joint Venture. *Methods. Buy-Sell Agreements. Restrictions on Competition.* Conclusion.

8 **Tax Planning for Joint Ventures,** *Douglas M. Mancino* 102
Introduction. Choice of Business Entity: *Contractual Model. Partnerships. Corporations. S Corporations. Selected Comparisons of Tax Advantages. Observations.* Operational Tax Considerations: *Cost Recovery Deductions. "At Risk" Limitations.* The Tax Reform Act of 1986 and Joint Ventures: *Passive Investment Loss Limitation. Limitation on Use of Cash Method of Accounting. Taxable Year Rules.* Alternative Depreciation System: *Tax-Exempt Entity Defined. Tax-Exempt Use Property. Treatment of Tax-Exempt Use of Real Property. Service Contract Rules. Special Rules Applicable to Partnerships and For Profit Subsidiaries. Joint Ventures and Tax-Exempt Status. Inurement. Private Benefit. Use of Corporate Subsidiaries. Planning Concerns.* Joint Ventures and the Unrelated Business Income Tax: *Contract Joint*

Ventures. Corporate Joint Ventures. Partnerships.
Conclusion.

9 Fraud and Abuse Implications of Joint Ventures,
Cary M. Adams   **129**
Introduction. Medicare and Medicaid Antifraud and Abuse
Laws. Basic Provisions. Exceptions for Discounts and
Employees. Interpreting the Statutes. Fraud and Abuse
Concerns in Joint Ventures. State Antikickback and
Related Laws. Diversity of State Law Provisions. *Conflicts
between State and Federal Laws.* Conclusion. Reference.

10 Antitrust Planning for Joint Ventures,
Douglas M. Mancino   **143**
Introduction. Overview of Federal Antitrust Laws:
*Sherman Act Section 1. Sherman Act Section 2. Clayton
Act Section 7. Robinson-Patman Act. Federal Trade
Commission Act Section 5. Penalties.* Potential Challenges
to Joint Venture Formation. Antitrust Issues Affecting
Joint Venture Operations: *Per Se Violations. Nonprice
Predation. Vertical Market Allocations. Collateral
Restraints. Spillover Collusion. Price Discrimination
Laws.* State Antitrust Laws. Conclusion.

Section IV Feasibility, Finance, and Operations   **159**

11 Market Analysis for Joint Ventures,
Douglas D. Gregory   **161**
Introduction. Business Concept. Segment/Size Market.
Market Attractiveness. Internal Economics. Key Success
Requirements. Joint Venture Economics. Conclusion.

12 Financing Joint Ventures, *Richard A. Baehr*   **170**
Introduction. The Financial Planning Process. Screening
Financial Alternatives: *Amount of Capital. Size of
Investment. Term of Financing. Control. Timing and
Costs. Evaluation of Process.* Surveying Alternative
Sources of Funds: *Debt Financing. Pooled Equipment
Financings. Industrial Development Bonds. Future of Tax
Exempt Debt. Taxable Debt. Lease Financing. Bond
Financing. Convertible Debt. Equity Financings. Public
Offerings. Venture Capital. Preferred Stock. Venture
Capital Companies. Self-Financing and Limited
Partnerships.* Selection Process. Development of a

Business Plan. The Future of Hospital-Physician Joint Venture Financing.

13 The Venture Capital Company, *Douglas M. Mancino*　**184**
Introduction. Advantages. Disadvantages. Organization and Management. Conclusion.

14 Enlisting Physician Participation, *Enzo V. DiGiacomo*　**190**
Introduction. Three Levels of Medical Staff. General Benefits. Making It Happen. The First Meeting. Opposition. Conclusion.

15 Operational Problems in Joint Venture Management,
Gary Meller　**196**
Introduction. Issues of Ownership: *Reporting Requirements. Influence and Votes. Reward and Responsibility. Jealousy and Interference. Unresolved Conflict from Negotiations.* Issues of Control: *Ownership versus Control. Confusion in Goals. Unempowered Managers. Managing Up and Down. The Runaway Success.* Issues Related to Allocation of Resources: *The Starving Subsidiary. Make versus Buy Decisions. A Huge Part of a Tiny Firm.* Issues of Timing: *How Long to Give It. Market Responsiveness. Planning Horizons. Looking Ahead.* Issues Related to Corporate Culture: *"They Are Not Like Us". "They Don't Like Us". "We Don't Answer to Them". "What Happened to Your Tie".* Joint Ventures in Other Industries: *International Joint Ventures. Real Estate Joint Ventures. Financial Joint Ventures. Manufacturing Joint Ventures. The Nonprofit Sector.* Historical Results. The "New" Joint Venture. References.

Section V　Perspectives on Joint Ventures　**211**

16 A Physician's Perspective on Joint Ventures,
Michael L. McCullough　**213**
Introduction. Creating a Physician Organization: *Credentialing and Utilization Review. Selecting an Investment Vehicle.* Choosing a Partner. Shareholders Agreement. Implementation of the Joint Venture. Conclusion.

17 The Chief Executive Officer's Perspective on Joint Ventures, *Douglas D. Hawthorne*　**220**

Introduction. Consistency with Strategic Plan. Structuring
the Venture. Importance of a Business Plan. Establishing a
Track Record with the First Venture. Long-Term
Implications. Conclusion.

18 A Trustee's Perspective on Joint Ventures,
Arthur D. Aston   224
The Medical Office Building Joint Venture. The
Ambulatory Surgery Center Joint Venture. Alternative
Delivery Systems. Changing Medical Staff–Hospital
Relations. General Observations.

Section VI Case Studies   231

19 Ambulatory Surgery Centers, *Wesley B. Thompson*   233
Introduction. Intermountain Health Care, Inc. and IHC
Professional Services, Inc. Roseland Surgical Center Joint
Venture. The Center. Key Capital Requirements. PSI's
Acquisition of Its Interest in RSC. Relationship of the
Center to PSI's Strategic Plan. Why a Joint Venture? The
Legal Structure and Financing of RSC. Financial Returns.
Impact on Physicians–PSI Relationships. Successes,
Disappointments, and Future Implications of the Joint
Venture. Lessons Learned. Epilogue.

20 Diagnostic Imaging Centers, *Ronald B. Barkley*   243
Introduction. Modesto 9800 CT Limited Partnership.
Central Valley Imaging Center. Conclusion.

21 Health Maintenance Organizations, *John K. Springer*   254
Introduction. Physician-Hospital Workshops. Gatekeepers.
Fees. Structure and Governance. Conclusion.

Section VII Commentary and Conclusions   261

22 A Look at the Future of Joint Ventures,
Douglas M. Mancino and Linda A. Burns   263

Index   267

1

Joint Venture Defined

Linda A. Burns, M.H.A.
Douglas M. Mancino, J.D.

Almost any agreement or undertaking between a hospital and a physician can be described as a "joint venture." As long as the agreement or undertaking links the economic welfare of both parties, such a description is at least partially accurate.

While such a loose definition may be appropriate to describe various relationships hospitals and physicians may establish generally, more precision is required in most business contexts. To begin with, characterization of a relationship between a hospital and a physician will have political consequences within a hospital's organizational structure and strategic consequences for the marketplace in which the hospital and physician operate. To describe a hospital's relationship with a particular physician as a joint venture often is to imply that special treatment is being afforded to that physician. In addition, such characterization suggests that the hospital-physician relationship stands apart from the typical relationship the physician has with the hospital as a member of the active medical staff.

The characterization of a relationship between a hospital and a physician as a joint venture also has business implications. A joint venture implies that the hospital and physician have at least partially integrated their businesses and have established common goals toward the achievement of joint economic gain. Such integration often means that each party has given up or forgone exclusive control over the business or project that is the subject of a joint venture. Some degree of economic interdependence is created between the parties that suggests a sharing of the opportunity for profit as well as the risk of loss.

Characterization of a relationship between a hospital and a physician as a joint venture will also have significant legal consequences, although mere characterization as a joint venture is almost useless in most legal contexts. For the most part, a greater degree of precision is required for legal purposes to determine the proper characterization of a relationship between a hospital and a physician. A relationship that might be characterized as a joint venture for tax purposes may be treated differently for antitrust or securities law purposes.

1

Similarly, proper characterization may be of extreme importance if a question arises concerning the liability of the hospital or the physician for the negligence or malpractice of the venture itself or of its hospital or physician owners.

We deliberately have not undertaken to provide a narrow definition of a joint venture in this book. Rather, we have recognized that the classification of a relationship as a joint venture is dictated more by the needs of the parties and the local marketplace than by the facility of having a stringent definition for comparison. However, most joint ventures have certain basic characteristics that distinguish them from traditional hospital-medical staff relationships:

1. A joint venture involves a relationship between a hospital and physician that is separate and distinct from the medical staff-hospital relationship. This relationship may take the legal form of a contract, a separate partnership, or a separate corporation.
2. A joint venture requires the hospital and the physician to make an investment in a common enterprise that is distinct from and in addition to the hospital-medical staff relationship. This may be an investment of capital, services, technology, or some other asset.
3. A joint venture requires sharing of control in ways not previously common among hospitals and physicians. The degree that control is shared between the joint venturers will vary with the type of business and legal form selected. However, whether the joint venture is a mere contractual arrangement, a corporation, or a partnership in which control is shared among the venturers, the hospital can be expected to share control over the enterprise with physicians and the physicians can be expected to share control with the hospital.

These three general characteristics endow a relationship between a hospital and a physician with features different from the traditional hospital-medical staff relationship. Specific circumstances should govern the relationship, but if hospitals and physicians analyze their relationships utilizing the forgoing characteristics, we believe that the analysis of the benefits, risks, and implications of hospital-physician joint ventures will be more readily apparent.

Joint ventures in the healthcare field have become a means of accomplishing strategic, business, and financial objectives for a variety of reasons. They also represent an acknowledgment that the relationships between hospitals and physicians have become more complex than in the past. The need to establish a more definitive relationship independent of the hospital-medical staff relationship covering a substantial period of time has its own inherent problems. Hospitals and physicians are burdened with the responsibility of defining their mutual obligations, sometimes exhaustively. This requires an ability to anticipate future contingencies while recognizing that it is practically impossible to identify and resolve all contingencies. In addition, it requires that hospitals and physicians control their own natural opportunism, which is likely to be exaggerated by the discrepancy in knowledge between the parties. Further, joint ventures will require reconciliation of conflicting agendas, time frames, goals, and economic capabilities. Finally, all joint ventures will require anticipation and ultimate resolution of potential conflicts among the joint venturers, such as the timing or amount of contributions of capital or services, allocations or distributions of profits, personnel, marketing, or other operational issues. Conflict resolution will be an important part of any joint venture.

Despite inherent definitional problems and operational difficulties, joint ventures can be productive business relationships. By creating opportunities in which financial risk, return, control, and commitments are shared, joint ventures present an opportunity for hospitals and physicians to exploit the current environment in a manner beneficial to both parties.

In summary, the precise definition of a joint venture is less important than the objectives pursued by the concerted activity between hospitals and physicians. A joint venture is, in many respects, a relationship that is created of necessity. With this in mind, the remaining chapters endeavor to present an overview of all facets of joint ventures designed to enable physicians and hospitals alike to focus their attention on this method of doing business.

I

MARKETPLACE DYNAMICS

2

Changing Hospital-Physician Relationships: Joint Ventures as Strategic Alliances

Linda A. Burns, M.H.A.
Douglas M. Mancino, J.D.

INTRODUCTION

Changes are occurring in almost every sector of the healthcare industry at an unprecedented pace. These changes have stimulated various responses that have and will continue to have significant short- and long-term effects on hospitals and physicians and on their relationships to one another. Now, the instability created by the rapidity with which such changes have occurred—and the swiftness with which responses have been formulated and implemented—have increased the tension that always has existed between hospitals and physicians. In the future, the changes that have occurred and are occurring are likely to result in a fundamental restructuring of the delivery and financing of medical and hospital services throughout the United States.

This chapter reviews various changes that have occurred in the healthcare industry in the financing and delivery of hospital and medical care. This chapter concludes with the proposition that hospital-physician joint ventures are one of many appropriate strategies for dealing with such changes.

THE UNEASY PARTNERSHIP

The healthcare marketplace was at one time a fairly simple environment. The services provided by hospitals were fairly clearly identifiable as were the professional services provided by physicians and other professions. While there were areas of overlapping interest, hospitals and physicians each had their own independent products and services. Further, these independent products and services were largely not influenced by federal and state governments, private insurers, and consumers. Only health planning and licensing laws and the rules and regulations pertaining to public and private reimbursement or payment for such services influenced these independent interests.

Physicians individually and collectively have sought to remain independent of control by hospitals and others over their professional judgments and practices because of their professional status. Hospitals have managed to retain a degree of independence from physicians due to their substantial resources and their ability to offer services, personnel, equipment, and facilities that attract physicians without impinging upon their independence.

Generally, in the past, the financing of hospital and medical services perpetuated the independence of hospitals and physicians. Physicians were under few constraints as to the amount of charges they made for professional services, while hospitals similarly were being paid on a cost basis that placed little financial risk on them for overutilization. Thus, the forms of payment for medical and hospital services in the United States focused more on a complex maze of seemingly unrelated and individual services and have up until recently ignored the fact that the cost of patient care is determined by the combined actions and decisions of physicians and hospitals.

CHANGES AFFECTING HOSPITALS

During the past five years, numerous changes have occurred in the competitive and financial environment that have had a profound impact on the way hospitals are managed and relate to physicians. These changes have been chronicled in numerous other places and will not be dealt with in detail here. Rather, what follows is simply a brief review of the significant changes.

Perhaps the most significant change affecting hospitals in recent years was the enactment of the prospective payment system for Medicare beneficiaries in 1983, which for the first time in history placed government payments to hospitals for treatment of Medicare inpatients on a predetermined charge basis rather than on a cost-reimbursement basis. While many hospitals have been favorably affected by the enactment of the prospective payment system since operating incomes of many hospitals have actually risen, few hospital executives expect this trend to continue. Indeed, most think that the government payment climate will continue to become even more constricted and that it will be even more difficult for hospitals to survive economically unless they become part of larger financing and delivery networks.

Changes in the Medicare payment mechanism have begun altering the traditional hospital-physician relationship. Until recently, the traditional physician-patient relationship was relatively insulated from daily interference, and physicians were unrestricted in their ability to utilize the resources of hospitals to treat their patients. Hospitals, at the same time, had little incentive to control the utilization of their resources by physicians because they were paid for their services on a cost-reimbursement basis.

Now that acute care hospitals are subject to payment policies that place them at substantial financial risk for a physician's behavior, hospitals are beginning to devise means to place physicians under similar incentives. While federal programs have not yet been restructured to place physicians at financial risk for their behavior, hospitals clearly are moving in that direction because of the significant, if not determinative, impact physicians have on the actual cost per discharge. Moreover, as hospitals expand into more highly competitive outpatient services, such as ambulatory surgery and diagnostic imaging, where control of costs is crucial to economic success, it is increasingly incumbent upon them to place physicians in a position where they are accountable for control of costs and can participate in any profits that are derived from the reduction of costs. In other words, systems must be created to provide motivation to both parties to accomplish a common goal, namely the provision of high-quality hospital and medical care at a reasonable cost in a competitive environment.

Even in the absence of direct financial incentives, hospital-physician interdependence is quickly replacing the independence and autonomy that both parties have enjoyed over the years. The day is quickly passing when physicians can be unconcerned about the cost of hospital care for their patients. An affiliation with an expensive hospital can eliminate a physician's patient base and undermine his practice. Likewise, hospitals must be increasingly concerned about the impact of physicians on their costs of delivering such care.

CHANGES AFFECTING PHYSICIANS

As hospitals have been affected by excess capacity, physicians have been affected by the growing surplus of physicians, the increased costs of medical education, and competition.

In 1980, the Graduate Medical Education National Advisory Committee concluded that there would be 70,000 excess physicians by the year 1990 and 145,000 excess physicians by the year 2000. Four years later, the Bureau of Health Professions, U.S. Department of Health and Human Services, estimated that the surplus would be approximately 35,300 physicians by 1990 and 51,800 physicians by the year 2000.

While there still is a great deal of debate as to whether there is a true physician surplus and, if so, the effects of such surplus, there is little question as to the current economic environment affecting physicians. According to data published by the American Medical Association, the typical American physician has experienced a 25 percent reduction in his or her office visit volume, while the number of physicians per 100,000 of population has increased dramatically. Though the typical American is visiting the doctor less each year than he or she was only 10 years ago, this decline is likely to be accelerated by the aggressive development and expansion of health maintenance organizations, preferred provider arrangements, and other alternative health delivery systems.

Moreover, 1983 marked the first time in history that the actual nominal physician income declined even though, on an inflation-adjusted basis, physician income has been falling since at least 1970.

At the same time, the costs of medical education have increased dramatically as has the extent of medical student borrowing. According to one recent survey, the average debt of graduating medical students in 1984 was $26,500 as compared to $17,200 in 1980 and $5,000 in 1971. There is much debate about the impact of growing medical education indebtedness on such issues as choice of specialty and location of medical practice. One impact, however, is relatively clear: Physicians will need to enter into practices or develop employment relationships that will enable them not only to pay off the substantial medical education debts, but also to enjoy a standard of living that is commensurate with their expectations at the start of medical school.

GROWTH OF HEALTH MAINTENANCE ORGANIZATIONS

From 1981 to 1985, the number of health maintenance organizations has grown to 393, a 62 percent increase. The number of members during the same period increased to 18.9 million, a 98 percent increase.[1] Unlike the traditional hospital-physician relationship, health maintenance organizations typically make hospitals and physicians accountable for the provision of medical and hospital services by placing responsibility for overutilization or excessive costs on them. As a consequence, physicians and hospitals have been required to combine their resources to deliver hospital and medical care in a more efficient and economic manner.

Five years ago, in many hospitals the mere mention of the words *health maintenance organization* at a medical staff meeting meant immediate banishment of the hospital administrator and institutionalization of the physician who dared raise that issue. Today, by contrast, hospitals and physicians are scrambling to develop their own health maintenance organizations, to affiliate with the growing number of national health maintenance organizations, to form individual practice associations that will contract for the professional component of the health maintenance organization's services, and to contract with preferred provider organizations.

GROWING POWER OF GROUP PURCHASERS

Large employers and other purchasers of healthcare on a group basis have been in existence for a number of years. It has not been until recent years, however, that such group purchasers recognized the power that they had, individually as well as collectively, to control the spiraling costs of healthcare. In recent years, group purchasers have emerged as active, more informed, and more sophisticated buyers of medical and hospital services. A by-product of this is that the economic interests of physicians and hospitals are becoming more closely linked in dealing with group purchasers. It is much less likely today than it might have been five years ago for physicians to admit and treat patients without regard to the costs of the care being provided by the hospital. Similarly, hospitals up until recently have had little incentive to control the costs of medical care provided to persons whose care was paid for by group purchasers. Hospitals were often paid on a cost basis or were paid on a charge basis that resulted in a substantial payment in excess of the actual costs of delivery of care.

Today, when it is becoming increasingly prevalent for the services of hospitals and physicians to be purchased as a package, the failure to meet the expectations of group purchasers will lead to lost patient volumes, particularly if other more cost-effective options are available to the group purchasers.

TECHNOLOGICAL CHANGE

The rapid development of diagnostic and therapeutic technology continues to have an impact on hospitals and physicians. The growth of laser technology, for example, has enabled many procedures to be performed on an outpatient basis that previously required lengthy hospital stays. New technology has also spurred the growth of ambulatory surgery, even before amendments to the Medicare program in 1980 provided increased incentives to hospitals and physicians to perform many procedures on an outpatient basis. While in 1979 approximately 14 percent of hospitals' surgical procedures were performed on an outpatient basis, more than 28 percent of surgical procedures were performed on an outpatient basis by 1984, and most industry observers predict that anywhere from 40 to 60 percent of all surgical procedures can currently be performed on an outpatient basis.[2]

In addition, the development of noninvasive diagnostic and therapeutic techniques has enabled many other procedures to be performed in a nonhospital setting. This has set the stage for the development of freestanding imaging centers and the purchase of lower cost diagnostic and therapeutic equipment for use in physicians' offices.

THE CHANGING ROLE OF THE CONSUMER

Hospitals and physicians are becoming increasingly conscious of marketing their services to prospective patients. Once passively doing whatever they were told, patients are now customers—they want to be involved in decisions; they want convenience; they are increasingly concerned about the issue of price; and they no longer accept the notion that "doctor knows best."

Patients are beginning to select hospitals and physicians on the basis of price, convenience, and compatibility with predetermined conceptions of how the care is expected to be delivered. Further, employers are subjecting patients to greater deductibles, copayments, and coinsurance provisions, thereby making them increasingly accountable for healthcare expenditures. This growing accountability of patients for the economic consequences of their decisions, as well as the increasing sophistication of patients in the selection of physicians and health decisions that are being made, has altered the nature of medical competition, hospital competition, and physician-hospital competition.

THE EFFECTS OF CHANGE ON HOSPITALS AND PHYSICIANS

The changes in the delivery and financing of hospital and medical care have radically altered the way both groups do business. Hospitals have responded to the economic challenges by increasing their emphasis on outpatient services; broadening their markets to provide a wider range of ambulatory and other types of care; developing, acquiring, or becoming affiliated with one or more alternative delivery systems; and, ultimately, restructuring themselves into organizations that will assume responsibility within their marketplace for the financing and delivery of healthcare services in a vertically integrated manner. Physicians have also responded to changes affecting them professionally and financially by becoming more marketing-oriented, expanding the number and scope of services performed on an in-office basis, affiliating with alternative delivery systems, and competing aggressively for many of the same patients for which hospitals are competing.

Hospitals and physicians also have demonstrated that they do respond to economic incentives. Hospitals have been extraordinarily responsive to the economic incentives contained in the prospective payment system as well as the economic incentives that large employers and other large purchasers of healthcare services have placed on them. Through the swift adoption of preferred provider arrangements, the ability to work with physicians to modify practice patterns to encourage earlier discharges, and other techniques, hospitals have been able to operate well, generally speaking, from an economic standpoint in spite of the increased pressure placed on them to control costs and provide increased levels of services for the same amount of revenues.

Both hospitals and physicians have also seen the need for improved management in their business operations. Hospitals have placed greater emphasis on managing their businesses, determining their "product lines" and marketing them, cutting out unprofitable services, and undertaking business development activities that previously had not existed.

Physicians also are placing greater emphasis on practice management. A growing number of physician groups have hired professional managers; they place greater emphasis on billing practices and marketing activities; and they have penetrated other markets that previously had been in the province of hospitals, such as ambulatory surgery, urgent and ambulatory care, home health, durable medical equipment, and diagnostic imaging.

EMERGENCE OF NEW STRATEGIC RELATIONSHIPS

The slowing of growth in the healthcare industry has resulted in increased stress in hospital-physician relationships. Hospitals are increasingly being asked to provide the same or increased levels of services ·with fewer resources. This is forcing hospitals and their physicians to prioritize their needs and to do without or with fewer things. Similarly, the supply of new physicians, new entrepreneurial practice styles, and new hospital strategies will result in winners and losers among physicians and medical groups. The likelihood that some physicians will be survivors and others will be casualties exacerbates already existing problems.

Further, hospitals and physicians individually are seeking to optimize their own conditions through innovative practice opportunities, expansion, and vertical integration. In an expansionary economy, there is often enough room to permit all of the parties to benefit from this approach. In the nonexpansionary healthcare economy that currently exists, however, as each party seeks to improve its own conditions, much of this improvement will be at the expense of other components within the system. Thus, positive and negative aspects of change are merely compounding already existing problems and will affect more parties.

What has become apparent to most hospitals and physicians is that the traditional hospital-physician relationship must change. With the various environmental factors giving rise to greater opportunities for conflict between hospitals and physicians, such changes also give rise to a need for increased cooperation. The essentially economically independent operations of hospitals and physicians have become economically interdependent. In many instances, cooperation rather than competition has become the preferred means of survival.

Hospital-physician joint ventures, in many respects, provide a framework for hospitals and physicians to predict the long- and short-term consequences of a particular action and to effect the types of compromise of individual goals for the sake of better overall performance in the future. However, joint ventures are merely one means to the achievement of the various ends that hospitals and physicians seek. There clearly will remain numerous areas where the interests of hospitals and physicians will diverge and where it will be clearly advantageous for both players to maintain their independence. Nevertheless, there are increasingly greater numbers of opportunities in which cooperation rather than conflict will be required. For example, the beginnings of a merging of private healthcare financing, largely represented by HMOs and PPOs, and the healthcare delivery system, represented largely by hospitals and physicians, will continue to demand greater degrees of integration than previously extant in the healthcare field.

While there is little question that there will be a growing number of areas where the debate between hospitals and physicians is likely to be acrimonious, there are also a growing number of opportunities where physicians and hospitals are likely to have mutual interests at stake. If there is a potential for synergy between the hospitals and physicians, then a joint venture should be utilized. Nevertheless, it must continually be acknowledged that joint ventures are simply a means of accomplishing strategies that require interaction toward the broader purposes they both serve and that both have interdependence and mutual dependency in achieving the objectives of the organizations and individuals.

Notes

[1] *HMO Summary 1985* (Excelsior, Minn.: Interstudy, 1985), p. 1.
[2] American Hospital Association, Annual Surveys, 1980 and 1985.

3

Why Engage in Joint Ventures?

Linda A. Burns, M.H.A.
Douglas M. Mancino, J.D.

INTRODUCTION

Joint ventures are simply one means of attaining strategic, economic, or business objectives that hospitals or physicians could not attain as quickly, as profitability, or at all by themselves. To joint venture a business or project in the healthcare industry successfully requires an understanding of the reasons why joint ventures may be a preferred means of accomplishing those objectives.

We start with the premise that a joint venture is unsuitable if a hospital or a physician could undertake a project or operate a business successfully alone and if nothing of value could be added to the project or business by another party. Going into a business alone or forgoing an opportunity to bring a partner into a business implies that the single party can withstand the competitive challenge of the spurned partner. Consequently, this chapter focuses on the reasons why hospitals and physicians form joint ventures. It is important to note that hospitals and physicians will be motivated to joint venture projects or businesses by many forces, and each joint venturer is likely to have several motivations.

SOURCES OF CAPITAL

Some of the most common motivations for joint venturing are to obtain sources of capital, to increase returns on capital investment, and to reduce the riskiness of the investment.

Hospitals engage in joint ventures to obtain capital for several different reasons. The first is to reduce or shift the risk of costly capital expenditures to the potential users of new equipment or facilities. Faced with the prospect of

15

being unable to recover the full cost of capital through governmental and private insurance programs, hospitals are wary of making large capital expenditures for new technology unless some assurance can be provided that such technology will be used at levels adequate to provide the desired rate of return on their investment. The growing numbers of joint ventures being created to acquire magnetic resonance imaging (MRI) technology underscores the importance of this objective for many hospitals.

The costs of MRI technology are substantial, ranging from $1 million to in excess of $3 million. Because of uncertainty concerning reimbursement and demand, many hospitals have elected to acquire such technology through joint ventures with their radiologists and other physician specialists who are most likely to use MRI technology. In so doing, the hospital obtains capital to acquire the technology and provide the service, while the physicians provide the capital and have a service available for their patients that otherwise might not be conveniently available. The physicians also have an economic incentive (or, to put it another way, are at risk) to utilize the MRI technology acquired by the joint venture, rather than send their patients to an MRI center established by a competing hospital or physician.

Physicians also are likely to employ joint ventures to access capital markets because, unlike hospitals, physicians typically have less resources available to invest in new businesses, to expand existing businesses, and to acquire necessary capital for such businesses. Conventional sources of capital, such as bank loans or venture capital, may be alternatives to a joint venture with a hospital. Bank loans, however, are likely to entail significant risks to physicians' personal assets (including substantially greater equity than the physician is willing to part with), and venture capital often results in loss of control.

Hospitals are less likely than physicians to use joint ventures solely to acquire capital, because they generally have stronger financial positions and access to other, often lower cost, capital through debt and equity markets. However, hospitals may wish to use joint ventures to acquire capital in order to provide "off balance sheet" financing and thereby preserve debt capacity or other capital access capabilities for other programs. This objective is manifest in the development and operation of medical office buildings.

Hospitals have long recognized that one or more medical office buildings on or adjacent to their campuses will probably result in increased utilization of inpatient and outpatient facilities and ancillary services. Thus, hospitals typically have constructed or purchased office buildings directly for use by members of their medical staff. As an alternative, a growing number of hospitals are using joint ventures to accomplish the same objective.

Through hospital-sponsored general or limited partnerships, the hospital will acquire capital from physicians to construct or acquire the medical office building and obtain commitments from the investors to lease space in the building on a long-term basis. By utilizing this form of joint venture, the hospital on the one hand has acquired capital from the physicians, while on the other hand has physicians on or near campus without substantially impairing its balance sheet. Thus, the hospital will have preserved its debt capacity for other hospital-related purposes and will not have substantial capital tied up in a low-return, high-cost medical office building. The physicians, having put up the capital for the medical office building, should quickly recognize that a healthy hospital adjacent to their medical office building will increase the investment potential of the medical office building. Therefore, both parties will have achieved their common objectives in a way that probably neither could have achieved independently.

Franchising is another means of acquiring capital for expansion of a product line using the capital of others while at the same time retaining a return on the initial idea or service. Franchising is discussed in detail in Chapter 7.

ACQUIRE PROFESSIONAL SKILLS OR TECHNICAL EXPERTISE

The acquisition of professional skills or technical expertise is a commonly offered reason for utilizing joint ventures inside and outside of the healthcare industry.

Hospitals have found that shortages of management talent or professional expertise make it increasingly difficult to expand existing healthcare services or product lines to meet business needs or competitive challenges. Consequently, joint ventures can be a means of obtaining the complementary professional skills, market knowledge, or technical expertise necessary for the hospital successfully to expand an existing market or enter a new market for healthcare services. By obtaining the professional or technical expertise through joint ventures, both parties are able to become stronger competitors in the market more quickly and are more likely to avoid the costly start-up mistakes in a new business.

Where there is a shortage of professional or managerial talent for a particular line of business, the joint venture may be the only feasible alternative because short-term consulting arrangements or long-term employment contracts may be undesirable or unacceptable. A physician with skills in operating an industrial medicine program, for example, may be willing to become a joint venturer with a hospital to develop or expand an industrial medicine program, while that physician would not be willing to become an employee of the hospital.

Physicians may also see joint venturing as a means of acquiring skills or technical expertise that are otherwise unavailable or too costly. It is increasingly common for physicians to approach hospitals with partially developed business ideas or plans that require additional professional or technical expertise to bring such ideas to fruition. A physician may be willing to joint venture the business with the hospital in order to take advantage of the skills or expertise that the hospital may have, whether such skills are managerial, financial, marketing, or otherwise.

INCREASE UTILIZATION AND OBTAIN REFERRALS

Up until recent years, the relationships between hospitals and physicians have been predicated on complementary interests. The hospitals needed the physicians to refer patients to their facilities and to utilize their ancillary services. The physicians needed hospitals to provide the facilities and technologies necessary to enable the physicians to practice medicine and provide professional services. As discussed in Chapter 2, this relationship has been rocked by the changes in technology and increased competition and the price pressures resulting from both. For this reason, hospitals and physicians are forming joint ventures to formalize referral patterns and to share risks of underutilization. Access to utilization is today as important as or more important than access to capital from the standpoint of future financial viability of hospitals and physicians.

Joint ventures present an opportunity for physicians and hospitals to combine their risk capital in a single economic enterprise. As a result, both parties will have a vested financial interest in the success of the business of the venture. A properly structured joint venture will provide appropriate economic incentives to physicians and hospitals to utilize the services or facilities of the joint venture, rather than comparable services provided by someone else. Similarly, joint ventures present an opportunity to expand referral patterns. If physicians other than the direct users of a facility or service are permitted to invest in the joint venture, those physicians have an economic incentive to select the joint venture or other physicians who have invested in the joint venture for referrals where medically appropriate.

It is generally recognized that, with certain exceptions discussed in Chapters 6, 7, and 9, it is not illegal or unethical for physicians or hospitals to refer patients to a facility in which they have an economic interest as long as they are not compensated for such referrals and the fact of their ownership is disclosed to the patient. Although discussed in more detail in those chapters, it is important to note that participation in profits and losses of a joint venture generally must be in proportion to investment, and the joint venture must take steps to ensure that the facilities or services of the joint venture are utilized only where medically appropriate and in the best interest of the patient.

RETAIN MARKET SHARE

Increasing availability of technology and shifting emphasis from inpatient to outpatient treatment of patients have made it easier for physicians and other businesses to gain shares of markets previously the exclusive domain of hospitals at hospitals' expense. Since 1983 there has been a tremendous increase in the number of new entrants in profitable segments of the healthcare industry, such as the home health business, durable medical equipment sales and leasing, outpatient diagnostic services, ambulatory surgery, and other traditional hospital markets.

At the same time, a growing number of physician entrepreneurs are competing directly with hospitals for outpatient surgery business, clinical laboratory services, and outpatient diagnostic testing. Thus, hospitals are finding it necessary to joint venture many of these activities with physicians on the theory that if they do not joint venture they will lose more of their market share than if they do joint venture the activity.

Physicians also have seen a growing number of entrepreneurs and hospital management companies competing more directly with them than at any time in the past. The introduction of urgent care centers and convenience clinics, the growth of group practices, the burgeoning growth of health maintenance organizations (HMOs), and similar incursions into the primary and ambulatory care markets by hospitals and other businesses have resulted in a loss of market share by many solo physicians throughout the United States.

INCREASE MARKET SHARE

A joint venture may be a means to increase market share by a hospital or a physician. Healthcare planners have typically thought of markets in geographic terms, for a hospital as a whole. Increasingly, however, hospital executives are looking at market share of individual clinical services or product lines and how to increase market share irrespective of geographic boundaries. Through joint venturing with physicians in new markets, hospitals may expand market share while shifting or reducing the risk of failure to physicians who may play an important role in the success or failure of the venture's business. Also, many physicians may find it better to joint venture an HMO, an urgent care center, or a primary care center because, if they do not, they risk the loss of substantial market share.

EXPEDIENCY

Joint ventures often result from a unique set of circumstances designed to take advantage of a special situation. Many hospital chief executive officers have had physicians on their staff tell them of their plans to develop freestanding ambulatory surgery centers or diagnostic centers. Then the hospital faces the immediate decision of whether to compete or to joint venture such a center in order to minimize loss of market share or capture additional market share. Thus, expediency may dictate the use of a joint venture over other forms of exploiting the business opportunity.

Similarly, joint ventures may be a means of developing or expanding a line of business more quickly and with less risk. In these circumstances, the ability to enter a market quickly and achieve a dominant position may be well worth the price of giving up a portion of the profits or control to another party.

CONCLUSION

Joint ventures in the healthcare industry have, thus far, tended to be project specific. Hospital-physician joint ventures are no exception and have been generally designed to facilitate separate management and cooperation along with specific lines, rather than full integration of the businesses of the hospital and physicians.

In attempting to describe the various and complex motivations that hospitals and physicians have for joint venturing healthcare projects and businesses, it should be readily apparent that there is no way to rank the reasons in any order of importance. Rather, only certain broad conclusions can be drawn from the foregoing information.

For hospitals, joint ventures first must be consistent with the corporate strategy of the hospital as a whole and for specific clinical programs. Second, successful joint ventures should tend to emphasize the strengths of the hospital rather than be used to enter into high-risk businesses with physicians. Very few hospital managers or boards are willing to risk jeopardizing their medical staff relationships with ventures that have a low probability of success. Third, joint ventures are appropriate only when the circumstances uniquely support the use of a joint venture rather than an alternative form of relationship with physicians. Finally, the most successful joint ventures will result from the careful screening of the prospective partner's capabilities and motivations and prior agreement as to the appropriate goals and operational requirements of the joint venture.

Physicians desiring to participate in a joint venture also must assess the desirability of it against their own business or practice requirements. While it is more probable that joint ventures will yield capital and management efficiency for physicians that are unattainable in other forms of expansion, this must be weighed against the loss of autonomy and control that is likely to be associated with the joint venture opportunity.

Hospitals and physicians face many choices when selecting, planning for, and operating joint ventures. Careful identification and assessment of their own reasons for pursuing a joint venture will be a critical first step in deciding to participate in one.

4

Identifying and Classifying Joint Venture Opportunities

Linda A. Burns, M.H.A.

INTRODUCTION

The topic "joint venture" has two components: first, the notion of mutuality or "jointness" and, second, the idea of an investment in a business or "venture." The purpose of this chapter is to identify the broad range of services that are candidates for business ventures in healthcare, particularly those whose riskiness might be reduced and whose overall rate of return might be enhanced by involvement of both hospitals and physicians as coinvestors.

Chapter 1 defined a joint venture and Chapter 2 reviewed the changes in the healthcare industry that are giving rise to the competitive advantages that hospital and physicians can reap by becoming business partners in healthcare. Assuming that a hospital and its physicians are interested in undertaking a joint business investment, what business ventures can be developed from the clinical and administrative services currently offered by hospitals, physicians, insurers, or suppliers? What new businesses arise from the introduction of new technology, modifications of payment policies, unilateral action of a competitor, shifting preferences of consumers, and deregulation?

The possible set of new ventures or current services and facilities that can be converted to joint ventures varies from institution to institution and across geographic markets. A partial listing of services and facilities appears in Table 4–1.

Besides consulting a laundry listing of possible venture opportunities, one way of identifying ventures that may be suitable for development by hospitals in conjunction with physicians is an analysis of overlapping domains. Figure 4–1 illustrates the mapping of the traditional domains of hospitals, physicians,

TABLE 4–1 Listing of Joint Venture Opportunities

Primary care centers	Freestanding surgery centers
Minor emergency centers	Occupation/industrial medicine programs and
Health maintenance organizations	clinics
Preferred provider organizations	Wellness centers
Third party claims administration	Home health services
Utilization review	Durable medical equipment sales and leasing
Retirement living (retirement housing)	Geriatric assessment center
Nursing homes	Geriatric programs
Skilled nursing facilities	Sports medicine programs
Freestanding psychiatric hospitals	Physical therapy programs
Outpatient psychiatric centers	Cardiac catheterization laboratories
Substance abuse programs	Outpatient cancer treatment centers
Freestanding rehabilitation hospital	Mobile diagnostic services
Outpatient rehabilitation facility	(CT, mammography, MRI)
Contract management services for hospitals	Fitness centers
Purchase or lease of entire hospital facilities	Health clubs
Freestanding diagnostic centers	Medical office buildings
Freestanding women's health centers	Cardiac rehabilitation programs
Reference laboratories	Apartments
Birthing centers	Lithotripters

FIGURE 4–1 Identification of Joint Venture Opportunities by Overlapping Domains

and insurers, suggesting that synergy can be increased by investing in ventures where a competitive advantage can be achieved through a joint venture.

Most of the business opportunities suitable for joint ventures are noninpatient care services. Substantial opportunities exist in outpatient physician care, outpatient diagnostic and treatment services, and managing the health insurance premium dollar. These opportunities represent a diversification from the core business of acute inpatient care for hospitals.

Still another way to conceptualize these business opportunities is to envision a diversification chain. A diversification chain of opportunities for hospitals is illustrated in Figure 4–2.

This chain permits a hospital or its parent corporation to see how the proposed business fits strategically with its core business of acute inpatient care. The concept also helps to make explicit that different management skills are necessary as the business changes from acute inpatient care to outpatient care or insurance products. The farther away the business venture is from inpatient care, the greater the likelihood that the key business skills and management experiences will be different.

FIGURE 4–2 Chain of Diversification Opportunities for Hospitals

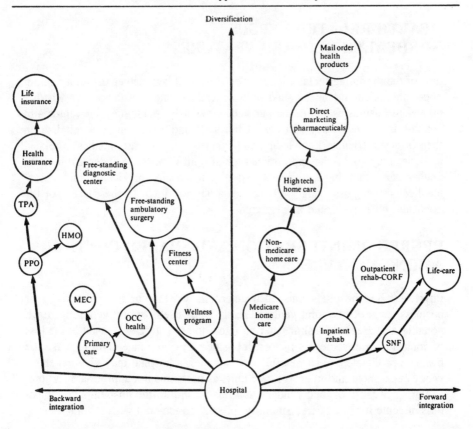

Each joint venture opportunity can be classified according to a number of variables:

- Health-related business versus nonhealth-related businesses.
- Market risk.
- Degree of integration and sharing of control among venturers.
- Management experience.
- Capital intensity.
- Expected return on investment.
- Who will be involved as investors.
- Existing services versus new services.

If a hospital's strategic plan calls for the development of new businesses as joint ventures or the conversion of existing services and facilities to a joint venture structure, the executive management of the hospital or parent corporation and board are well-advised to use these variables in classifying the various joint ventures proposed. By discussing these variables, managers and board members will permit a speedier development of the joint venture and will educate themselves about the implications of any joint venture oportunity. Developing and using a classification scheme will assist hospitals and physicians in evaluating the risks associated with joint ventures.

HEALTH-RELATED VERSUS NONHEALTH-RELATED VENTURES

One of the preliminary classification decisions will be whether the joint venture opportunities should be pursued only in health-related businesses or whether nonhealth businesses should be pursued. Obviously, pursuing joint ventures in health-related businesses will permit hospitals and physicians to capitalize on their prior experience, knowledge, and expertise. In contrast, nonhealth-related activities may not be the appropriate type of joint ventures to undertake because neither party may have sufficient expertise to ensure success. In such cases, another partner possessing skills and experience critical to the success of the nonhealth business would be preferred.

DEGREE OF INTEGRATION AND SHARED CONTROL AMONG VENTURERS

Physicians and hospitals must also determine whether or not the activity or business sought to be joint ventured really lends itself to joint venturing. Each potential venturer must ask if entering into a joint venture will result in the loss of control over key success factors in business or dilute incentives to make the business profitable and successful. For example, a hospital may view its emergency department and intensive care units as programs not appropriate for joint venturing because of their fundamental relationship to the hospital's core business of acute inpatient care. Similarly, physicians may not wish to joint venture their office practices since that would require them to become, in effect, employees of the joint venture; the arrangement would be intrusive to the physician's office-based care. However, both parties may see opportunities in joint venturing selected ambulatory services and facilities, such as ambulatory surgery, reference laboratories, and diagnostic imaging services, which are principally thought of as hospital services. Likewise, some physicians, particularly surgeons and medical subspecialists, may not be threatened by joint venturing freestanding emergency treatment centers or primary care centers that do not infringe upon their private office practices. Thus, from an analytical standpoint, all parties must first identify those services or business activities that lend themselves to joint venturing.

After identifying the businesses that lend themselves to joint ventures and deciding the degree to which the individual or organization will require or permit the integration of another party, the next step is to classify joint ventures by several characteristics to determine what services or capital are required of both parties. Further, this classification scheme will help in evaluating the risks associated with particular activities.

CAPITAL INTENSITY

One of the fundamental issues that should be analyzed early on is the degree of capital intensity of the joint venture. This determination will enable the parties quickly to assess if or to what extent capital is available from existing sources. By identifying the capital needs of the venture at the outset, the potential venturers will be able to make fundamental decisions such as whether they will only enter into capital-intensive activities in a joint venture with another party or whether they will only engage in low-capital intensive joint businesses in joint ventures. As illustrated in the case study involving the CT scanner in Chapter 20, one of the reasons that the hospital elected to enter into a joint venture for the new GE 9800 was because it would validate the demand for the services and ensure that the potential users and referrers to such service would be at risk.

The following illustration shows examples of high-capital intensive and low-capital business opportunities.

Proposed Business Activity	Projected Start-Up Costs
CT scanner	$900,000
Full imaging center	$2.5 million
40,000-square-foot medical office building	$4 million
Emergency care center in leasehold space	$150,000
Reference laboratory	$1 million
100-bed acute care hospital	$8–$10 million
Home health agency	$100,000
Medical office building	$40,000–$25 million
Ambulatory surgery center *.134,188*	$2.5 million–$4 million

EXPECTED RETURN ON INVESTMENT

Another variable affecting the selection of joint venture business and their probabilities for success will be the likely profitability of the business when conducted by a joint venture. By classifying joint ventures according to their expected return on investment, investors are forecasting not only the value of future cash flows from the ventures, but also the degree of probability that the forecasted cash flows will be achieved. Just because a freestanding ambulatory surgery center is highly profitable in one location, that is, its return on investment is high, does not mean that the same venture will achieve the same or similar return on investment in another location. The probability of achieving the return may be different due to local market characteristics such as the degree of competition.

In general, the riskier the investment (i.e., the lower the probability of achieving a given return), the greater the return should be to attract investors. A hospital can balance its portfolio of investments in joint ventures by assessing the risk-adjusted rate of return on individual businesses and selecting ventures whose individual performance is likely to reduce the hospital's overall risk. For example, certain types of high-volume, low-margin businesses, such as urgent care centers and primary care centers, have in the past been thought of as suitable opportunities for joint venturing. However, actual experience suggests that because of the low margins, high level of competition, and economic structure of a primary care practice, these are probably better operated by physicians unless hospitals choose to subsidize their operations for the referrals that they generate. Thus, the interests of a physician for profitability may be quite the opposite of those of the hospital which may place a higher premium on inpatient referrals. As an alternative to joint venturing in this type of circumstance, the hospitals and the physicians may simply choose to market jointly rather than to integrate hospital business with the joint venture business, the physician business, and the urgent care center.

In contrast to urgent care centers, ambulatory surgery centers have much higher margins (assuming sufficient volume levels are achieved) and thus lend themselves to joint venturing. They can be sufficiently profitable so that both parties can get adequate rates of return on investment while achieving other business or programmatic objectives.

WHO WILL BE INVOLVED?

When planning joint ventures, the parties must determine who will be permitted to participate. Strategic as well as political considerations will have an effect on those determinations. For example, it would be appropriate for a hospital to involve surgeons in an ambulatory surgery joint venture while perhaps excluding pathologists and radiologists. Similarly, in an imaging center, particularly one that uses magnetic resonance imaging techniques, it may be appropriate to have radiologists involved along with neurologists and orthopedists, whereas the ear, nose, and throat specialists or obstetricians would not play an important role.

Other types of joint ventures lend themselves to broad participation, such as the development of a health maintenance organization, a venture capital company, or a preferred provider organization. In these instances, broad participation will increase the likelihood of success and acceptance. In contrast, the development of an urgent care center does not readily lend itself to broad participation but in fact is typically very narrowly limited to primary care or emergency medicine specialists.

Regardless of the business activity, however, though we are discussing the broad topic of hospital-physician joint ventures, clearly not all physicians can be placed into one monolithic group. The business of the joint venture and the strategic business plan for it need to be refined so that the physicians selected will result in the greatest degree of potential success. Experience to date indicates that the business of the joint venture, rather than personal or political preferences, should dictate the types of physicians involved.

EXISTING SERVICES VERSUS NEW SERVICES

Many hospitals are pursuing joint ventures with physicians by taking existing programs or services and converting them to joint venture opportunities. This strategy serves two fundamental purposes. The first is to reposition an existing line of business to enhance its ability to sustain or increase profitability or to maintain or increase market share. The second is to create new financial incentives by bringing in physicians who otherwise would be mere users of the services. This will increase the economic interdependence of the parties and in some cases prevent physicians from establishing competing programs on their own. This strategy is designed to make a business partner out of your potential competitor.

New business activities may be developed for a variety of reasons. For example, the development of a health maintenance organization with members of the medical staff may enhance the competitive posture of both the hospital and physicians vis-à-vis major purchasers of hospital care. On the other hand, the development of a new skilled nursing facility in partnership with physicians may be a strategy to capitalize on the opportunities created by the so-called graying of America and the increased need to provide specialized services to the elderly rather than a program designed simply to accomplish either a hospital-related or a physician-related objective.

CONCLUSION

Classification of joint ventures is important to help sort out and relate each joint venture opportunity with the specific objective or objectives being sought.

Sometimes joint ventures represent an opportunity to obtain capital from another source for a particular service. In others, a joint venture approach may be a method of neutralizing a competitor or turning that competitor into a business partner. Still, a joint venture might be a way to combine specific talents of two or more parties to make a given clinical program or business a success.

5

Step-by-Step Approach for Developing and Implementing a Joint Venture

Linda A. Burns, M.H.A.

INTRODUCTION

The decision to team up is not an easy one. Nevertheless, hospitals and physicians can derive significant economic and other benefits through mutual participation in owning and operating healthcare facilities and programs. In the process of developing and implementing a joint venture, the venture participants must answer a number of questions regarding the advisability and feasibility of the joint venture.

This chapter describes a step-by-step process that hospitals and physicians can follow to develop and implement a joint venture. It serves as the introduction to succeeding chapters describing in detail the market assessments, financing alternatives, and legal issues which must be addressed in developing and implementing joint ventures between hospitals and physicians. Moreover, this chapter discusses the qualifications of individuals who should constitute the project team that is charged with developing and implementing a joint venture.

ORGANIZING FOR JOINT VENTURE DEVELOPMENT

Launching and managing new clinical programs and facilities in partnership with physicians requires that healthcare organizations reexamine their organizational structures and decision-making processes. Hospital chief executive officers should ask the question: Are the current organizational structure and operational decision-making process compatible with or suitable for developing and implementing joint ventures?

FIGURE 5–1 Functional Hospital Organization Structure

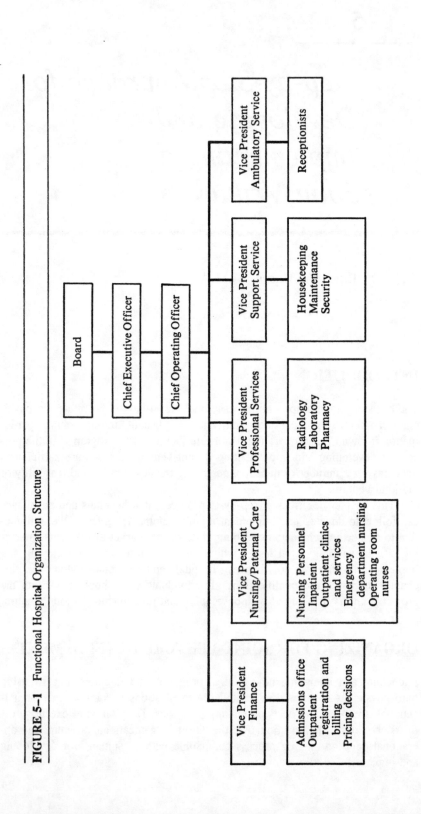

In times of dramatic and rapid industry restructuring, organizations need flexibility and organizational slack so that opportunities for reconfiguring existing health services or offering new ones can be identified and capitalized on. Organizations that exhibit rigid bureaucratic structures and decision making and that are organized along functional lines are at a competitive disadvantage during times of industry restructuring compared with organizations that are flexible and organized according to clinical product lines and markets.

Historically, hospitals have been organized according to functional areas as illustrated in Figure 5–1. As more health services are shifted from an inpatient setting to an outpatient setting, this traditional organization structure must change in order for the organization to enable its managers to achieve a delivery system oriented to outpatients.

Similarly, business development activities and joint venture activities require an organizational context and structure that permit new ways of structuring and operating health services. While the design of organizational structures must take into account an individual institution's idiosyncrasies, the responsibilities of the board and CEO remain to design a structure that permits the organization to achieve its strategic objectives. Establishing new corporate legal entities for joint ventures without changing the underlying decision-making process to grant the venture managers more autonomy will decrease the likelihood of success for the new venture.

A variety of organizational structures are emerging in hospitals and their related entities. One example of these appears in Figure 5–2.

Increasingly, hospitals or their parent corporations are creating senior management positions with responsibility for business development or joint venture development for the constellation of health services companies or medical centers. These individuals frequently possess a vice president or senior vice president title and may report directly to the president and chief executive officer of the healthcare system or the parent corporation. These individuals should have

FIGURE 5–2 Matrix Structure for Core Inpatient Business and Strategic Business Unit Structure for Diversified Services and New Businesses

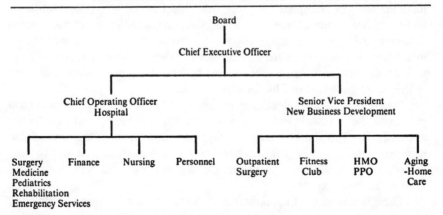

the capabilities to develop and analyze business plans and generate business ideas and joint venture opportunities. They should possess more than just an analyst's abilities though; they should be doers. They should be experienced in developing and implementing new clinical programs. In addition, they should be individuals who like to work with and who communicate well with physicians.

SCREENING NEW VENTURES

Developing joint ventures for various clinical programs and facilities should be part of an institution's overall business strategy. Because a hospital can anticipate using joint ventures as an approach to developing new or reconfiguring existing health services, businesses, or clinical product lines, hospitals are advised to establish a process for screening and evaluating joint venture and other business opportunities.

Because joint venture development and new business development activities frequently raise key questions and issues about the degree of risk that the hospital should undertake and the types of businesses to engage in, the hospital or its parent corporation is advised to establish a joint venture or business screening committee. This committee functions as a quasi board or an actual board if the activity is proposed in a separate corporation. The committee could include a member or two from the parent corporation's board of directors. Also, it is wise to include other individuals from the community who may not be interested in serving full terms on the hospital board but who can bring business experience to this joint venture committee. These individuals may include bankers involved in lending money to new businesses or expanding businesses, a local venture capitalist or real estate developer, and successful entrepreneurs.

The committee, working with the vice president of business development, should develop a series of criteria which outline the scope of business or joint venture opportunities about which the hospital or healthcare organization is interested. These criteria can be general, but at the very least they should stipulate the amount of capital per project that the hospital or its organization is willing to invest, the degree of financial risk, and whether or not the hospital is interested in joint venturing only service businesses that are closely related to the core business of acute inpatient care, other health-related services, or services that are not related to traditional hospital services. Examples of these criteria were discussed in Chapter 4.

Finally, the business development executive can publicize to managers and physicians the process by which joint venture opportunities would be screened and analyzed. This communicates to physicians and others in the organization who may wish to pursue joint ventures the types of analyses that will be conducted, and will also serve to protect the organization from being stampeded into an ill-advised venture.

There is no dearth of opportunities for joint ventures between hospitals and physicians. More often than not the problem is one of focusing on the most promising opportunities and executing them well. Because the amount of managers' and physicians' time to evaluate and implement a joint venture is substantial, hospitals and physicians are advised to use the screening criteria described earlier to weed out ventures that may not fit their particular criteria.

STEP-BY-STEP PROCESS FOR DEVELOPING JOINT VENTURES

The business development process is a methodical step-by-step process which is intended to reduce the likelihood of a business failure. Although the popular

---

FIGURE 5–3 Joint Venture Development and Implementation Process

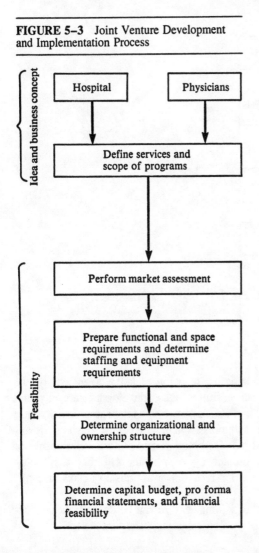

FIGURE 5-3 *(concluded)*

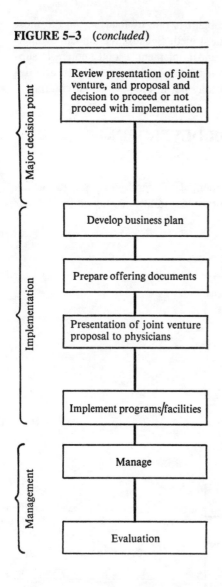

image of an entrepreneur is a hip-shooting decision maker who invests on the basis of "gut feel," in reality, successful business developers carefully and fully define the business proposal and its market, financial structure, risks, and management before proceeding with the investment. Successful business development requires that investors and managers understand the interrelationship of all these factors in contributing to the success of a business, rather than focusing on financial structure without market research or appraisal of risks or availability of competent management.

Some of the steps in developing a joint venture can be carried out concurrently. For example, attorneys can begin investigating various regulations that may be pertinent to the joint venture structure, such as applicability of certificate of need and corporate practice of medicine laws, while consultants are performing market assessments. The entire process of developing a joint venture is illustrated in Figure 5–3.

Step 1 Determine Services and Scope of Program to Be Joint Ventured

Ideas for joint ventures will frequently be posed as, "Let's establish a women's health program," without a clear definition of the scope of clinical services that would constitute the program. Therefore, a necessary first step in developing a joint venture is to determine the exact scope of services or programs which will form the business. For example, women's health services can be restricted primarily to routine office obstetrics and gynecology services or can include nutrition programs, mammography screening, psychological counseling, gynecologic surgery, primary care for women, and infertility services.

During this step the people involved in developing the joint venture should discuss with the physicians and hospital managers the geographic market the program would serve or could serve, the nature of the competitors, and physicians' practice patterns. In addition, the managers should discuss the relationship of the proposed programs or businesses with other strategic initiatives of the hospital and the relationship of the program to the competitive strategy of the hospital.

As a result of these determinations, the joint venture team should have a clearer definition of the scope of the joint venture and the potential benefits to be gained from the joint venture initiative. The definition of the program will serve as the basis for the market assessment.

Step 2 Is the Proposed Business of the Joint Venture Program Consistent with the Strategic Plan?

After the scope of the joint venture program or facility has been defined, managers and physicians should ask the question: Is this proposed business consistent with the hospital's or parent corporation's strategic plan? This means, does this venture fit with the overall strategy for the hospital and its related services and the strategy for market penetration in certain geographic markets or particular consumers or other physicians who may use the service? If the answer is negative, then the joint venture proposal should be jettisoned then and there. No subsequent efforts should be devoted to pursuing the business. Only a substantial change in the strategy of the organization would warrant reconsideration of the business. Thus, this question poses the first screen that a joint venture opportunity should pass before proceeding to the succeeding steps where detailed analyses are performed.

Step 3 Perform Market Assessment

This step determines whether or not an adequate market exists for the proposed services or facilities of the joint venture and to determine the features of the program, service, or facility that should be incorporated into the joint venture. The analysis of the market should include both quantitative and qualitative factors.

The quantitative analyses for a health services joint venture should include a demand assessment using the following information:

- Historical use rates.
- Projections of physician office visits.
- Utilization of existing services at the hospital.
- National and regional incidence rates for various diseases and conditions.

The qualitative analyses, which would be used to augment the demand projections, could include interviews with physicians to gauge their interest as well as market research including focus groups and consumer telephone surveys. The market assessment should include an identification of current or potential competitors and the characteristics of the competitors' programs.

As a result of these analyses, the joint venture team can determine the services and features that should be part of the program package. Utilization projections for these services, based on both qualitative and quantitative analyses, can then be prepared for use in the next step. In addition, a strategy for entering the market and introducing the program should be devised as part of the market analyses.

Step 4 Prepare Functional and Space Program and Staffing and Equipment Requirements for the Program

Based on the utilization projections and findings from the market assessment, detailed functional and space programs for the program and facilities can be prepared. These functional and space programs should include the following:

- Delineation of workstations.
- Staffing requirements.
- Zoning/proximity requirements.
- Room-by-room space requirements.
- Gross space requirements.
- Equipment requirements.

Step 5 Determine Organizational and Ownership Structure

Here the decision to team up or not is made. During this step the ownership structure and organizational structure will be determined. The preceding steps would be the same regardless of whether or not the program is to be financed and managed as a joint venture. Analyses during this step include an evaluation of alternative organizational models and legal entities.

Factors that should be taken into account in the analysis include:

- Legal implications.
- Reimbursement implications.
- Interest of physicians in investing in the venture.

Should a joint venture structure be desired, the legal issues to be included in the analyses are:

- Antitrust issues pertaining to the structure and proposed operations of a joint venture.
- Review of contractual and other documents that may affect the joint venture.
- Noncompetitive clauses.
- Bond financing covenants.
- Ground lease.

A full discussion of the legal issues appears in Chapter 7 through 10.

At this stage of the development, legal counsel with specialized skills in hospital-physician joint ventures and new business management is necessary.

Step 6   Determine Capital Budget, Pro Forma Financial Statements, and Financial Feasibility for the Joint Venture

During this step, the project team assesses the financial feasibility of the joint venture. To do this, the joint venture team must first develop a capital budget. Then, in consultation with management, an appropriate financing vehicle should be selected and a source and use of funds statement should be developed.

In preparing the pro forma financial statements, the team should identify an appropriate charge structure, determine operating expenses, and prepare a pro forma income statement for the project. Sensitivity analyses should be performed together with projections for best case, worst case, and most probable case scenarios. An analysis of pricing strategies should be part of the financial feasibility analysis. This is particularly important if the joint venture program will be offered to HMOs and PPOs on a contractual basis.

A written analysis of the financial feasibility should be developed including:

- Description of assumptions.
- Rationale and methodology used.
- Capital budget.
- Sources and uses of funds.
- Forecasted statements of revenues and expenses.
- Forecasted cash flow.
- Forecasted balance sheet.
- Notes to financial statements.

Step 7   Present Joint Venture Proposal and Decide Whether or Not to Proceed with Implementation

The joint venture team should prepare a written report of the market and financial analyses and present the findings and their recommendations to the board or the new venture committee. A decision to proceed or not should be made.

Step 8   Develop Business Plan

A business plan describing the competitive position and proposed strategy of the proposed joint venture should be developed. At a minimum, the written plan should include:

- Description of the joint venture program and its competitive strategy.
- Analysis of competitors.
- Market research.
- Marketing plan, including entry strategy.
- Operations plan, including staffing patterns and space requirements.
- Risk factors.
- Management.
- Financial statements.
- Financing plan and ownership structure.

A special section of the business plan should be devoted to risk factors and their likelihood of preventing the business from achieving its financial and programmatic objective. As part of the discussion of risk factors, the business plan should include provisions that outline an exit strategy. The plan should specify under what conditions the business would be discontinued.

The purpose of the business plan is to provide a roadmap of how the business will be structured, its services and products, its operations plan, and its competitive strategy. The business plan is the one document that summarizes the business concept and operating objectives and plans. The plan provides a written record of the logic of the business and identifies the key success factors in the proposed business.

Step 9   Prepare Legal Documents, Offering Documents, Securities Registration, and Other Documents

Upon confirmation of the joint venture structure and financing, the legal work pertaining to the offering circular for the joint venture and all other documents necessary or appropriate for the joint venture should be commenced. In the event that the investment is required to be registered or qualified with the Securities Exchange Commission and/or state department of securities, appropriate applications should be prepared. Chapter 7 describes these issues in more detail. In addition, tax opinions may be required. Preparation should commence on the organization documents for the legal structure, corporation or partnership. Other legal work involves description documents, professional service contracts, facility leases, loan documentation, and Internal Revenue Service rulings. Attorneys knowledgeable and experienced in the development and implementation of joint ventures should be part of the project team.

Step 10 Present Joint Venture Proposal to Prospective Physician Investors

Formal presentations of the joint venture idea and structure should be made to interested physicians in one-on-one as well as group settings.

Step 11 Implement Program

Assuming that sufficient interest exists among potential investors and that the offering will be adequately subscribed, the project team should proceed with carrying out the business plan. The manager of the venture should be hired, along with specialized assistance from outside professionals to launch the program and take it through its start-up stage.

As is true for any service business, the key ingredient to success is proper execution of the business concept. All decisions regarding the marketing, operations, and financial management of the program should be vested with the manager.

Step 12 Evaluate Performance Program/Joint Venture

The managers and governing board of the joint venture should monitor the development and performance of the business. Actual performance should be compared with the expected performance described in the business plan. Having a detailed business plan will permit the managers to better understand the source of the business's failure to meet projected utilization, financial, or consumer satisfaction targets.

In any new business, changes in course are necessary to respond to changes in the market external to the business. New businesses especially require continued in-depth management attention in order to succeed. Frequently, specialized external expertise is required to rectify an operating problem or to devise a change in competitive strategy. An elegant structure and adequate capital will not guarantee success. Ongoing management also is a critical element.

JOINT VENTURE/BUSINESS DEVELOPMENT TEAM

Because of the specialized skills necessary to design and launch new businesses as joint ventures, hospitals and physicians are advised to assemble and use project teams who can assist them in implementing a joint venture. Even hos-

TABLE 5-1 Identification of Members of Joint Venture Project Team and Description of Functions*

Team Member	Role	Source
Project leader	Manages process of developing joint venture and assures that key decision points are reviewed with board and/or hospital management	Internal vice president of business development or external consultants
Feasibility analysts	Perform market assessments, prepare space and staff requirements, determine financial feasibility and risk factors	Internal staff or external consultant
Attorneys	Assist in evaluation of ownership and organizational options and prepare legal documents to execute joint venture	External legal counsel
Physician leader	Communicates goals of joint venture and assures that clinical issues are addressed	Internal; can be augmented with external physician consultant
Architects	Design of space	External
Equipment planners		External
Construction managers		External

*Assumes the joint venture project is a health services program that involves construction of a facility and acquisition of major equipment.

pitals that have implemented three to five joint ventures will not necessarily possess the type and mix of specialized expertise for their next one. Thus, external consultants may be necessary, not just for their expertise, but also to conduct the increased managerial work and analysis that accompany joint venture development.

In addition, the hospital, through its vice president of business development or through the use of an outside consultant, should designate a project leader. This individual will coordinate the work of internal and external consultants, attorneys, and architects, and will see that the project's timetable is adhered to. Moving a joint venture project expeditiously through idea conceptualization to implementation can garner advantages in the local marketplace vis-à-vis competition and, at the same time, build credibility with physicians by proving that the managers can execute and implement the deal. A listing of the members of a joint venture project team appears in Table 5-1.

II

ETHICAL CONSIDERATIONS

6

Ethical Considerations of Hospital-Physician Joint Ventures

Norman Fost, M.D., M.P.H.

"Doctors cut, burn and torture the sick, and then demand of them an undeserved fee for such services."

Heraclitus, On the Universe, *513* B.C.

"A physician who heals for nothing is worth nothing."

The Talmud

"[It] is a murderous absurdity . . . to give a surgeon a pecuniary interest in cutting off your leg. . . . And the more appalling the mutilation, the more the mutilator is paid . . . except when he does it to a poor person for practice."

G.B. Shaw, The Doctor's Dilemma

INTRODUCTION

Concern about physicians making money from treating the sick is not new.[1] While no one expects physicians to work for nothing, there is great debate about the proper limits to their incomes and the ways their income is generated. The recent growth in the number and types of joint ventures between physicians and hospitals is only the most recent development. Ethical concerns about such joint ventures grow in general from a vague discomfort about physicians seeking profits and in particular from whether or not they should be permitted to earn a profit from services that they do not administer directly. The central ethical issue is the potential harm that may come to patients because of the physician's conflicting interest in his or her own material well-being and the interests of patients.

This chapter reviews the historical aspects of this problem and analyzes several specific ethical questions raised by hospital-physician joint ventures:

- Do these new ways of making profits constitute a different or more serious threat to patient interests than traditional methods used by physicians to earn income?
- Are there fundamental ethical differences between medicine and other professions and businesses?
- As physicians shift to a more businesslike orientation, are patient interests likely to be compromised?

Because the growth of joint ventures is so recent, there is not yet a body of experience with specific ethical dilemmas and controversies raised by them. Therefore, consideration of ethical issues must necessarily be somewhat theoretical to anticipate the problems and objections that might arise in the future. The major purpose of this chapter is to sensitize the joint venturer and others to those issues and to make some modest proposals on how to avoid some of the more obvious pitfalls.

PHYSICIAN SELF-INTEREST IS NOT NEW

"Where your treasure is, there your heart shall be."

Old Testament, Matthew VI:21

"It is asking more than human perfection to assume that a judgment may not be influenced unconsciously by pressing financial need."

E.P. Lehman, 28 Surgery 595 (1950)

The practice of medicine has always been fraught with the incessant conflict between self-interest and altruism.[2] This conflict is at the heart of the fee-for-service system. This tension need not be attributed to willful profiteering. It is unavoidable as long as physicians have the discretion to choose among acceptable options with different rewards. These unconscious influences are aggravated when the physician's personal needs are great. The high level of indebtedness of current medical school graduates, for example, may partly explain the rise in interest in augmenting practice income with "secondary income," that is, income from other sources than personal services provided by the physician. "Need" of course is a subjective notion tied to one's expectations. Physicians who do not earn enough to support the lifestyle they expect may feel themselves to be in "need."

There are other recent changes in American medicine affecting practice patterns besides personal need that pit physician self-interest against patient interests. Health maintenance organizations (HMOs) present physicians with a motive to compromise patient interests in the name of preserving or promoting personal well-being. While HMOs may bring financial benefits to patients by reducing costs, they do so by giving physicians incentives to provide the least amount of or least expensive healthcare that they can justify. The same phenomenon occurs when payments for hospital services are fixed prospectively, as occurs in the Medicare prospective payment system which pays hospitals by diagnosis-related groups (DRGs). The savings in these cases do not go directly into the physician's pocket, but if his salary is tied to the financial well-being of his HMO or hospital, he will quickly learn that there is a relationship between his income and his medical decisions. The risks to patients in these cases, in contrast to the fee-for-service system, are from too little care rather than too much. It is unclear which risk is more serious.

It is not just financial reward that affects physician behavior. Academicians earning a fixed salary know that their status, influence, promotion, and ultimately their income are affected by the generation of hospital fees and practice income. The principal investigator of a clinical trial requiring recruitment of large numbers of patients has incentives to distort, however mildly, the relative benefits and risks in offering such experimental treatments to patients. Indeed, the physician is most likely to select treatments or drugs to study on the basis of decisions made by federal funding agencies or pharmaceutical companies.[3] The rewards include a secure source of salary, support for a secretary or research assistant who can facilitate other aspects of the investigator's career, and the possibility or promise of invitations to travel and lecture in faraway places, sometimes for handsome honoraria.

These considerations affect not only physician decisions regarding identifiable patients, but also institutional decisions to offer or market certain services. The development and advertising of hospital-based programs for mass genetic screening, physical fitness, eating disorders, and so on are obviously predicated on a belief that they offer health benefits to consumers, but they also depend on an expectation that they will bring additional revenues to the institution. The simple decision regarding where to establish one's practice or hospital or ambulatory surgery center is usually not predicated primarily on population needs, but on prospects for income and market share. Conflicts between self-interest and patient interests and the potential for adverse effects of decision making are sometimes unavoidable.

PROFIT AND NONPROFIT DISTINCTIONS MAY BE OVERDRAWN

A major concern about joint ventures is that they constitute or reflect an undesirable shift in physician and hospital interest in maximizing profits. Much ado has been made over the rapid growth of for-profit healthcare institutions.[4] The distinctive financial feature of such organizations is that excess income can be distributed to owners or stockholders. In a not-for-profit or "voluntary" hospital, excess income must be reinvested for improving patient care services. The claim is that the not-for-profit hospital is more likely to be more patient-oriented. This claim is at the least unsubstantiated, and there are reasons for believing it may be wrong.

Both kinds of hospitals have various mixtures of altruism and self-interest. Both are certainly allowed to make a profit on their activities in the sense that income may exceed expenses, usually without limit. The not-for-profit hospital depends on having income (from all sources, including gifts) exceed expenses at the risk of closing its doors. It therefore has powerful incentives to limit unprofitable services and develop and promote profitable services independent of their health benefits.

Similarly, most physicians are profit-seeking entities, regardless of the setting in which they work; income must exceed expenses, preferably by a wide margin. Long before joint ventures, physician decisions were heavily influenced by their effect on personal income.

Relman has suggested that there is a fundamental difference between primary income derived directly from personal services delivered to a patient and secondary income derived from the services of others.[5] In the latter, physicians profit without having a personal relationship with patients who contribute to their income. This distance, it is feared, may reduce the altruistic component of their decisions because of the absence of a personal relationship with the patient. Relman has strenuously urged physicians to separate themselves clearly from the healthcare industry and disavow any entrepreneurial interests.[6]

The most probable adverse effect of a shift toward for-profit institutions, particularly if they come to dominate the healthcare scene, may be a broad societal effect rather than a change in the behavior of individual physicians. This "macro" concern is that the growth of a profit-orientation will reduce access to services by the poor.

To understand the ethical concern about physicians becoming more involved in traditional business relationships, it is important to review briefly the alleged ethical differences between medicine and other businesses and professions.

ETHICAL DIFFERENCES BETWEEN MEDICINE AND OTHER BUSINESSES/PROFESSIONS

Veatch's review of the alleged difference in moral codes of physicians as compared with business executives and other professionals suggest that there is not a bright line separating the two.[7] In some instances, there may be more of a commitment to formal ethical principles—such as truth-telling—in the business world. In others, such as serving the poor, physicians appear more likely to place moral concerns ahead of self-interest. Some of these examples will be reviewed primarily to show the ambiguity of the problem and the difficulty in asserting that medicine has established a clear claim as a uniquely altruistic or "moral" profession.

Provision of Essential Services, Regardless of Ability to Pay

Medicine is not alone in providing a service or product that is among the necessities of life. The baker, the builder, and the clothier also provide basic needs, but they have not traditionally felt an obligation to personally subsidize those in need, nor does the public expect them to. In contrast, there is a long tradition, supported by law in the United States, of physicians and hospitals providing necessary services to patients appearing in their offices or emergency rooms, regardless of ability to pay. There is no analogous expectation that the bakery should dispense free bread to the hungry or malnourished. The duty to provide food, shelter, and clothing has generally been perceived as a duty of the community or society as a whole, not of the smaller society or a profession of providers.

Pragmatic considerations may partly account for this. The number of true emergencies presented to an emergency room or physician's office is a manageable one. In contrast, bakeries or construction companies cannot typically afford to provide for all the needy in their communities. Nonetheless, physicians have been perceived as different, and this perception may be undermined if they ally themselves with hospitals or other businesses that turn away certain patients in the name of economic efficiency.

Supplying Competitors with the Latest Information

The business executive rejoices when competitors persist in using outdated information, whether it involves selling outmoded products or failing to offer the most current services. The physician, in contrast, is flattered to have the opportunity to spread the latest news, whether in the form of publication in a scholarly or educational journal or a state-of-the-art talk on "how-to-do-it."

It may be that the physician's behavior is not motivated by concern for patients or altruism toward colleagues or competitors. For the academician, publication is the basis for personal advancement. For the speaker at a local or regional conference, the motivation is sometimes explicitly for purposes of public relations in the hope of increasing referrals.

This difference in behavior, therefore, may simply be due to a different structure of rewards rather than any inherent ethical moral differences in altruistic or beneficent motive. There is a wide perception, nonetheless, that the physician model better serves the public interest.

Enticement of Needless Consumption

The encouragement through advertising of consumption, particularly of frivolous or even unhealthy products such as tobacco and alcohol, has been a persisting cloud over discussions of the morality of American business. Medicine, it is claimed, in contrast seeks only to make people healthier.

While better health is the advertised benefit of medical services, it is debatable whether it is the actual result. And, more importantly, it is debatable whether better health is the primary motive for marketing such services. While new drugs must be shown to have demonstrated and acceptable efficacy before marketing, this is so because of federal regulations, not because of healthful motives. New procedures such as coronary bypass surgery or programs such as mass genetic screening[8] are typically not studied before mass marketing. Even when allegedly efficacious preventive programs or interventions, such as annual physicals, are shown to have marginal benefits at very high costs, they may persist or expand. As with marketing of nonmedical goods and services, the costs of such services are not simply monetary, but include adverse effects on health.

Discouragement and Exclusion of Unprofitable Customers

It is expected that a retail business will seek a location with easy access for customers with discretionary income. Not-for-profit hospitals, in contrast, are more likely to be found in neighborhoods with high concentrations of indigent consumers and to offer services which are unprofitable. While the growth in public subsidies through Medicare and Medicaid mitigated the economic burdens, there has been a trend to build or relocate hospitals and shift services away from economically unfavorable environments.

Even before the recent growth in for-profit hospitals, it was customary for physicians to establish their practices in economically strategic locations. There was no pretense about the economic basis of such decisions. Patients did not seem to lose trust in their physician simply because the practice location was motivated by self-interest rather than community need or other altruistic factors. Paradoxically, the occasional physician who set up practice in the inner city to "take advantage" of public subsidies was often maligned as opportunistic. While some of this criticism related to fraudulent billing practices, it was easier to find fault with physicians who settled in a ghetto for crassly financial reasons even if they practiced within the rules, than to criticize their counterparts who chose careers in the suburbs for the same reasons.

The suburban doctor could even refuse to see Medicare or Medicaid patients because it was not personally cost-effective to handle the burden of paperwork for the financial return. The fully insured patients in the same office, if aware of such a policy, were as likely to approve as not, depending in part on their political ideology. But the realization that their doctor could allow personal financial gain to take priority over patient interests did not seem to undermine trust or respect in most cases.

Willingness to Lie

As Veatch has pointed out, the difference between physicians and business executives in this dimension is counterintuitive.[9] Whatever the actual practice, it is at least an axiom in codes of business ethics that the customer should be told the truth. In contrast, lying has long been advocated by physicians, whether in the use of placebos or more explicitly in disclosing bad news to terminally ill patients. It is beside the point that the business code of truth-telling was probably motivated by self-interest to protect the group from criticism and regulation. Self-interest, not altruism, is a hallmark of some professional codes of ethics.[10]

In summary, medicine can be distinguished from other businesses in some areas of moral importance, such as commitment to the poor. In others, such as sharing of new information, there is a difference but the complex motivation behind it leaves doubts as to its moral significance. In those areas involving more obvious marketing decisions and commitment to truth-telling, there may be more similarities than differences, or medicine may be seen in a more un-favorable light.

IS A BUSINESS ORIENTATION BAD FOR PATIENTS?

In the previous discussion, we asked if there was a clear difference between the attitudes and practices of physicians and business executives that would justify a claim by physicians to moral superiority. This question focused on the attitudes and behaviors of physicians as individuals, but that is not the whole story. A trend to organize medicine in a more businesslike way would have benefits and risks for patients apart from the effects on individual physicians. A consideration of the ethical implications of joint ventures must consider these consequences as well.

POSSIBLE BENEFITS OF A MORE BUSINESSLIKE TREND

Improved Efficiency and Reduced Costs

There is no question of the beneficial effects of HMOs and DRGs in controlling costs of medical care. Communities that were experiencing annual increases of 20 percent in such costs saw reductions in the rate of growth to less than one half of that within a year of a shift to prospective payment. These savings benefit individual consumers who pay premiums as well as taxpayers who un-derwrite public subsidies for healthcare costs. Prospective payment systems also give the underwriters of medical care financial incentives to promote healthier lifestyles among their clients.

Consumer Orientation

While consumers typically are ill-equipped to make informed choices about technical aspects of medical care, they know what services make them feel better. The recent trend toward more homelike obstetrical services was fueled by classic market phenomena.

The majority of visits to physicians are for problems that technical services cannot help. What patients want and need from their physicians is nontechnical help: understanding, listening, caring. Physicians working together with hospitals to improve the market for both are more likely to focus on consumer wants and needs even though the motivation to improve such services is self-interest.

New Sources of Capital

The evolving saga of the clinical testing of the artificial heart by Humana Inc. raises a host of ethical and social policy questions. It is too soon to draw conclusions as to its net effect on the interests of the American public. One of the benefits, however, has been to demonstrate that the private sector can be a source of funds for research and development. This occurs at a time when federal resources are threatened. Whether this particular investment turns out to be undesirable may be beside the point, unless it becomes apparent that private sector funding of research is systematically undesirable on ethical grounds. A long experience with research supported by pharmaceutical companies suggests that, like public support, private underwriting will be a mixture of good and bad.[11]

New Sources of Taxes

One of the most feared consequences of the for-profit trend is an adverse effect on access to services by the medically indigent, that is, those without insurance or eligibility for public programs. If one sees the duty to provide for such people as a general societal responsibility rather than a specific duty of hospitals or physicians, then the trend toward profit-making joint ventures could increase public funds through taxes. It is uncertain whether or not such taxes would actually be targeted for healthcare for the poor, but the joint venturer might reply that there is no particular reason why they should. If the needs of the indigent are a general responsibility, hospitals and physicians might have no more and no less responsibility than the baker or builder has to the hungry or to those without shelter.

POSSIBLE HAZARDS OF A BUSINESS ORIENTATION

Reduced Access by the Poor

It would seem unavoidable that a more businesslike orientation will aggravate the problem of access to healthcare services by persons in lower socioeconomic areas. At worst, there could be an increase in the number of sophisticated services that are available only or primarily to insured consumers. At the least, there could be a return to the two-tier system that prevailed before the enactment of the Medicare and Medicaid programs: the middle class served in comfortable, efficient community hospitals, the poor in underfunded, impersonal public hospitals and clinics. [12]

Loss of Academic Influence

Teaching hospitals may have special reasons to be concerned about the business orientation that joint ventures could bring. As hospitals come to be controlled by business interests, it is likely that academic concerns and the power of those with academic interests will diminish. Education and training programs are generally not cost effective. The physician-joint venturer may be less willing to tolerate students and residents in an ambulatory setting because of the added costs. The efficiency of delivering clinical services, hospital length of stay, and utilization of laboratory services in a prepaid system are all aggravated by allowing students and residents to participate. A comparison of the library collections in teaching versus nonteaching hospitals illustrates the point.

As educational considerations recede, the quality of peer review is also likely to diminish with potential adverse effects on quality of care. Hiring and promotion considerations in hospitals affiliated with medical schools, while nominally still controlled by academicians, could be increasingly influenced by economic considerations. The bright young investigator who is not clinically active, the iconoclastic teacher who is skeptical or critical of hospital practices, or the clinical ethicist who questions everything is less likely to be welcome in the business-oriented environment.

Concerns about competition are likely to work against those who favor making decisions in a reflective way. The marketplace requires speed and secrecy; academia values deliberate and open discussion. [13]

Compromises in Quality of Care

The effects of prepayment systems on clinical decisions have already been discussed. While encouraging hospitals to reduce costs, they give incentives to provide the least medical care possible, consistent with adequate quality. Opposing these forces are the integrity and commitment of physicians and others in the system. A reputation for poor care among physicians or laypersons could be financially disastrous. There are also the traditional legal constraints against malpractice. How these forces balance out will be the subject of much study in the coming decades, but a business orientation will create some pressures to compromise on quality.

Reduction in Unprofitable Services

It has already been noted that the business-oriented hospitals or clinics, like any other business, can be expected to locate in areas where unprofitable clients have reduced access. They can also be expected to reduce services that have low profit margins. As an example, the advent of HMOs has been accompanied in many instances by a reduction in mental health services or by a reduction of the quality of such services by transfers to social workers, nurses, or others whose salaries are lower than psychiatrists'.

Loss of Trust

Relman has argued that the most pernicious effect of the involvement of doctors in joint ventures will be the loss of trust by patients and those citizens and leaders involved in health policy. [14] This is based on the premise that there is a fundamental difference in the quality or degree of vested interest in the physician who earns money from secondary income, in constrast to the physician whose income is solely from direct one-to-one services.

Relman's concern appears to have two components: first, that physicians with secondary income *should* be trusted less, and second, that they *will* be trusted less, regardless of whether they ought to be. The first question is an empiric one, as yet unsupported by data. The second is a question of perception and probably is the more important since perceptions do not need to be rational to be influential. Relman argues that physicians will no longer have a major influence on policy because they will be perceived as arguing from self-interest rather than from their traditional concern for patient welfare.

Some would claim that this concern ignores evidence that physicians have always had a heavy amount of self-interest. The long campaign of organized medicine against government support for the medical needs of the elderly did not speak well for the profession. It can hardly be claimed to have sprung from altruism. [15] The admittedly powerful influence of the American Medical Association does not derive from the moral force of its arguments. It may be, however, that the AMA's political influence is dependent on public respect for the opinion of physicians and that the new trends could undermine such a base. Boldly stated, however, this might reduce to an argument that the trend toward a business orientation could make physicians less effective in pursuing their professional self-interests in the political arena. [16]

It is also possible that a trend toward a more contractual relationship between physician and patient will benefit patients. The physician's altruism often takes the form of paternalism and frustrates the increasing number of patients who want to participate more in decisions about their own healthcare. Seeing the physician as a business executive may free up some patients from the regressed, dependent attitude that inhibits aggressive, skeptical questioning. While some may yearn for the idyllic physician-patient relationship portrayed in a Norman Rockwell painting, for others the good old days were not so good and not what they want today. Patients probably want caring and concern more than paternalism masquerading as altruism. There is no incompatibility between caring and profits; indeed, the new physician, in a more competitive marketplace, may discover real incentives in displaying the qualities that patients have long been asking for. [17]

PRACTICAL IMPLICATIONS AND RECOMMENDATIONS

It is too early in the history of joint ventures for consensus to have developed on the policy implications of the ethical concerns discussed here. Indeed, there has been little time for analysis of the ethical issues. The Institute of Medicine has completed a study of the ethical implications of for-profit healthcare in general, [18] but this is only indirectly related to the issues surrounding joint ventures.

The recommendations summarized below are presented for consideration, not as conclusions. They constitute a range of policies the joint venturer might consider to avoid the appearance and reality of undue self-interest.

Prohibit "Kickbacks"

It is relatively easy to get consensus on this long-standing taboo, but it is difficult to define the practice. Federal law as well as state medical practice acts proscribe direct payments for referring a patient to another physician or facility. This is particularly egregious when the referring physician has an ownership interest in the facility.

The conceptual difference between a kickback and profit sharing is unclear. The joint venturer who owns a share of a diagnostic radiology facility clearly receives a rebate, however indirectly, from referring his patients there, but this is not so clearly proscribed. The law in this area is ambiguous and rapidly changing.

Codes of conduct do not help in clarifying the matter. The Code of Ethics of the American College of Physicians, for example, states:

The physician should avoid any business arrangement that might, because of personal gain, influence his decisions in patient care. [19]

On the surface, this would seem to preclude referring or admitting a patient to any facility in which the physician had a financial interest. It could even be interpreted to proscribe fee-for-service medical practice.

Require Full Disclosure of Physician Conflicts of Interest

The "publicity" test is a crude litmus test for the ethical acceptability of a position. If people are not willing to expose their views and practices, they may be suspect. Exceptions would include trade secrets and personal matters, but an established joint venture would not qualify for such exclusion. The

American Medical Association Judicial Council endorsed this principle. [20] Disclosure theoretically allows the patient to be more alert to physician conflicts of interest and to consider using an alternate provider. In the real world these considerations are unlikely to have important effects on physician or consumer behavior, so it is not clear what disclosure would practically accomplish.

As with the kickback rule, the boundaries of this principle will be difficult to define. Presumably the physician would not be expected to disclose ownership of stock in a publicly traded company whose products he prescribed.

Establish Vigorous and Regular Outside Review

The joint venturer who sincerely desires to maximize self-interest within the boundaries of moral acceptability can seek critical, periodic review from outside consultants including experts in medical ethics and representatives from the community.

Seek Consumer Input

While the details of the financial arrangements of the joint venture could be considered confidential, the partners can seek advice from consumers affected by their arrangements. It cannot be assumed that financial success implies consumer acceptance, since traditional marketplace principles do not generally apply in the selection of healthcare services.

Maintain a Commitment to the Indigent

It is arguable that healthcare providers do not have a special duty to provide medical care to the poor, but it would be morally praiseworthy to do so. It would also reduce the appearance, as well as the reality, of being motivated purely by personal gain. Some reasonable proportion of income or time could be committed to charitable services.

When Appropriate, Establish Guidelines for the Preservation of Academic Values

Institutions which have a teaching function can protect the integrity of that aspect by investing strong authority in someone who is explicitly *not* part of the joint venture. In a major academic setting, this would involve continuing the tenure process in some form isolated from those whose interests are explicitly business-oriented. In affiliated institutions, the subsidization of educational activities is another mechanism of providing a check on purely profit-seeking motives.

CONCLUSION

"There is nothing new under the sun."

Ecclesiastes

"Do not inquire as to why former days were better than these, for men have always inquired about this."

Ecclesiastes

It is undoubtedly true, as Albert Jonsen observed, that the practice of medicine has always endured a tension between altruism and self-interest. But old ethical problems are problems nonetheless. Whether or not the new ways of financing and delivery care and the involvement of physicians as joint venturers turns out to be, on balance, better or worse for our citizens is in part an empiric question. Time and study will tell. It is also, however, a perceptual question. If consumers and policy makers believe they can no longer trust physicians as much as they used to, in the office or in the legislature, then that too will have effects. But whether this declining influence will be good or bad is also a matter of conjecture. As a physician, I fear the loss of such influence and believe that citizens would be worse off. As a doctor watcher and critic of practices and policies in American healthcare, I can imagine that in many ways a decline in physician influence will be helpful.

The individual joint venturer can claim that broad social problems are his or her concern but not his or her primary responsibility, that they are the responsibility of everyone, and that physicians have much to contribute to the development of better social policy, but they are not ultimately responsible. But there is nothing inherent in joint venturing which precludes the physician taking an active role in promoting the resolution of some of the problems discussed here.

While joint venturers can hide behind a claim that the solution to broad social problems is not their specific obligation, it would be unwise to do so. From a standpoint of pure self-interest, as well as a real sign of continuing concern, it behooves the new physicians to make special efforts to manifest their altruistic side.

Joint ventures and the larger shift toward profit making in healthcare are probably beyond the point of no return. While some physicians may eschew such modes of making money, there are already enough committed that the debate will necessarily be over the limits to such activities. As with other controversies in the regulation of healthcare, physicians can serve the public and themselves best by taking a lead in addressing the ethical problems vigorously, rather than reacting to concerns and proposals that come from those outside the institution.[21]

Notes

[1] Daniel Wikler, "Forming an Ethical Response to For-Profit Health Care," *Business and Health* 2, no. 3 (January–February 1985), pp. 25–29.

[2] Albert Jonsen, "Watching the Doctor," *New England Journal of Medicine* 308 (1983) pp. 1531–35.

[3] D. D. Rutstein, "The Ethical Design of Human Experiments," in *Experimentation with Human Subjects*, ed. Paul Freund (New York: Braziller, 1970).

[4] B. H. Gray, "An Introduction to the New Health Care for Profit," in *The New Health Care for Profit: Doctors and Hospitals in a Competitive Environment*, ed. B. H. Gray (Washington, D.C.: National Academy Press, 1983).

[5] Arnold Relman, "The New Medical Industrial Complex," *New England Journal of Medicine*, 299 (1980), pp. 1012–14.

[6] Relman, "The Future of Medical Practice," *Health Affairs*, 2, no. 3 (1983), pp. 5–19.

[7] Robert Veatch, "Ethical Dilemmas of For-Profit Enterprise in Health Care," in *The New Health Care for Profit: Doctors and Hospitals in a Competitive Environment*, ed. B. H. Gray (Washington, D.C.: National Academy Press, 1983).

[8] Committee for the Study of Inborn Errors of Metabolism, *Genetic Screening: Programs, Principles and Research* (Washington, D.C.: National Academy of Sciences, 1975).

[9] Robert Veatch, "Ethical Dilemmas of For-Profit Enterprise in Health Care."

[10] Relman, "The New Medical Industrial Complex."

[11] D. Mechanic, "Rationing Health Care: Public Policy and the Medical Marketplace," *Hastings Center Report*, 6, no. 1 (1976), pp. 34–37.

[12] *For-Profit Health Care* (Washington, D.C.: National Academy Press, 1986), chap. 5.

[13] M. Tolchin, *"Studies Differ on Takeovers of Teaching Hospitals by Chains," New York Times*, July 18, 1985.

[14] Relman, "The New Medical Industrial Complex."

[15] C. Fried, "Equality and Rights in Medical Care," *Hastings Center Report*, 6, no. 1 (1976), pp. 29–34; D. Mechanic, "Rationing Health Care: Public Policy and the Medical Marketplace," *Hastings Center Report*, 6, no. 1 (1976), pp. 34–37.

[16] R. Numbers, *Almost Persuaded: American Physicians and Compulsory Health Insurance 1912–1920* (Baltimore: Johns Hopkins, 1978).

[17] N. Daniels, *Just Health Care* (New York: Cambridge Press, 1985).

[18] For-Profit Enterprise in Health Care (Washington, D.C.: National Academy Press, 1986).

[19] American College of Physicians, *Ethics Manual* (Philadelphia: American College of Physicians, 1984).

[20] American Medical Association, *Current Opinions of the Judicial Council*, 1984. Various state laws requiring disclosure of financial interests are described in Chapter 7 of this book.

[21] Much of what I have learned about this subject comes from discussions with Daniel Wikler, who also made extensive suggestions on the manuscript. He bears no responsibility for its deficiencies.

III

LEGAL CONSIDERATIONS

7

Legal and Regulatory Issues Affecting Joint Ventures

Douglas M. Mancino, J.D.

INTRODUCTION

From the legal and regulatory perspectives, hospital-physician joint ventures differ from most other types of healthcare ventures. The joinder of hospitals and physicians in a single economic enterprise raises many new and complex legal and regulatory issues that typically are not applicable to separate ventures by hospitals or physicians.

Hospital-physician joint ventures are subject to several layers of law and regulation, from the federal level—including federal tax and securities laws, the Medicare program's rules and regulations, and the Federal Trade Commission's rules governing franchises—to state and local laws and regulations such as health planning and capital expenditure laws, licensing laws, and state Medicaid program rules and regulations. These legal and regulatory provisions often overlap and occasionally conflict, adding to the complexities and uncertainties of establishing and operating hospital-physician joint ventures.

In addition, numerous forms of "private" regulation, such as the requirements of accreditation agencies and the requirements of insurance companies regarding compensation for services rendered to insureds, can affect the structure, financing, and operations of hospital-physician joint ventures.

Hospitals and physicians typically approach the legal and regulatory aspects of joint ventures on a transactional basis. Each venture usually requires the formation of a specific entity, and the parties tend to focus their attention on the nature of that entity. However, each proposed joint venture should be structured carefully to ensure that the legal entities and relationships created are consistent with the strategic and other long-term objectives of all parties.

The various legal and regulatory issues affecting joint ventures are discussed below in the context of the three stages of a joint venture's life cycle: the formation stage, the operating stage, and the dissolution stage. Before reviewing these issues, however, a general approach to the legal and regulatory issues pertaining to joint ventures is suggested. [1]

PUT IT IN WRITING

The laws of the various states contain very few statutory requirements applicable to joint ventures in general. For example, a general partnership can be formed with a handshake by the parties, and no written partnership agreement is even required. While limited partnerships and corporations require the adoption and execution of limited partnership agreements or articles of incorporation and bylaws, all of which need to be in writing, the limited partnership and general business corporation laws of most states merely prescribe the minimum requirements to form these types of entities.

While a handshake, an oral "understanding," or "boilerplate" articles of incorporation or bylaws may be as legal and binding as comprehensive written agreements prepared by a capable attorney, they may also sow the seeds of discord between the parties and may eventually lead to expensive, disruptive, and time-consuming lawsuits regarding the terms of the oral or incomplete agreement. The law reporters are filled with cases involving litigation among partners and between shareholders and corporations over unwritten terms and oral understandings.

For these reasons, it is essential that the parties to a joint venture negotiate and execute written agreements covering the significant business, economic, and tax aspects of the venture. Such written agreements should, at a minimum, address the following fundamental issues.

The Business and Business Opportunities

The agreements should define the business of the joint venture and address whether similar or related business opportunities must be presented to the coventurers for their consideration. The agreements also should state how conflicts of interest will be identified and resolved.

Capital Requirements

The agreements should identify the capital requirements of the joint venture and address such issues as the amount of capital to be contributed at the commencement of the joint venture, the amount of subsequent capital required to be contributed at later times during the life cycle of the joint venture, the manner in which further capital contributions may be compelled, and penalties for noncompliance with a capital call. Similar issues regarding indebtedness to be incurred by the joint venture, both at its formation and in the future, should also be addressed.

Profits and Losses

One of the basic elements of any joint venture agreement will be the determination of each venturer's interest in the profits and losses of the business. While general corporate law may make it easy to allocate profits and losses of a regular business corporation in accordance with share holdings, other joint venture forms such as partnerships and close corporations will require careful attention to the issue of how profits and losses will be allocated.

Closely related to the issue of profits and losses will be the factors that may be taken into account in determining profits and losses, such as whether or not profits attributable to appreciation in value of capital assets should be divided in the same proportion as profits from the operation of the joint venture.

Management

Issues concerning the management of the joint venture should be addressed. These issues will include (a) selection and removal of the board of directors of a corporate joint venture or of the general partner or the management committee of a partnership joint venture, (b) procedures to be followed to select or remove key management personnel, and (c) methods to resolve deadlocks, particularly in those cases where the interests or voting power of the hospital and the physicians are equal.

Distributions

The timing of distributions, such as dividends, should be addressed. When it comes to cash distributions, the venturers may not necessarily desire the same thing. The hospital general partner of a limited partnership, for example, may want the flexibility to withhold cash distributions to assure that the partnership will always have sufficient funds on hand to cover its debts. On the other hand, physician limited partners may require that cash be distributed at specific times, thus reducing the amount of their investment at risk. It may also be appropriate to regulate cash distributions according to their sources, such as from normal operations, capital transactions, and refinancings.

Books and Records

The joint venture documents should deal with such matters as bank accounts and investments and the authority of the parties with regard to them. The documents also should (a) require the maintenance of complete and accurate books of accounts and records relative to the joint venture business; (*b*) specify the method of accounting to be used (e.g., generally accepted accounting principles or a tax-based method of accounting); (*c*) require interim and year-end financial reports and the preparation of federal, state, local, and other tax returns; and (*d*) mandate the furnishing of relevant financial information to the joint venturers.

Withdrawals and Transfers

Provision should be made for the withdrawal of venturers and for the transfer of interests in the venture. Even if transfers of interests are generally prohibited, certain types of transfers are inevitable, such as those that will occur by law upon death or will typically be compelled by the venture documents as a result of the occurrence of other events, such as loss of license, medical staff privileges or malpractice insurance, disability, or acquisition of an interest in a competing enterprise.

Termination

Appropriate provision should be made for the termination of the joint venture and for the division and distribution of its assets upon dissolution. In this regard, the documents may include rights of first refusal or options to purchase fixed assets and other tangible and intangible property of the joint venture, and provisions regarding control over business records such as patient records, client lists, and proprietary financial and business information.

THE FORMATION STAGE OF A JOINT VENTURE

Authority to Enter into Joint Ventures

Early in the discussions of a joint venture, legal counsel to the hospital should examine the hospital's or the related organization's organizational documents to ensure that participation in the joint venture will not exceed the hospital's or the related organization's authority. In the case of community hospitals, this examination should probably include a review of the hospital's articles of incorporation and bylaws, as well as deeds and other instruments that may have been involved in the formation and operation of the hospital. In the case of public hospitals, this review may encompass not only the charter and bylaws of the hospital but also the underlying statutes, ordinances, or state constitutional provisions pertaining to the formation and operation of the public hospital.[2]

If one or more of these documents conflict with the hospital's desire to participate in the joint venture, it may be sufficient merely to modify its provisions. In other cases, it may be necessary for the hospital to form a separate entity to participate in the joint venture on the hospital's behalf.

Selection of a Legal Structure

Once the business of the joint venture has been identified, one of the first issues that must be addressed is the selection of the legal structure through which the joint venture will operate.

Joint ventures may take a variety of forms, ranging from a simple contract to a business corporation with a complex capital structure.[3] Each of the various possible forms will have its own legal, tax, and financial implications.[4] The form chosen for the venture should be the one that is best suited to facilitate achievement of the objectives of the hospital and physicians; in short, it should work for the venturers and not against them.

Contracts and Leases. A joint venture may consist of little more than a contract or lease between a hospital and a physician or physician group. The terms of the contract or lease might call for the hospital to provide the facilities (such as an ambulatory care center), equipment (such as an MRI scanner), and staff (such as technicians, nurses, and clerical personnel) for the joint venture, while providing for the physicians to perform professional services. Properly drafted contracts and leases can result in the swift implementation of joint ventures that will further the various strategic and business objectives of the participants.

Partnerships and Corporations. Typically, however, the terms of the joint venture will be more complex and will require formation of a separate legal entity, such as a corporation or partnership. Numerous legal and tax considerations are involved in the selection of the corporate or partnership forms generally. In addition, there are numerous variations on the basic corporate and partnership forms, such as general partnerships, limited partnerships, regular corporations, close corporations, and professional corporations, as well as corporations that are taxed as separate entities (C corporations) and corporations that are taxed in a manner similar to partnerships (S corporations). Table 7–1 summarizes and compares attributes of partnerships and corporations.

TABLE 7–1

Tax Attributes of Operations	Tax Attributes of Distributions	Liability	Management
General partnership			
Almost all income and loss passed through to partners at individual rates.	Generally tax-free, since partners taxed on operations.	General liability of all partners.	All partners in management; may be delegated by contract, but delegation doesn't affect liability.

TABLE 7–1 (*concluded*)

Tax Attributes of Operations	Tax Attributes of Distributions	Liability	Management
Limited partnership Almost all income and loss passed through to partners at individual rates.	Generally tax-free. See general partnership.	General liability of general partners; limited partners have limited liability. May limit liability of general partners by using corporate general partner or another limited partnership as general partner, but potential tax problem of limited partnership taxed as a corporation unless done properly.	Only general partners.
C corporation Income or loss taxed at corporate level.	Generally taxed as dividends.	Generally no investor liability; a creditor may pierce corporate veil under certain special circumstances.	Officers subject to direction of board of directors who are elected by shareholders.
Close corporation Income or loss taxed at corporate level.	Generally taxed as dividends.	Generally no investor liability; see C corporation.	Traditional corporate structure of management may be modified by contract; similar to partnership in terms of flexibility.
S corporation Most income and loss generally passed through to shareholders at individual rates; most states tax this entity as a corporation.	Tax-free to shareholders, if previously passed through and taxed to them; difficulties with flexibility (i.e., cannot allocate subordinated returns). Also, no more than 35 shareholders. No shareholder can be a corporation. Basis is better with partnerships, since nonrecourse loans can be basis to take losses against. Allocations of losses between investors also better with partnerships.	Same as other corporations	Same as other corporations

Contractual Issues Affecting Hospitals

Before completing the formation of a joint venture, the parties must carefully review contracts and agreements that might affect or be affected by the joint venture. Hospitals typically have numerous contractual obligations that may have an impact on the terms of the venture, such as those arising under financing agreements, contracts with vendors or suppliers, labor agreements, leases, and contracts with physicians. In addition, hospitals have their own medical staff structures and internal corporate procedures that may affect or be affected by joint ventures.

Financing Covenants. Debt financing has been one of the most commonly used methods of obtaining capital for hospital acquisition, renovation, and expansion. Most public and private financing arrangements will contain positive and negative covenants that will be of critical concern in the structure and financing of many joint ventures. Positive covenants require hospitals to do certain things, such as maintain certain financial ratios, retain tax exempt status, or continue to operate certain programs or services. Negative covenants restrict or prevent hospitals from doing certain things, such as transferring assets, incurring certain types of indebtedness, or selling assets at other than fair market value.

One of the typical negative covenants found in financing documents will be a covenant dealing with additional indebtedness. Debt covenants generally will prohibit a hospital from incurring additional debt, or certain types or classes of additional debt, without compliance with specified procedures and satisfaction of specified financial tests. For example, a debt convenant may affect the ability of a hospital to serve as the general partner of a limited partnership, particularly if the limited partnership will incur indebtedness for which the general partner may be wholly or partially responsible under state law or under agreements entered into by the partnership.

Debt covenants also need to be considered if the hospital will be required to guarantee or provide some other form of credit enhancement for any portion of the indebtedness of the joint venture. For example, if a guarantee is considered additional indebtedness, the hospital should negotiate special treatment for such a guarantee, such as requiring only a percentage of the guaranteed debt to be included in the maximum allowable debt or permitting such guarantees when the hospital has a specified minimum percentage interest in the joint venture, such as 50 percent or more.

Another typical negative covenant is one restricting the transfer of assets. Asset transfer covenants frequently prohibit all transfers of assets without adequate consideration, although some may permit limited transfers of assets, such as a specified percentage of the hospital's net book value, without lender approval. Asset transfer covenants also may restrict or prohibit a hospital from making investments (e.g., capital contributions) in corporations or partnerships the interests in which are not readily marketable. Other transactions affected by such negative covenants may include leases or sales of land or equipment.

Additional types of covenants may require the hospital to operate specific types of services or may limit a hospital's ability to engage in a competing enterprise, even if the hospital is a part owner of the enterprise.

Hospitals that may engage in joint ventures should anticipate these activities when negotiating financing covenants. If a specific joint venture is contemplated, the hospital may be able to exclude the joint venture from the financing covenants. If the hospital does not contemplate a specific joint venture, the hospital still may wish to negotiate sufficiently flexible language to permit it to undertake various joint ventures with limited or no restrictions.

Physician Contracts. Hospitals also have various types of contracts with physicians that may restrict the hospital from directly or indirectly engaging in certain types of joint ventures. For example, the following language, which was contained in a hospital-based radiology contract, quite clearly limits the hospital's ability to engage in a joint venture to develop a magnetic resonance imaging center:

> This Agreement shall be a mutual exclusive agreement for radiology services between XYZ Hospital and the radiologist and shall not be assigned by either party without the written consent of the other. The radiologist shall not establish a practice outside of the hospital without the written consent of the hospital. The hospital shall not establish a radiology practice outside of the hospital utilizing services of other professionals without the written consent of the radiologist.

Observations. The foregoing is by no means an exhaustive list of all of the contracts that may affect or be affected by joint ventures. Certain joint ventures may be affected by other contracts, such as labor agreements, pension plans, PPO and HMO contracts, Hill-Burton obligations, and management contracts. Where appropriate, these contracts should be reviewed and, if they will adversely affect the venture, modified or, if possible, terminated.

Contractual Issues Affecting Physicians

Physicians also are often parties to numerous contractual obligations. Physicians are likely to be employees of professional corporations or otherwise involved in group practices, through which they are subject to employment and other agreements that contain covenants not to compete or business opportunity provisions. Individual physicians and group practices also are likely to have outstanding financial obligations to public and private lenders that may restrict their ability to incur further debt or to assume further obligations. In addition, they may have contractual obligations at other hospitals that will inhibit their ability to perform their joint venture obligations. Participating physicians need to review these contracts early in the formation stage.

Control and Related Issues

In every joint venture, control issues are paramount. It is essential that the hospital and physician venturers each have a clear understanding as to how active each party will be in the management of the joint venture. For example, the active participation of an experienced hospital executive or a physician can be invaluable to the success of the joint venture, while the participation of the wrong person may be equally destructive. Moreover, natural rivalries and insecurities can make control or lack thereof central to the success or failure of a joint venture.

Once the business deal is structured, creativity should be used in tailoring the legal relationships to the objectives of the parties. Clarity of intent is of paramount importance. Those participating in the structuring and negotiating a joint venture should avoid the impulse to overburden the joint venture with unnecessary reporting requirements, positive and negative covenants, and similar restraints.

The form of the joint venture will directly affect the types of control that may be exercised. The form and extent of control generally can be clearly articulated with relative freedom in a contract or a lease. On the other hand, corporations and partnerships will require greater care because control may have liability implications and, in addition, state partnership and corporation laws as well as tax laws may have specific requirements that must be satisfied.

Some of the basic control issues will involve voting rights, selection or removal of the board of directors, management committee representation or observer rights, as well as veto, consultation, or approval rights regarding major decisions, operations issues, fundamental changes, and disposition of assets.

Franchising

Franchising is essentially a system of production and distribution of goods or services. Businesses engaged in franchising had revenues of more than $500 billion in 1985. While traditionally associated with automobile sales and service, gasoline service stations, and fast-food restaurants, franchising techniques are beginning to be used with great frequency in the healthcare field, particularly as restrictions on the use of commercial practices in professions, such as advertising, are being loosened. The types of healthcare franchises already in existence include a variety of franchises for health improvement (such as weight loss), primary and urgent care centers, practice management and advertising for dentists and physicians, referral and marketing services, prepaid dental and health plans, surgery centers, occupational health services, home health services, and nurse registries.[5]

A franchising business usually consists of an organization composed of supporting units that are created and administered by the franchisor in order to expand the production and distribution of products or services of uniform quality, format, and technique. The traditional type of franchise consists primarily of product distribution arrangements in which a franchisee is to some degree identified with a manufacturer's product or supplies. Automobile dealers, gasoline service stations, and soft drink bottlers fall into this category. However, a growing number of franchises are business format franchises. This latter type of franchise is characterized by an ongoing business relationship between the franchisor and the franchisee that includes not only products or services and a trademark but also the entire business format itself. That format may include a marketing strategy and plans, operating manuals and standards, quality control, and continuing two-way communications.[6]

The current level of interest in the use of franchising in the healthcare field may stem, in part, from the increased marketing orientation of the industry. As patients are treated more like customers and are dealt with on a more direct basis, franchising will have a greater appeal to marketing-oriented companies that are capable of building a strong image among consumers.

Knowledge of the scope of franchising laws also is important in order to avoid establishing an inadvertent franchise that may unnecessarily expose the venturers to liability or expensive and time-consuming registration requirements.

Franchise Regulation. Franchising is a significantly regulated method of doing business at both the federal and state levels. The Federal Trade Commission (FTC) has promulgated a regulation entitled "Disclosure Requirements and Prohibitions Concerning Franchising and Business Opportunity Ventures," which became effective on October 21, 1979.[7] California adopted the first statute regulating the offer and sale of franchises in 1970, and since that time 14 other states have adopted registration and/or disclosure statutes. In addition, most states have some type of statute that applies to franchises, such as business opportunity statutes. Consequently, before a hospital or a physician undertakes to use franchising, the FTC rule as well as the laws of the particular state or states in which such franchising business will be conducted need to be reviewed in order to ensure compliance with the applicable regulatory requirements.

The FTC Rule. When the FTC issued its regulations concerning franchises, the stated policy was to ensure that sufficient information, including information generally only available to the seller of franchises, be made available to prospective franchisees to enable them to make intelligent investment decisions as well as to preclude the types of high-pressure tactics that historically had been employed by some franchise salespersons.[8]

Under the FTC rule, a franchise is defined as one of two types of business relationships that generally have certain characteristics in common. The first type of franchise encompasses the traditional type of product and trade name franchise. This type of franchise is identified by the following three characteristics:

1. The franchisee sells goods or services that are supplied by the franchisor or persons affiliated with the franchisor.
2. The franchisor secures accounts for the franchisee or secures locations for sites for vending machines or rack displays or provides the services of a person able to do either.
3. The franchisee is required to make a payment of $500 or more to the

franchisor or a person affiliated with the franchisor within six months after the business opens.

The second type of franchise includes business format franchises. In general, this type of franchise will include an arrangement whereby the "franchisor exercises significant control over, or gives the franchisee significant assistance in the franchisee's method of operation."

Under the FTC rule, a franchisor must give prospective franchisees a disclosure document at the earlier of (*a*) the prospective franchisee's first personal meeting with the franchisor, or (*b*) 10 business days prior to the execution of any agreement, or (*c*) 10 business days before payment of any money by the franchisee to the franchisor.[9]

State Regulation of Franchises. As previously noted, a large percentage of the states have some form of regulation that affects either the offer and sale of a franchise or the relationship between a franchisor and franchisee. Each state must be approached with care to determine the specific requirements applicable to a proposed franchise.

The scope of jurisdiction in each state will depend initially on the particular definition of franchise adopted. Some states have enacted franchise definitions that are directed toward business format franchises. California, the first state to enact a law governing the registration and disclosure of franchise information, defines a "franchise" to mean a contract or agreement between two or more persons by which:

(1) A franchisee is granted the right to engage in the business of offering, selling or distributing goods or services under a marketing plan or system prescribed in substantial part by a franchisor; and

(2) The operation of the franchisee's business pursuant to such plan or system is substantially associated with the franchisor's trademark, service mark, trade name, logotype, advertising or other commercial symbol designating the franchisor or its affiliate; and

(3) The franchisee is required to pay, directly or indirectly, a franchise fee.[10]

Other states have taken a slightly different approach by looking at the community of interest that the franchisor and franchisee have in marketing goods or services and a common identity or appearance. For example, New Jersey, which regulates the relationship between franchisors and franchisees but not offers and sales of franchises, defines a "franchise" to mean:

a written arrangement for a definite or indefinite period, in which a person grants to another person a license to use a trade name, trade mark, service mark, or related characteristics, and in which there is a community of interest in the marketing of goods and services in wholesale, retail, by lease, agreement, or otherwise.[11]

Regardless of the statutory definition of franchise, the states have taken a variety of approaches to regulation of franchises. Although this is a very active area and continual monitoring of state legislation is necessary, the basic types of statutory schemes are described below.

Registration and Disclosure. States that have enacted registration and disclosure statutes require registration of franchises prior to any offer or sale and disclosure of certain prescribed information in a prospectus or offering circular which is delivered to the prospective franchisee within a prescribed period of time before the sale. These laws generally provide for automatic effectiveness of the registration statement for a specified period of time after filing, unless the regulatory body reviewing the registration statement issues an order delaying the effectiveness of such statement.[12]

Disclosure Only. A few states have laws requiring the disclosure of specific information to potential franchisees, but do not require the actual filing of a registration statement with a regulatory body.[13]

Unfair Practices. Roughly one third of the states regulate certain types of unfair trade practices, the definitions of which vary from state to state. These states require neither registration nor any particular disclosure.[14]

Business Opportunities. A large number of states have enacted legislation regulating business opportunity schemes. Although not directed specifically toward franchises, the broad definitions of business opportunities typically will include franchises as well as various other schemes involving manufacturing, sales or distributions of goods, and pyramid sales. These states also often require both registration and disclosure.[15]

Observations. Franchising is an effective and growing means of economic participation for a host of players in the healthcare industry, from individual physicians to multi-institutional healthcare systems aggressively pursuing diversification or market development. The advantages of sharing the knowledge of successful systems with those who have neither the resources nor the experience to develop their own are numerous and give franchising its vitality and relevance to the healthcare field.

Designing, implementing, and maintaining a successful franchise system is a significant undertaking. As healthcare professionals and organizations turn to franchising, increased attention will have to be paid to the complex and extensive federal and state rules and regulations governing the offer and sale of franchises and the relations between franchisors and franchisees.[16]

Certificate of Need and Section 1122 of the Social Security Act

Legislation in most states requires a certificate of need (CON) in order to establish or substantially expand certain healthcare facilities. The required approval is based on various criteria such as need, financial feasibility, impact on other healthcare providers, and access by indigents to the proposed services. In addition, Section 1122 of the Social Security Act requires approval of certain types of capital expenditures in those states under contract with the Health Care Financing Administration.

Health planning and capital expenditure regulation have been undergoing dramatic changes throughout the United States during the past five years. Some states are deregulating and have repealed, allowed to expire, or reduced the scope of their certificate of need laws. For example, CON laws were never enacted or have expired in Arizona, Idaho, Louisiana, Minnesota, New Mexico, and Utah. Capital expenditure reviews are performed under Section 1122 of the Social Security Act in each of those states except Utah and Arizona. Several other states have raised one or more CON review thresholds above the federal maximum levels. Other states, such as California, have substantially reduced the scope of projects covered by their CON laws and have increased expenditure thresholds.

While some states are in a deregulatory mode, others are expanding the scope of CON laws and several have imposed moratoriums on the granting of CONs. For example, Maine and Rhode Island have enacted capital expenditure legislation, and in Ohio a moratorium on all CON applications expired on July 1, 1984, and a revised CON law allowing the imposition of unrelated conditions on CON approvals was implemented. Recently, a bill providing for a two-year moratorium on new hospital beds and new construction in Tennessee was defeated.[17]

Joint ventures may be affected by CON laws in several ways. First, a number of states apply CON regulations to projects that are not sponsored by hospitals. For example, most states require a CON for freestanding ambulatory surgery centers. However, some states, such as California and Ohio, exempt from CON requirements surgery centers operated as physicians' offices.[18]

Second, a small number of states require CON review for some or all of the capital expenditures for diagnostic equipment. In Montana, for example, any service proposed to be offered by a physician is reviewable if the service would be reviewable if offered by a hospital.[19] In Missouri, purchases of major medical equipment require a CON regardless of ownership.[20]

Finally, a growing number of states are attempting to control the development of alternative delivery systems, such as freestanding emergency treatment centers. Ohio, for example, requires CON approval for freestanding emergency facilities. The Ohio CON law defines such facilities as any facility, other than a hospital-based emergency department, that accepts patients from ambulatory delivery on a regular basis, employs the word *emergency* or a derivative thereof in its name or title, or otherwise holds itself out as accepting or treating life or limb threatening conditions.[21] Vermont goes even further and requires CON review if the facility includes a service or facility beyond those of a "normal" physician's office.[22]

Regulation of Securities

The offer and sale of interests in joint ventures often involve the offer and sale of securities. If an interest in a joint venture is deemed a security, it becomes subject to comprehensive regulatory and disclosure provisions of the federal Securities Act of 1933 (1933 Act) and, frequently, the provisions of the Securities Exchange Act of 1934 (1934 Act).[23] Under the 1933 Act, it is illegal without an exemption for any person, directly or indirectly, to use interstate commerce or the mails to offer or sell a security unless a registration statement has been filed with the Securities and Exchange Commission (SEC) and has become effective.[24]

Security Defined. The term *security* is defined very broadly under Section 2(1) of the 1933 Act.[25] The definition includes "stock," "investment contract," and "participation in any profit sharing arrangement," as well as other security instruments.

Of critical importance in the joint venture context is that the term *security* is defined in sufficiently broad and general terms so as to include many types of investments and financial transactions that may be involved in the development of a hospital-physician joint venture. Indeed, in the landmark case of *SEC v. W. J. Howey Co.*,[26] the United States Supreme Court held that the test of whether a particular contract, transaction, or scheme constitutes an "investment contract," within the definition of security in Section 2(1) of the 1933 Act, "is whether the scheme involves an investment of money in a common enterprise with profits to come solely from the efforts of others."[27] The Court elaborated on the test by stating that "[i]f that test be satisfied, it is immaterial whether the enterprise is speculative or non-speculative or whether there is a sale of property with or without intrinsic value."[28]

Stock. One of the most obvious types of securities is stock of a corporation. Unless there are unusual circumstances, it generally should be assumed that common or preferred stock of an incorporated joint venture will constitute securities and thus will be subject to the registration, fraud, and other pertinent provisions of the 1933 and 1934 Acts. Nevertheless, there may be circumstances in which stock issued by a business or not-for-profit corporation will not be treated as a security for purposes of the 1933 and 1934 Acts.

In *United Housing Foundation, Inc.* v. *Forman*,[29] the United States Supreme Court dealt with the question of whether shares of stock in a nonprofit housing cooperative were securities within the meaning of the 1933 and 1934 Acts. In reaching its decision, the Court quoted the following principle from an earlier case:

> [I]n searching for the meaning and scope of the word "security" in the Act[s], form should be disregarded for substance and the emphasis should be on economic reality.[30]

In *United Housing Foundation, Inc.* v. *Forman*, the Supreme Court held that shares of common stock in a cooperative housing project, which were required to be purchased by tenants in the housing project, did not constitute "stock" within the meaning of Section 2(1) of the 1933 Act because the shares did not possess the characteristics traditionally associated with stock.[31] The

Court also addressed the question of whether the shares constituted an "investment contract" within the meaning of Section 2(1). In applying the *Howey* test, the Court said:

> The touchstone is the presence of an investment in a common venture premised on a reasonable expectation of profits to be derived from the entrepreneurial or managerial efforts of others. By profits, the Court has meant either capital appreciation resulting from the development of the initial investment, . . . or a participation in earnings resulting from the use of investors' funds. . . . In such cases the investor is "attracted solely by the prospects of a return" on his investment. . . . By contrast, when a purchaser is motivated by a desire to use or consume the item purchased—"to occupy the land or to develop it themselves," . . . the securities laws do not apply.[32]

The Court concluded that, although the tenants had a remote possibility of rental reduction through their ownership of the common stock, there was not an "expectation of profit" in the sense found necessary in *Howey*. Therefore, since the purchasers of stock in the cooperative merely sought to obtain inexpensive housing, the shares of stock were not "investment contracts" within the meaning of Section 2(1). In short, in *United Housing Foundation, Inc.* v. *Forman,* the Court rejected a literal interpretation of the definition of security in favor of one that "turn[s] on the economic realities underlying a transaction, and not on the name appended thereto."[33]

The SEC has issued two no-action letters concerning the question of whether securities were involved in two hospital-physician joint ventures.[34] In the first no-action letter, a hospital and members of its medical staff planned to form a corporation that would become associated with a preferred provider organization (PPO).[35] Although the PPO itself would be a wholly owned subsidiary of the hospital, a separate business corporation would be formed to select the physician providers and evaluate their performance in the program. A stock corporation owned by the physician providers had been determined to be the most appropriate form of organization to perform the functions of selecting physician providers and evaluating their performance, because it would enable the physician providers to exercise control over the corporation's leadership and policies and, unlike other forms of organization, would limit the liability of each physician provider for the acts of other providers. Stock would be sold to active members of the hospital staff who would enter into physician provider agreements with the corporation. The stock would be subject to restrictions of transferability, and the bylaws would prohibit dividends from being paid. Each physician provider would be offered one share of stock at a nominal price, and expenses of the corporation would be paid from interest on the proceeds from the sale of the stock plus annual administrative fees paid by physician providers. Neither the corporation nor the ownership of its shares would be held out as a financial investment or profit-making venture. Based on these representations, the SEC staff said that it would not recommend any enforcement action to the Commission if the corporation sold its stock without registration in the manner described on the ground that the shares of stock were not "securities" within the meaning of the 1933 Act.

The SEC has also issued a no-action letter concerning a "medical staff–hospital joint venture known as a MeSH organization."[36] MeSH Central, Inc., was proposed to be organized as a general business corporation under Missouri law. Fifty percent of the stock would be purchased by the hospital and 50 percent would be sold to physicians. Each participating physician would be required to purchase one share of stock for $500, with a possible assessment of $500. The SEC staff agreed that the MeSH's stock was not required to be registered under the 1933 Act because the shares would not have the usual attributes of stock. Counsel asserted that "shareholders in MeSH Central, Inc. will neither be entitled to capital appreciation resulting from the developing of the initial investment, nor to a participation in earnings resulting from the use of investor funds." In granting no-action relief, the staff noted particularly that the stock in the MeSH could be resold only to the corporation at its original cost; if the corporation was liquidated or dissolved, the stock would be redeemed at cost and any excess funds would be used for charitable purposes; no dividends would be paid on the stock. It is significant to note, however, that the no-action letter specifically stated that individual ventures sponsored by MeSH Central, Inc. could be treated as involving the offer or sale of securities and would therefore be subject to the securities laws.

Memberships. Hospital-physician joint ventures sometimes are formed using not-for-profit membership corporations as the vehicle through which the joint venture will be conducted. In such cases, memberships are issued to the hospital and the physicians evidencing their rights to voting and other matters pertaining to the corporation. Memberships in not-for-profit corporations may constitute securities, depending on the particular facts surrounding their issuance and the nature of the operations of the not-for-profit corporation itself. Although the SEC has not specifically dealt with this question in the context of hospital-physician joint ventures, the SEC has considered the issue of whether memberships constitute securities in other contexts, particularly memberships in not-for-profit corporations formed solely for social or recreational purposes such as country clubs and health clubs.

In those cases where membership conferred no rights to income or profits of the club but merely conferred the right to use the club facilities after payment of membership fees and dues, the SEC staff has concluded that such memberships would not be securities for purposes of the 1933 Act.[37] In such cases, the SEC has frequently stated that, "[i]n arriving at this position, we have noted particularly that: (1) the memberships are not transferable or assignable with the exception of repurchases by [the club] from members at a price equal to such members' original purchase price, and (2) members will not share in the profits or losses of the club."[38] On the other hand, in those instances where the club proposed to issue memberships that could be transferred for profit, the SEC has been unable to conclude that the memberships might not be deemed to be securities.[39]

Limited Partnerships. Interests in limited partnerships will in almost every instance be regarded as securities for purposes of the 1933 Act.[40] In most cases in which a limited partnership will be used for a hospital-physician joint venture, the purpose of the limited partnership will be to operate a business or acquire assets and to derive profits from such business or assets that will accrue to the limited partners.

General Partnerships and Joint Ventures. Interests in general partnerships and joint ventures also may constitute securities when the purchasers of the interests are expected to be passive investors and control is vested in persons other than the investor. As stated by the Fifth Circuit in *Williamson* v. *Tucker*, "The mere fact that an investment takes the form of a general partnership or joint venture does not inevitably insulate it from the reach of the federal securities laws."[41]

Other Arrangements. The scope of the definition of a security can be quite broad, particularly when it involves the raising of funds to be managed by a third party for profit. Thus, contracts, leases, and similar types of arrangements may be treated as securities depending on the particular context.

Federal Registration and Exemptions. Due to the time and expense involved, offerings of joint venture securities are usually structured to avoid the federal registration requirements. If, however, registration is required or desired (e.g., to create a public market for the securities), registrations may take place on Form S-1 or Form S-18 (maximum $7.5 million). Failure to register securities when required can have severe consequences, including giving rise to a right of rescission, damages, and other civil and criminal penalties.

In practice, the offer and sale of securities in most joint ventures are structured to qualify for exemption from registration under one of several transaction exemptions generally available to joint ventures issuing their own securities:

1. The intrastate exemption found in Section 3(a)(11) of the 1933 Act and in SEC Rule 147 thereunder.
2. The private offering exemption found in Section 4(2) of the 1933 Act and in SEC Rule 506 thereunder.
3. The small offering exemptions found in Sections 3(b) and 4(6) of the 1933 Act and in SEC Rules 504 and 505 and Regulation A thereunder.

In order to be eligible for the intrastate exemption under Section 3(a)(11), noncorporate joint venture issuers, such as general and limited partnerships, must be residents of, and corporate issuers must be incorporated within, the state in which *all* potential *offerees* reside. If an offer is made to even one out-of-state resident, the exemption will be denied. In addition, the joint venture issuer must be "doing business" and, under Rule 147, at least 80 percent of the financing proceeds must be used in the state. Section 3(a)(11) offerings are not limited as to size, nor do they require any specific disclosures of information.[42]

Section 4(2) of the 1933 Act exempts from registration "transactions by an issuer not involving any public offering" of securities.[43] Section 4(2) does not define when a nonpublic offering of securities occurs, and thus the courts have looked at various factors such as the number and sophistication of the offerees, the information available to offerees, the relationship between the offeror and the offerees, the method used to market the securities, and other factors to ascertain whether a nonpublic offering is involved.[44]

The SEC has issued Rule 506 of Regulation D pursuant to section 4(2).[45] Under Rule 506, the issuer can sell its securities to an unlimited number of accredited investors and to not more than 35 unaccredited investors. An accredited investor, defined in Rule 501, is generally a person with a substantial income or net worth who has or has access to advisers with knowledge and expertise on financial matters. Rule 506 also specifies the type of information that must be provided to a prospective investor and prohibits the use of general advertising to solicit purchasers.

Under Section 3(b) of the 1933 Act, the SEC is empowered to exempt from registration transactions with an aggregate public offering price of up to $5 million. Pursuant to this authority, the SEC has promulgated, and there currently are in effect, Regulation A (Rules 251 through 264),[46] Rules 504 and 505 of Regulation D,[47] and other rules not generally relevant to joint ventures.

Under Regulation A, corporate issuers of securities, which have their principal business operations in the United States or Canada, can make public offerings of securities without registration 10 days after the filing with the appropriate regional office of the SEC of an offering statement on Form 1-A. Regulation A also contains provisions modeled on the "tombstone ad," preliminary prospectus, and postoffering reporting rules. Regulation A also provides that no offering circular is required with respect to an offering of not more than $100,000 by a nonpromotional company, except for filing (not the use) of the nonfinancial information normally required in an offering circular.

The Rule 504 exemption is available to all issuer offerings other than an offering by a reporting company or an investment company. Accordingly, it can be used by most types of hospital-physician joint ventures. Under Rule 504, the amount of the offering during a 12-month period is limited to $500,000. There is no limitation on the number of shareholders of the issuer upon completion of the offering or restrictions on the payment of commissions. Nor does Rule 504 require the use of a specific disclosure document, although there may be a disclosure requirement under applicable state laws.

Rule 505 can be utilized for offerings by an issuer including, among others, corporations and limited partnerships. Under Rule 505, an issuer cannot raise more than $5 million during a 12-month period. Under Rule 505, an offering can be made to an unlimited number of offerees provided there are no more than 35 nonaccredited investors. In calculating the number of nonaccredited investors, a corporation, partnership, or other entity is counted as one purchaser unless it organized for the specific purpose of acquiring the securities being offered, in which event each beneficial owner of an equity interest is counted.

Finally, Section 4(6) of the 1933 Act provides an exemption from registration for transactions involving offers or sales by an issuer solely to one or more accredited investors if the aggregate offering price of an issue of securities offered in reliance on Section 4(6) does not exceed $5 million, if there is no advertising or public solicitation in connection with the transaction by the issuer or anyone acting on the issuers behalf, and if a notice is filed with the SEC.[48] Generally speaking, Section 4(6) is not likely to be used when compliance with one of the other exemptions is available.

State Regulation of Securities. In addition to federal regulations, every state and the District of Columbia regulate transactions in securities pursuant to "blue sky laws." State registration requirements and exemptions from registration typically will be of great significance in the joint venture context inasmuch as most joint venture offerings will be structured to qualify for one or more exemptions from federal registration.

There are many differences between state and federal securities laws that an issuer must take into account in connection with a hospital-physician joint venture. First, despite the use of language defining a "security" that is very similar to the federal definition, most states have adopted minor, and in some cases major, variations from this definition.[49] Second, even as to those aspects of the federal definition of securities that have been adopted by the states, there may be significant differences in interpretation. For example, while the United States Supreme Court held that an interest in a cooperative apartment complex represented by a "stock certificate" did not constitute a security within the meaning of the federal securities laws,[50] the state courts have generally not moved in this direction and are likely to treat any transfer for value of an interest in a corporation represented by a stock certificate as involving a sale of securities.

Another major difference between the state and federal securities laws has to do with the application of the registration provisions. The federal acts are only directed toward the original distribution of securities, that is, when the issuer sells them to the first purchaser. Under the state securities acts, however, a registration must be effected or an exemption must be found each time the security is sold.[51] In other words, the federal laws are designed to deal with the primary or first distribution of securities, while the state securities acts regulate both the initial distribution of and the secondary market in securities.

State blue sky laws fall into two general classifications, disclosure and merit. Disclosure statutes generally require promoters to give full disclosure of all material facts to investors on the theory that investors are capable of protecting themselves if given sufficient information.[52] Merit statutes seek to determine whether or not the offering is "fair, just, and equitable" to investors before an issuer is allowed to offer or sell the securities to the public on the theory that investments in securities entail a degree of business knowledge and expertise that most investors do not possess.[53]

Every state securities law requires the registration of securities offered or sold in that state with the state's division or department of securities. As with the federal securities laws, however, state securities laws often exempt certain types of transactions in securities from their registration requirements. Approximately one half of the states and the District of Columbia have adopted exemptions compatible with Rules 505 and 506 of Regulation D. Consequently, offerings of securities made in reliance on the Rule 505 or 506 federal exemption have an appropriate exemption in such states. Approximately eight states have exemptions based on the number of purchasers within the state over a specified period of time, generally 12 months. Approximately 11 states exempt only those offerings of securities made in compliance with the Rule 506 exemption. A small number of states grant exemptions for offers to limited numbers of persons or limit their exemptions to isolated transactions.[54]

Fraud and Other Liabilities.   Whether an offer or sale of securities is registered or exempt from federal and/or state securities laws, issuers still have the responsibility not to offer or sell a security by means of material fraudulent misstatements or omissions. Numerous provisions of the 1933 and 1934 Acts and of state securities acts impose liability on issuers of securities and those who participate in the issuance of securities.[55] Because of their disclosure responsibilities, issuers of joint venture interests relying on exemptions routinely prepare disclosure documents in the form of private placement memoranda or offering circulars even if not otherwise required by statute or regulation.

Broker-Dealer Regulation.   Hospitals and physicians that issue or participate in the issuance of securities of joint ventures need to be aware of the federal and state broker-dealer registration or licensing requirements.[56]

In order to operate as a broker or dealer under federal law, a firm must first register with the SEC. Indeed, it is unlawful to effect transactions in securities unless registered or exempt from registration. If a firm must be registered, the 1934 Act requires, with certain exceptions, brokers and dealers to be members of the National Association of Securities Dealers and compliance with both the regulations promulgated under the 1934 Act and the rules of the National Association of Securities Dealers.

In practice, the sponsors of hospital-physician joint ventures will qualify for the intrastate or issuer exemptions from the federal broker-dealer registration requirements. However, state blue sky laws generally prohibit transacting business in a particular state as a "broker-dealer" or as an "agent." Frequently, sponsors of joint ventures will qualify for an "issuer" exemption from state broker-dealer registration at least with respect to a limited number of joint venture offerings. In others registration will be required, and those persons selling joint venture interest will have to be licensed as securities salesmen.

Civil and criminal penalties are applicable where a sponsor of a joint venture is required but fails to register or become licensed to sell securities. These can include injunctions, criminal sanctions, damage suits, and contract recissions through actions instituted by the SEC, the U.S. Department of Justice, state securities regulators, or private parties to the transactions.

Ethical Considerations

An important and frequently raised issue that needs to be addressed in the organizational phase is whether participation in the joint venture will comply with the ethical requirements of various state and national professional organizations. These issues are discussed in more depth in Chapter 6.

The Judicial Council of the American Medical Association has concluded that a physician may own or have a financial interest in health facilities, such as a freestanding surgery center or emergency clinic, but imposes on the physician an affirmative ethical obligation to disclose the fact of his ownership interest to his patient prior to admission or utilization.[57]

The AMA House of Delegates at its 1984 annual meeting adopted a board report on "Physician Conflict of Interest" and asked the Judicial Council to develop guidelines relating to conflict of interest with emphasis on disclosure of ownership of health facilities. In December 1984, the Judicial Council presented Report C, which sets forth conflict guidelines. The following is excerpted from that report.

> The Judicial Council has long been concerned with ethical issues relating to conflict of interest. The Judicial Council's opinions on *Health Facility Ownership by Physician* (4.04), *Fee Splitting* (6.03), *Drugs and Devices: Prescribing* (8.06), and *Laboratory Services* (8.08) embody the basic principles relating to the resolution of conflicts of interest faced by physicians. The Judicial Council has long recognized that a physician who derives economic benefits from commercial ventures involving his or her patients has an interest that potentially may conflict with the physician's practice of medicine and service of the patient's medical interests. *It is unethical for a physician to use his fiduciary relationship to abuse, exploit, or deceive the patient for the physician's personal gain, including profit from a commercial venture.*
>
> *Physician ownership interest in a commercial venture with the potential for abuse is not in itself unethical.* Physicians are free to enter lawful contractual relationships, including the acquisition of ownership interests in health facilities or equipment or pharmaceuticals. However, the potential conflict of interest must be addressed by the following:
>
> > (1) the physician has an affirmative ethical obligation to disclose to the patient or referring colleagues his or her ownership interest in the facility or therapy prior to utilization;
> >
> > (2) the physician may not exploit the patient in any way, as by *inappropriate* or *unnecessary utilization;*
> >
> > (3) the physician's activities must be in *strict conformance* with the law;

(4) the patient should have *free choice* either to use the physician's proprietary facility or therapy or to seek the needed medical services elsewhere; and

(5) when a physician's commercial interest conflicts so greatly with the patient's interest as to be incompatible, the physician should make alternative arrangements for the care of the patient.[58]

At the 1984 interim meeting of the AMA, a resolution on joint ventures was debated that would require joint ventures to be done with the approval of the voting medical staff, with each physician on the medical staff having the opportunity to participate in the venture. The resolution also addressed other concerns and was referred to the AMA Board of Trustees for further study.

State medical societies have generally adopted the AMA position, although each state society should be consulted concerning its particular position.

Special Problems of Public Hospitals

Public hospitals and affiliated institutions must take into account a variety of legal issues in the development of joint ventures that are applicable specifically to public hospitals. This section discusses many of these issues in a brief fashion. It should be noted, however, that as with other issues raised in this chapter, specific reference must be made to state law.

Sovereign Immunity. The common and statutory law governing sovereign immunity for tort actions, its waiver and the limitations on it is in disarray and confusion in many states. Several states have completely eliminated sovereign immunity, making public hospitals liable for tort actions. Others, such as Florida, provide for limited sovereign immunity from liability from personal injuries which is available to the state and its "agencies or subdivisions."[59] Even in Florida, however, the status of public hospitals is the subject of current litigation before the Florida Supreme Court.[60]

In those states which continue to have a doctrine of sovereign immunity, it is unlikely that the protection offered by that doctrine could be extended to a separate joint venture, whether it is a partnership or corporation.

Gift of Public Funds. Another state constitutional doctrine frequently raised in connection with joint ventures is the prohibition against the loan, gift, or use of the funds or credit of public hospitals. A few states, such as Oklahoma, interpret the gift of public funds prohibition quite restrictively, using it to place severe restraints on the extent to which public hospitals can engage in joint ventures.[61] On the other hand, several states, such as Florida and California, have concluded, both judicially through case law and legislatively by statute, that certain "public purpose" exceptions to the prohibition should be recognized.[62] Thus, in these states public hospitals are permitted to enter into certain transactions with nongovernmental entities as long as a public purpose is served.

The potential application of the gift of public funds prohibition to joint ventures may arise in a number of different circumstances. Clearly, a loan or outright transfer of funds to a joint venture may fall under such prohibition.[63] In addition, if a public hospital serves as a general partner of a general or limited partnership and as a result assumes unlimited liability for debts and liabilities of the partnership, it could be deemed to be extending the credit of the public entity.[64] Further, loan guarantees and similar forms of credit enhancement also may be deemed to be an improper extension of credit by the public hospital to the joint venture.

Stock Ownership Prohibition. A majority of the states also have enacted prohibitions against the ownership of stock in business corporations.[65] In some instances, it is not entirely clear whether or not this would extend to an equity ownership interest in an unincorporated joint venture, such as a general or limited partnership.

Open Meeting Laws. A number of states have enacted open meeting or "sunshine" laws that require public entities to conduct meetings at which official actions are to be taken in the open and frequently state that actions taken at meetings that do not comply with the sunshine law will not be considered binding. The Florida Supreme Court, for example, has observed that the Florida government in the sunshine law is to be construed "so as to frustrate all evasive devices," noting that "the Legislature intended to extend application of the 'open meeting' concept so as to bind every 'board or commission' of the state, or of any country or political subdivision over which it has dominion or control."[66]

The application of sunshine laws to joint ventures will undoubtedly require a careful analysis of the degree of ownership retained directly or indirectly by the public entity, the advisory or decisional capacity with respect to the joint venture that is maintained by the public entity, the relationship of the activities undertaken by the joint venture to the public entity's public purposes, and whether, taken together, the characteristics of the joint venture indicate that it is subject to the dominion and control of the public entity.

Public Records Law. A number of states have also enacted public records laws, providing that all documents made in connection with the transaction of the official business of a state agency must be open to the public. Many states have suggested that public records laws comprehend all private corporations acting "on behalf of" any public agency in addition to governmental units. Factors affecting the applicability of the public records requirements to joint venturers may include (1) whether the joint venture performs a governmental function, (2) the level of governmental funding, (3) the extent of governmental involvement or regulation, and (4) whether the joint venture was sponsored by the public hospital.

Geographical Restrictions. Many public hospitals are subject to geographical restrictions on their operations arising from the state legislation creating them. These restrictions might serve not only to prohibit the location of facilities outside the geographical confines set forth in the enabling legislation, but also may prohibit a public hospital from participating in some joint ventures, such as HMOs, PPOs, or other alternative delivery systems that are located in or draw their patients from areas beyond the identified boundaries.

Procurement Procedures. Public hospitals generally must comply with certain statutory procedures in the procurement of certain supplies, equipment, facilities, and construction contracts. While these requirements are intended to encourage purchases at competitive prices, the procedures themselves can at times result in needless delay and complexity when decisions must be made quickly to meet market conditions.

Observations. Public hospitals are subjected to many of the same environmental pressures as nonpublic hospitals, whether for-profit or not-for-profit. Many public hospitals are already developing strategies that focus on broadening their role from that of providing inpatient care and passively financing indigent care to developing new products, marketing, providing a full range of services, and financing health care services with an assumption and management of the economic risk. When these activities involve the establishment of joint ventures, careful attention must be paid to the special rules applicable to public hospitals.

THE OPERATIONAL PHASE OF A JOINT VENTURE

Once the joint venture vehicle has been selected, contractual terms and conditions have been negotiated, and purchase or construction of necessary facilities and equipment has been completed, it will be necessary to address several regulatory and legal issues that will affect the operation and financing of the joint venture.

Licensure Requirements

Activities undertaken by joint ventures often are subject to state licensing statutes applicable to hospitals as well as those applicable to freestanding entities. Licensing statutes generally regulate the character and competence of the provider and its staff, its financial resources, the fitness and adequacy of the facility, its medical or technical personnel, and its procedures. The activity of the joint venture therefore must be analyzed to determine whether separate licensure is required, whether the activity can be conducted under a hospital's license, whether the activity can be conducted under a physician's license, or whether the activity can be conducted without a license.

If a license is required by state law, compliance with the licensing requirements may be necessary in order to receive payment under certain types of payment and reimbursement programs. For example, if an ambulatory surgery center must be licensed under state law, the Medicare program will require the ambulatory surgery center to be licensed as a condition of obtaining Medicare reimbursement for a facility charge. On the other hand, if an ambulatory surgery center is not required to be licensed under state law, then no license will be required by the Medicare program.[67]

In other instances, even if the activity of the joint venture is not required to be licensed, the venture may not be eligible for payment unless it obtains a license. In California, for example, the Medi-Cal (Medicaid) program will not pay a facility charge to *unlicensed* ambulatory surgery centers, even though ambulatory surgery centers operated as physicians' offices are exempt from license requirements.[68] Similarly, insurance companies and other private payors may not pay facility charges to unlicensed facilities.

Many types of hospital-physician joint ventures will be subject to licensing requirements. For example, laboratories, pharmacies, and home health agencies generally will be subject to separate licensing requirements. In addition, most states will require the licensure of freestanding ambulatory surgery centers.[69] A few states, however, such as California and Ohio, exempt freestanding ambulatory surgery centers from licensure if such centers are operated as physicians' offices.[70]

In a growing number of states, freestanding emergency care facilities also must be licensed. For example, Connecticut requires that freestanding emergency care facilities be licensed and defines such facilities as:

[A]n establishment, place or facility which may be a public or private organization, structurally distinct and separate from a hospital, staffed, equipped, operated, and identified for the public to provide prompt emergency medical care.[71]

Payment for Services

The most important issue arising in the operating stage of a joint venture is how the joint venture will be paid for the services that it renders. Payment for services (technical, facility, and/or professional) rendered by joint ventures will affect decisions such as the type of entity to be selected, the nature of the participants, financial feasibility, the possible legal relationships between and among the participants, and numerous other issues. Indeed, every joint venture must be structured to take into account the availability and requirements of various governmental and private payment systems.

Ambulatory Surgery. The Medicare program will pay physicians 100 percent of reasonable charges for services in an ambulatory surgery center if assignment is accepted but only 80 percent of reasonable charges for hospital-based surgery. In addition, ambulatory surgery centers will be paid a facility fee if they meet the conditions of coverage and have entered into an agreement with the Health Care Financing Administration. Hospital-based ambulatory surgery centers are eligible for reasonable cost reimbursement. In addition, freestanding ambulatory surgery centers (including hospital-based ASCs) are eligible to be paid a predetermined facility charge that will vary depending on the category into which the procedure falls.[72] Thus, the structure of the surgery center joint venture will dictate the availability of this form of payment.

The Medicaid programs in many states also have developed payment schedules that favor treatment in ambulatory surgery centers. In some cases, those programs will only pay for certain procedures that are performed in a qualified ambulatory surgery center.

Finally, Blue Cross and Blue Shield plans and other insurance companies have developed their own payment systems for ambulatory surgery. The programs vary widely in regard to their conditions of participation, covered procedures, and other requirements. In certain states, such as Michigan, ambulatory surgery joint ventures are not feasible due to the inability of physician-owned ambulatory surgery centers to obtain Blue Cross reimbursement for facility charges.[73]

Other Services.   Third-party payment for services provided in other types of freestanding healthcare facilities appears to vary from state to state (and in some cases from city to city), depending on whether the payor is the employer or insurer, and depends greatly on the laws of the states. Payors may create additional conditions for payment such as Medicare participation, accreditation, or affiliation with a hospital. Restrictions may also be placed on certain services or procedures provided in the freestanding setting. State laws and regulations may even require the facilities to go through a certificate of need process. The physician's fee, however, is usually paid regardless of where the care is provided.

As of this writing, ambulatory care centers, emergency care centers, and urgent care centers typically accept cash or credit cards only and are not eligible for a separate facility charge. Payment for professional, technical, or facility charges provided by other types of joint ventures, such as diagnostic imaging, home health, radiation therapy, and cardiac catheterization laboratories, is often complex and will depend on the legal relationship of the joint venture to a hospital or to the physicians.

Quality Assurance and Peer Review

Joint ventures involving the provision of medical services need to have appropriate mechanisms in place for quality assurance and peer review. In some instances, a quality assurance and peer review program will be required by licensing laws or as a condition of participation in a third-party payment program.[74] In addition, having such a mechanism will help protect the joint venture from liability for harm resulting to patients for negligence or mistakes of physicians who practice at the facility and will enable the entity to prevent or remove from practice at the facility physicians who are disruptive or unqualified.

The potential liability of the joint venture for the actions of physicians who use its facility is a logical extension of a number of cases holding hospitals liable under the theory of corporate liability. The same logic supporting liability in the case of hospitals is likely to be applied to facilities such as freestanding ambulatory surgery centers, primary care centers, and other types of hospital-physician joint ventures.

There are numerous issues that must be taken into account in establishing a quality assurance and peer review program. These include:

1. The "fair procedure" requirements (similar to but not quite as strong as due process) imposed on hospitals by case law because of the importance of the right to practice in a hospital to a physician's professional livelihood would probably not be applicable to freestanding surgery centers, imaging centers, and similar types of hospital-physician joint ventures. At some point in time, however, these protections might be extended to such entities. In any case, the rule that is almost certain to be applicable to these types of joint ventures is that, as private associations, such entities must at least follow their own rules in denying membership or access or when revoking or limiting privileges.

2. Another significant issue will be the protection of confidentiality of peer review or quality assurance actions. Unlike hospitals and medical societies, there do not appear to be any states that have extended such confidentiality to the deliberations conducted by joint ventures.

3. Joint ventures appear to have no responsibility to provide information to licensing agencies, nor do they appear to have the opportunity to obtain information from licensing agencies concerning physicians. Again, however, the laws of a specific state will govern and should be consulted to ascertain the status of the law.

Corporate Practice of Medicine and Division of Fees

Two recurring and interrelated issues that arise in considering various structures for organizing and operating a joint venture are:

1. Whether or not the structure or method of operation raises corporate practice of medicine questions.
2. Whether or not the structure or method of operation would result in an improper division of fees received for medical services rendered.

Corporate Practice of Medicine.   Almost every state has a rule against the "corporate practice of medicine." The basis for the rule is the general concept that the practice of medicine is a profession that can only be served by a natural person duly licensed by the state. Where the corporate practice of medicine doctrine exists, it is usually applied for the stated purpose of preventing control over professional judgment, commercial exploitation or other dominance of the professional practice and the consequent lowering of professional standards, and the division of loyalty of the professional practitioner.

The corporate practice of medicine originated in the formative years of the medical profession:

The other form of business involvement in medical care, the sale of services of to public, was known as the "corporate practice" of medicine, and it developed on an even more limited scale. A series of legal decisions shortly after the turn of the century effectively precluded the emergence of profit-making medical care corporations in most jurisdictions. Between 1905 and 1917, courts in several states ruled that corporations could not engage in the commercial practice of medicine, even if they employed licensed physicians, on the grounds that a corporation could not be licensed to practice and that commercialism in medicine violated "sound public policy." These decisions were not models of rigorous legal reasoning. They were not applied to the employment of company doctors nor to for-profit hospitals, where the logic of the argument should have carried them. Yet no one made much of a fuss. Respectable opinion did not favor "commercialism" in medicine.[75]

This perhaps outdated doctrine continues to be recognized in a number of states and has significant implications for hospital-physician joint ventures in those states.

The practice of medicine by a corporation for profit, other than a professional corporation, is prohibited expressly by statute in a few states.[76] In those states, the acts of a physician employee would be deemed to be acts of the corporate employer.[77]

Many hospitals, clinics, and universities throughout the United States operate as not-for-profit corporations and employ salaried physicians. In several states, not-for-profit corporations often are exempted from the general prohibition against the corporate practice of medicine either by statute or by practice.[78] Other states make no distinction between not-for-profit and for-profit corporations.[79] The Ohio attorney general, for example, has repeatedly and unequivocally stated that "[i]t has been well settled in Ohio that a corporation whether organized for profit or not for profit, may not engage in the practice of medicine."[80] Certain other states have hinted at limited, but ambiguous, exceptions for nonprofit organizations in their court decisions and attorney general opinions.[81]

In the context of contractual joint ventures, the corporate practice of medicine may arise if the compensation payable to the physician for professional services is either fixed, such as an hourly rate, or is based on a percentage of net earnings or net income. If compensation is fixed, the physician may be regarded as an employee; if it is based on net earnings or income, the physician may be deemed to be a joint venturer with the for-profit or not-for-profit corporation.[82] In either case, the corporation could be deemed to be unlawfully engaged in the practice of medicine. To avoid this problem, the compensation formulas in many contractual joint ventures are structured as percentages of gross revenues, net revenues, or gross collections, adjusted only for certain items such as contractual allowances and bad debts. While it is difficult to generalize, many joint ventures structured in this manner should pass corporate practice of medicine scrutiny as long as the compensation paid to the joint venture is reasonably commensurate with the value of the goods, services, facilities, or equipment provided to the physician.[83]

While the corporate practice of medicine prohibition is largely unenforced in many states, it must be recognized that severe sanctions may be imposed on violators. The violation of a state licensing statute is usually a criminal offense, and sanctions may be imposed against the physicians as well as the corporate and partnership joint ventures involved with physicians. In addition, a physician may, in many cases, have his license revoked or suspended.

Finally, it should be noted that in many states the corporate practice of medicine doctrine frequently has been extended to other licensed health professionals, such as dentists, podiatrists, clinical psychologists, chiropractors, and physical therapists.[84]

Division of Fees. Closely related to the corporate practice of medicine doctrine is the issue of whether the joint venture relationship may result in an improper division of fees. In many states, the prohibition against fee splitting is directed only at arrangements between two or more physicians who agree to split fees in exchange for referrals. However, the medical practice acts of several states contain broader prohibitions against fee splitting and thus may apply to financial arrangements contemplated by a joint venture. Ohio, for example, authorizes the state medical board to revoke or suspend the license of a physician for,

> Any division of fees or charges, or any agreement or arrangement to share fees or charges, made by any person licensed to practice medicine and surgery . . . with any other person so licensed, or with any other person.[85]

In this instance, the meaning of the term *division of fees or charges* refers to something other than the division of fees with respect to the referral of patients since that activity is expressly prohibited elsewhere. In fact, the Ohio attorney general dealt with an arrangement between a hospital and a radiologist pursuant to which the hospital paid the physician a fixed percent of the net income of the X-ray department. He concluded that the physician would be illegally engaged in the division of fees, and thus guilty of gross unprofessional conduct justifying revocation of his license, if the amounts received by the hospital exceeded fair compensation for the use of hospital facilities and for the nonprofessional services performed by the hospital.[86]

Other states, such as California, also equate violations of the prohibition against the corporate practice of medicine with illegal fee splitting, even if the exact statutory basis for such treatment is somewhat uncertain.[87]

Observations. The corporate practice of medicine and fee splitting prohibitions should be of great concern to all hospitals and physicians as they structure joint ventures. Care must be used to avoid clear-cut violations of either prohibition. Where the applicability of the rules is uncertain, difficult decisions must be made and some risks must be assumed. Unfortunately, the precise level of risk is more uncertain than the law because many states are lax in enforcement of these prohibitions and several have gone so far as to look the other way while more and more hospitals are effectively placing physicians on their payrolls.

Despite this apparent divergence in many states between the law and the actual practice and due to the risk that a successful venture might be challenged or that investors in an unsuccessful joint venture might exploit these issues in litigation against the promoters of the venture, all joint ventures should be structured to minimize the risk of violating these legal principles, and any significant remaining risk should be disclosed in writing to the investors.

Accreditation

Ambulatory care programs conducted by joint ventures need to consider the accreditation requirements of various private organizations. In some cases, the joint venture may voluntarily seek accreditation in hopes of gaining increased acceptance from the public, the government, and insurance companies. In other cases, the very structure or operation of the joint venture may, intentionally or not, require compliance with certain accreditation standards. Joint ventures should be planned to take into account accreditation standards and requirements, and sponsors of such joint ventures should, at the earliest stage, decide which accreditations will be sought and which accreditation requirements should, if possible, be avoided.

JCAH Accreditation. Ambulatory care services provided by or under the sponsorship of a hospital generally *must* satisfy the accreditation requirements of the Joint Commission on Accreditation of Hospitals (JCAH) if the hospital itself is to obtain or retain its overall JCAH accreditation. These requirements will apply to ambulatory care centers, urgent care centers, and ambulatory surgery centers if these services are offered through a formally organized department/service or through other organized departments/services of the hospital.[88]

It is uncertain whether these requirements apply to separately incorporated affiliates of a hospital. Moreover, while the JCAH hospital accreditation standards should not be applicable to truly separate joint ventures, contractual forms of joint ventures should be carefully structured in order to avoid subjecting such joint ventures to the JCAH hospital requirements, depending on the objectives of the parties.

In addition, the JCAH also will voluntarily accredit freestanding ambulatory care programs, including community health centers, group practices, health maintenance organizations, urgent care centers, ambulatory surgery centers, and emergency centers. To be eligible, the organization or program must be in operation and actively caring for patients for at least six months prior to the survey. Accreditation is awarded for three years.[89]

AAAHC Accreditation. A voluntary survey accreditation process also is available through the Accreditation Association for Ambulatory Health Care, Inc. (AAAHC).[90] Accreditation by AAAHC is available to organizations providing ambulatory healthcare for at least six months at the time of the survey.

Specific requirements are established for the various types of ambulatory care activities conducted.

NAFAC Accreditation.   The National Association for Ambulatory Care does not separately accredit emergency care or urgent care centers. Rather, such organizations are accredited, if at all, by the AAAHC.[91]

Observations.   Accreditation is an important consideration in many joint ventures. In some cases, compliance with voluntary accreditation requirements may eliminate the need to comply with state licensing or control. Accreditation also may enable the joint venture to be automatically "deemed" to be in compliance with the conditions of participation of various payment or reimbursement programs, such as for an ambulatory surgery center under the Medicare program. In other instances, private insurers may be willing to pay a facility charge only to accredited facilities. Finally, accreditation may serve as a marketing tool by creating the impression that the accredited facility provides a higher level or quality of care.[92]

Professional and Other Liability Concerns

The emergence of joint ventures in the direct delivery of healthcare services will undoubtedly give rise to new theories of liability applicable to the joint venture and its participants. However, many of the fundamental principles of liability can be found in existing case law.[93]

When planning to become involved in a joint venture, special care must be exercised with regard to the choice of legal entity used to conduct the business. As previously indicated, the choice of entity may affect the legal liability of the participants for the actions of the venture itself or of physicians or other healthcare professionals providing services in connection with the joint venture.

First, the traditional theories of respondeat superior liability will, of course, be applicable to joint ventures. Thus, joint ventures will be liable for the negligent actions of their employees such as nurses and technical personnel in connection with the delivery of healthcare services.

In addition, the liability of a joint venture for the actions of independent contractors, such as physicians performing surgery in an ambulatory surgery center, is likely to develop in a manner similar to the liability of hospitals for the negligent actions of independent contractor members of their medical staffs. Physicians are especially sensitive to the concerns of malpractice, particularly malpractice exposure from physicians other than themselves who may be coventurers in particular transactions. Therefore, corporate negligence issues that arise in connection with credentialing, quality assurance, utilization review, and peer review are likely to be of paramount importance in the joint venture context.

Potential liability for negligent or fraudulent misrepresentations also may arise because of the types of advertising or public relations engaged in by the joint ventures. For example, the name of a joint venture, such as one including the words *urgent care* or *emergicare,* may suggest that the joint venture is capable of dealing with life-threatening or other acute medical conditions that in reality are beyond its capabilities. Analogous case law that developed in the emergency room setting establishes principles of liability in such circumstances, and such theories of liability may well become applicable to joint ventures.

In these situations, many joint ventures require that patients be transferred to another facility, such as to a hospital emergency room. To the extent that such transfers are made, the joint venture must ensure that it has guidelines for identifying those medical conditions it is equipped to handle and those it is not. It may be advisable to enter into formal transfer agreements with appropriate nearby hospitals in many cases, and in certain instances, such transfer agreements may be mandated by state or federal law. For example, the Rhode Island Department of Health mandates a freestanding emergency center to have a written transfer agreement with a licensed hospital having full emergency services for the provision of care to patients needing hospital services, inpatient care, or immediate specialty consultation.[94] Connecticut also requires a written transfer agreement for freestanding emergency care facilities.[95] Similarly, the Medicare conditions of coverage for ambulatory surgery centers require a freestanding ambulatory surgery center, whether licensed or operated as an unlicensed physician's office, to have a written transfer agreement with a proper facility.[96]

As hospitals and physicians develop new forms of patient care delivery systems, new types of liability issues are likely to emerge. Great care and planning will be required to minimize the venture's risks in this area. Current legal developments should be carefully monitored and evaluated and appropriate organizational and procedural responses devised in order to deal with them.

Ownership Limitations and Disclosure Requirements

Many states and the federal government have enacted laws or promulgated regulations governing the ownership by physicians of interests in healthcare facilities and in businesses that provide ancillary services to patients, such as laboratories, pharmacies, and imaging centers. The principal concern of most of these statutes is that the existence of such ownership interests may improperly influence the physicians' exercise of their independent professional judgment in making referrals or in utilization.

Disclosure of Ownership. Many states require physicians and hospitals to disclose to patients their ownership interests in facilities to which such patients are referred by them. For example, California makes it unlawful for physicians, dentists, and certain other professionals to refer patients to clinical laboratories in which they have a "membership, proprietary interest, or co-ownership in any form, or has any profit-sharing arrangement," unless at the time of making the referral the professionals disclose their financial interest to the patient in writing and advise the patient that he or she might choose another clinical laboratory to have the work performed.[97] The California legislature intended that this statute would discourage unnecessary and untoward referrals motivated by economic considerations principally by requiring disclosure to and knowledge by patients of those interests.[98]

In 1984, California enacted another statute that expanded the scope of the health professional ownership disclosure requirements to virtually any type of joint venture that is logically connected to or needed in the professional-patient relationship.[99]

In 1986, Arizona amended its Medical Practice Act to make it unprofessional conduct if a physician:

> Knowingly failing to disclose to a patient on a form prescribed by the board which is dated and signed by the patient or guardian acknowledging that the patient or guardian has read and understands that the doctor has a direct pecuniary interest in a separate diagnostic or treatment agency or in non-routine goods or services which the patient is being prescribed and if the prescribed treatment, goods or services are available on a competitive basis. This subdivision does not apply to a referral by one doctor of medicine to another doctor of medicine within a group of doctors of medicine practicing together.

Limitations on Ownership. The federal government and other states have taken the approach of limiting by statute, regulation, or administrative discretion the *extent* of physician ownership in certain types of healthcare facilities. The apparent rationale for these limits is that a physician's economic interest will inherently compromise such physician's professional judgment unless the ownership interest is relatively small.

Under the Medicare program, for example, the attending physician must establish a plan of treatment, certify the need, and recertify need every 60 days before the Medicare program will reimburse a home health agency for home health services rendered. However, a physician who has a significant ownership or a significant financial or contractual relationship with the home health agency is *prohibited* from certifying treatment plans for patients served by that agency with only limited exceptions.[100]

Ownership Prohibitions. Some states have decided that the potential risks of conflicting interests are so great, in certain cases, that physician ownership of certain types of health facilities should be flatly prohibited or that a physician-owned facility should be prohibited from billing a particular program for its services.

Many states, for example, make it unlawful for physicians to own interests in pharmacies.[101] The Connecticut Department of Health Services no longer grants certificates of need to ambulatory surgery centers that are owned by physicians who will use or refer patients to it.[102] The Michigan attorney general has concluded that it is illegal for physicians to own an interest in a clinical laboratory in Michigan,[103] and this prohibition may apply to other types of joint ventures.

Pennsylvania has taken a slightly different approach. By regulation adopted in late 1983, the Pennsylvania Department of Public Welfare made the following ruling applicable *only* to Medicaid providers:

> A participating practitioner or professional corporation may not refer a Medical Assistance recipient to an independent laboratory, pharmacy, radiology or other ancillary medical service in which the practitioner or professional corporation has an ownership interest.[104]

Although this regulation does not carry a criminal sanction, it establishes a basis for revocation of the practitioner's or professional corporation's provider agreement. Moreover, it only applies to facilities that provide ancillary services and, thus, does not apply to ambulatory surgery centers and other direct providers of care.

Observations.   Hospitals and physicians should be aware of enacted and pending federal and state laws and regulations that require disclosure or that prohibit or limit ownership of interests in various health facilities and ancillary services. Some of these provisions will extend to contracts and leases as well as to stock or partnership interests. Further, such laws and regulations can be expected to change, particularly if abuses arise with frequency or great publicity. Therefore, it is always appropriate to anticipate and plan for such changes in preparing joint venture agreements.

THE DISSOLUTION STAGE OF A JOINT VENTURE

Participants in a hospital-physician joint venture will, from time to time, desire or be required to withdraw from the joint venture, or they may desire to terminate and dissolve the joint venture. The need for the joint venture may simply end, and the parties may decide that it is in their best interests to terminate their relationship. In other cases, the project acquired or the business operated by the joint venture may run its course, the assets and activities of the venture will be sold, and the proceeds will be distributed to the venturers.

Some joint ventures will be business failures, and it will be necessary to unwind the joint venture and distribute its net assets and liabilities among the joint venturers. New areas of investment with higher potential returns may be developed, thus prompting a need or desire to dissolve the joint venture for reasons other than business failure. In other cases, management deadlocks, lack of cooperation, or growing mistrust among the joint venturers may give rise to the need to terminate the joint venture and distribute its assets.

External events also may give rise to a need for voluntary or involuntary withdrawal of some or all of the participants from the joint venture. Some joint ventures will end because of unfavorable business or legal developments, such as the enactment of a law that makes it illegal for physicians to have an ownership interest in a particular type of joint venture. Others will end because of a physician's death or disability or loss of license or medical staff privileges.

Regardless of the reason or circumstance giving rise to a need for the withdrawal of a venturer or the termination of the venture, it is essential that all of these issues be dealt with, to the extent relevant, at the time of formation. By planning for all reasonably foreseeable eventualities at the outset, controversy can be minimized and expensive and unpredictable litigation can be avoided.

Methods

Several methods are available for dealing with the voluntary or involuntary withdrawal of venturers or the termination of the venture itself. The specific method or methods selected should be tailored to the purposes sought to be accomplished, such as maintenance of control, provision of liquidity, the orderly transfer of ownership interests, and tax or other business objectives. These include:

- Termination of the joint venture and liquidation of its assets at the request of either venturer.
- A negotiated right to withdraw from the venture upon providing notice to the other venturer. If the nonwithdrawing party desires to continue the business, the nonwithdrawing party will be entitled to purchase the interest of the withdrawing party. If both parties wish to discontinue the venture, then the assets or business of the venture are sold and the proceeds are distributed to the venturers.
- A venturer or class of venturers may retain the right to require another venturer to purchase his/her or their interests upon the happening of certain events or the passage of an agreed period of time, for an agreed upon value. The venture itself or one of the venturers will retain a right to purchase the interest of another venturer if such person receives a bona fide offer to purchase such interest from a third party.

The foregoing methods dealing with the withdrawal of a venturer or the termination of the venture itself are by no means all-inclusive. The specific method or methods selected will depend on a number of variables, including the nature of the business or property of the venture, the business interests of the venturers in the continued operation of the venture, and whether the venture consists of physical assets that are capable of being resold or can be operated as an ongoing business.

Buy-Sell Agreements

Most joint ventures will utilize some form of buy-sell agreement to deal with the orderly sale or transfer of joint venture interests, particularly those of the physician participants. The coverage and provisions of the buy-sell agreement will depend on the type of joint venture, the participants, and the business objectives of the venturers. Some of the more typical issues addressed in a buy-sell agreement are described below.

Restrictions on Encumbering Joint Venture Interests. Typically, most buy-sell agreements will attempt to prevent a venturer from encumbering his or her interest in the venture. If that interest is encumbered to secure a debt, and if the venturer defaulted, a third party could attempt to levy on the interest.

An absolute prohibition against the encumbrance of a joint venture interest will, notwithstanding the business reasons supporting its use, foreclose some of the participants from a large potential source of credit and might be void as an unreasonable restraint on alienation. Therefore, the venturers should, at a minimum, consider whether other alternatives may be more appropriate in a particular context. For example, rights of first refusal may serve as a reasonable compromise between the desire to prevent interests in the joint venture from falling into the hands of a creditor, while at the same time permitting a venturer to utilize his or her interest in the venture to secure a loan from a third party.

Restrictions on Transfers. Most buy-sell agreements generally will prohibit all voluntary and involuntary transfers of joint venture interests. In order to prevent such blanket prohibitions from being disregarded as being unreasonable restraints on alienation, most buy-sell agreements also will provide that either the venture itself or the other venturers will have the first right to purchase the joint venture interest for substantially the same price and on substantially the same terms as are made available by third parties. A typical buy-sell agreement will provide the appropriate mechanisms for the offer of a venturer's interest to the venture itself or to the other venturers as well as identify the terms and conditions on which the purchase would be made.

Restrictions Tied to Medical Practice. Physician investors in most joint ventures will be selected for strategic reasons associated with the business of the venture. Frequently, one criterion will be medical staff membership. Legally, provisions in a buy-sell agreement requiring a resale of a venture interest incident to medical staff–related events should be enforceable, unless the forced sale amounts to a forfeiture.

Most buy-sell agreements in hospital-physician joint ventures provide for events of termination that include loss of staff membership at a specified hospital, voluntary or involuntary withdrawal from the active practice of medicine, and, in a growing number of cases, termination of malpractice insurance. Regardless of the reasons giving rise to such events of termination, the buy-sell agreement must provide for reasonably objective reasons giving rise to such rights and also must provide for a reasonable valuation of the interests that are required to be sold to the joint venture or to the other venturers or that may be purchased by the venture or the other venturers at their discretion.

Estate Planning Restrictions. In addition to restrictions tied to the medical practice of a particular physician participant in a joint venture, other events such as death, disability, divorce, and bankruptcy need to be addressed in the buy-sell agreement. As in the case of restrictions tied to medical practice, estate planning restrictions will require the joint venture or the other venture participants to purchase the interest of a venturer who dies, becomes disabled, is divorced, or becomes bankrupt. In other cases, the buy-sell agreement may obligate the venture or the coventurers to purchase the interests in such events. Special care also must be used in community property states to comply with the rules concerning disposition of community property interests.

Other Options. Some joint ventures require special treatment because of unique circumstances surrounding the venture or the venturers themselves.

One tool for dealing with these special situations is a "put." Basically, a put gives a venturer the right to insist that the venture of the coventurers purchase some or all of his or her interest. A put may be useful for minority venturers whose interests are small and may be negatively affected by the actions of the majority venturers. A put may also be important for passive stockholders in an S corporation, since they pay tax on all of the net earnings whether or not dividends are actually distributed. The use of a put in such cases may help ensure that the venture distributes sufficient cash to enable a shareholder to pay his or her taxes on the distributive share of income.

Another approach that may be of use in special circumstances is a "call." A call is a right to purchase additional interests from the venture itself, from the other venturers, or from both. Like a put, a call can be used to protect a venturer's rights in case of changes in control or management, but a call is more likely to be useful in protecting majority venturers from dealing with dissension among the minority venturers and for dealing with potential deadlocks.

Valuation. Regardless of type and scope of restrictions contained in a buy-sell agreement, the buy-sell agreement should provide for a method of valuing joint venture interests. One approach is to fix a price in the buy-sell agreement itself or to agree to revalue the joint venture interests annually. As an alternative, the buy-sell agreement may provide for the selection and use of appraisers. Buy-sell agreements also may contain various types of valuation formulas, such as book value, book value adjusted for the appreciation of certain types of assets, capitalization of earnings, capitalization of excess earnings, and so forth.

Regardless of the approach, however, it is extremely important to determine what method or methods of valuation will result in the most appropriate measure of value and what methods can be implemented with the least amount of cost and controversy.

Restrictions on Competition

The parties to a joint venture need to address the issue of competition during the operating stage of the joint venture, as well as after the withdrawal of a venturer or the dissolution of the joint venture itself. These types of issues generally relate to competition, solicitation of employees, and use of confidential information.

Noncompetition Agreements. Noncompetition agreements generally fall into two categories, those related to employment by the joint venture and those incident to the sale of an interest in the joint venture.

Employment-related noncompetition agreements have traditionally been disfavored by the courts. Generally, courts will enforce employment-related noncompetition agreements only if they further a legitimate business interest, are for a reasonable duration, and cover only a limited geographic area. In a few states, employment-related noncompetition agreements will be void or voidable. California, for example, will void an employment-related noncompetition agreement, while Michigan will void any contract that prevents a person from practicing a profession. Other states (e.g., Colorado and Louisiana) have restricted the circumstances in which employment-related noncompetition agreements will be enforceable. Such agreements also are reviewable under Section 1 of the Sherman Act as potential unlawful restraints of trade.

The courts have, however, tended to look more favorably on noncompetition agreements associated with the sale of an interest in the business, such as shares in a corporation or a partnership interest. As long as such restrictions are reasonably related to the conduct of the business itself, such noncompetition agreements should be enforceable.

Nonsolicitation and Nonservicing Agreements. Except in unusual circumstances, a withdrawn venturer will be entitled to solicit former customers or clients of the venture itself and will be entitled to provide services to them. Nonsolicitation and nonservicing agreements do not prevent a withdrawn venturer from competing with the joint venture, but rather prohibit the withdrawn venturer from soliciting or servicing the joint venture's clients or customers. Generally speaking, the courts are receptive to enforcing nonsolicitation and nonservicing convenants, since they are typically more reasonable in scope and more directly related to the conduct of the business.

The use of nonsolicitation convenants in connection with a hospital-physician joint venture is especially useful in those cases where the success of the venture depends on special contacts or customers. Such agreements are likely to be of less use and perhaps will be less enforceable, however, if the business of the joint venture does not involve particular clients or customer loyalties, such as the operation of a primary care center.

Use of Confidential Information. It is quite common for joint ventures to restrict the use of confidential information obtained by a venturer during the course of his or her involvement with the joint venture. These types of agreements are generally enforceable by the courts provided that the type of information deemed to be confidential truly is unique and not generally available and the joint venture has taken reasonable steps to prevent its general dissemination. Typical types of confidential information protected will include customer and client lists, operating policies and procedures, pricing information, and business strategy information. Confidential information also will include corporate trade secrets such as proprietary formulas.

CONCLUSION

The laws and regulations that affect hospital-physician joint ventures create a complicated maze through which their sponsors and participants must navigate carefully. This task is made difficult by the many layers of, and frequently inconsistent, laws and regulations affecting them. Further complexity is added by the formal and informal practices of private regulators, such as accreditation agencies, insurance companies, and lenders. While joint ventures in the health-care field are relatively new, many of the legal relationships created are traditional, and a substantial body of well-developed legal principles will affect them.

This chapter has considered a broad range of legal and regulatory issues and the present thinking concerning them. During the coming years, new legal and regulatory problems will arise and new solutions to existing problems will become apparent. It should be relatively clear, however, that joint ventures between hospitals and physicians are not uncomplicated transactions to negotiate or document, except in their simplest form. Each party is likely to be assuming risks that are at least partially dependent on the professional or financial contributions of the other party; thus, joint ventures are likely to require a great degree of care and consumption of time and resources to establish and operate successfully.

Notes

[1] The federal and state laws and regulations affecting hospital-physician joint ventures are extensive and often complex. These laws and regulations, as well as the procedures and requirements of private agencies, constantly change. This chapter is intended to serve as an overview of the principal legal and regulatory issues; it is not intended to be an exhaustive or all-inclusive treatment of such issues.

[2] For example, the Georgia Supreme Court has held that there was "*no* legislative authorization—express or implied—for [Tift County Hospital Authority to establish] an enterprise which offers durable medical equipment for sale or rent to the general public." *Tift County Hospital Authority v. MRS of Tifton, GA, Inc.*, 255 Ga. 164, 335 S.E.2d 546, 547 (1985). This decision would clearly prevent the establishment of a durable medical equipment joint venture by that hospital. *See also* the discussion in this chapter concerning the special legal considerations affecting public and governmental hospitals.

[3] For a more detailed discussion of these issues, see D. M. Mancino, "Hospital-Physician Joint Ventures: Some Crucial Considerations," *Hospital Progress* 65, no. 1 (January 1984), p. 30; R. H. Rosenfield, "Market Forces Set Off Skyrocketing Interest in Hospital-Doctor Ventures," *Modern Healthcare* 14, no. 6 (May 1, 1984), p. 70.

[4] The tax aspects of the various forms of joint ventures are discussed in detail in Chapter 8.

[5] *See generally,* United States Department of Commerce, *Franchise Opportunities Handbook,* October 1985, pp. 113–17, 280–92.

[6] Ibid., p. xxvii.

[7] The FTC rule is set forth in 16 C.F.R. §§ 436.1–436.3 (1985). The FTC also has proposed rules dealing specifically with ophthalmic franchises. 50 Fed. Reg. 598 (Jan. 4, 1985) (to be codified at 16 C.F.R. Part 456).

[8] 43 Fed. Reg. 59,614 (Dec. 21, 1978).

[9] 16 C.F.R. § 436.1 (1985).

[10]Cal. Corp. Code § 31005 (West Supp. 1986).

[11]N.J. Stat. Ann. § 56:10-3 (West Supp. 1985).

[12]See, for example, the franchise laws of California, Illinois, Indiana, Maryland, Minnesota, New York, North Dakota, Rhode Island, South Dakota, Virginia, Washington, and Wisconsin.

[13]See, for example, the franchise laws of Florida, Hawaii, Michigan, and Oregon.

[14]See, for example, the unfair practice laws of Arkansas, Connecticut, Delaware, Florida, Hawaii, Indiana, Kentucky, Maryland, Michigan, Minnesota, Mississippi, Missouri, Nebraska, New Jersey, Virginia, and Washington.

[15]See, for example, the business opportunity statutes in California, Connecticut, Florida, Georgia, Illinois, Indiana, Iowa, Kentucky, Louisiana, Maine, Maryland, Michigan, Minnesota, Nebraska, New Hampshire, New York, North Dakota, Oklahoma, Oregon, South Dakota, Rhode Island, Texas, Utah, Virginia, Washington, and Wisconsin.

[16]Of necessity, this discussion does not cover the numerous other issues raised by franchising, such as contract considerations, territorial restrictions, pricing issues, advertising concerns, antitrust aspects, and transfers and terminations.

[17]For a discussion of the status of CON and Section 1122, *see generally* Hill-Chinn, L., *Status Report: Health Planning and Capital Expenditure Regulation,* 7(25) HEALTH L. VIGIL Special Supp. 1 (Am Hosp Ass'n, Dec. 7, 1984).

[18]Cal. Health & Safety Code § 437.10 (West Supp. 1986); Ohio Rev. Code § 3702.51 (Baldwin Supp. 1985).

[19]Mont. Code Ann. § 50-5-301(d) (1985).

[20]Mo. Ann. Stat. § 197.300 (Vernon Supp. 1986).

[21]Ohio Rev. Code § 3702.51 (Baldwin Supp. 1985); Ohio Admin. Code § 3701-12-01.

[22]Vt. Stat. Ann. tit. 18, § 2404 (1982).

[23]Securities Act of 1933, 15 U.S.C. §§ 77a–77bb; Securities Exchange Act of 1934, 15 U.S.C. § 78(a).

[24]Securities Act of 1933, § 5, 15 U.S.C. §§ 77c(a)–78kk (1982).

[25]15 U.S.C. § 77b(1) (1982). The definition of securities under the 1934 Act is virtually identical. 15 U.S.C. § 78c(a)(10) (1982).

[26]328 U.S. 293 (1946).

[27]Ibid., p. 301.

[28]Ibid.

[29]421 U.S. 837 (1975).

[30]Ibid., p. 848 (*citing Tcherepnin v. Knight,* 389 U.S. 332, 336 [1967]).

[31]Ibid., p. 851.

[32]Ibid., pp. 852–53.

[33]Ibid., p. 849.

[34]The SEC staff will, upon request, issue interpretative opinions on various issues, known as "no-action" letters. While not legally binding on the SEC, no-action letters are highly useful and popular tools.

[35]No-action letter regarding Central Florida Medical Associates, Inc. (available April 22, 1985).

[36]No-action letter regarding St. John's Mercy Medical Center (available May 29, 1985).

[37]*See* no-action letter regarding Seaview Country Club Assocs. (available 1981); no action letter regarding Woodmont Country Club, Inc. (May 4, 1979).

[38]*See* no-action letter regarding Glen Arven Country Club, Inc. (July 13, 1985).

[39]*See* no-action letter regarding Argosy Travel Club (available July 9, 1975); *see also Silver Hills Country Club v. Sobieski,* 55 Cal.2d 811, 361 P.2d 906, 13 Cal. Rptr. 186 (1961).

[40]Limited partnerships are usually held to be securities, *e.g., Goodman v. Epstein,* 582 F.2d 388 (7th Cir. 1979), *cert. denied,* 440 U.S. 939 (1979). But there may be exceptions, *e.g., Frazier v. Manson,* 484 F. Supp. 449 (N.D. Tex. 1980), *aff'd,* 651 F.2d 1078 (5th Cir. 1981).

[41]645 F.2d 404, 422 (5th Cir.), *cert. denied,* 454 U.S. 897 (1981); *but cf. Pagwan v Silverstein,* 265 F. Supp. 898 (S.D.N.Y. 1967) (general partnership interest is security under 1933 Act);

N.Y. Admin. Code tit. 13, § 80.1(j)(4) (1968) (general partnership and joint venture interests are securities).

[42] Securities Act of 1933, § 3(a)(11); 15 U.S.C. § 77c(a)(11) (1982); 17 C.F.R. § 230.147 (1985).

[43] 15 U.S.C. § 77d(2) (1982).

[44] *E.g., SEC v. Ralston Purina Co.*, 346 U.S. 119 (1953); SEC Release No. 33-4552, 1 Fed. Sec. L. Rep. (CCH) ¶ 2770 (Nov. 6, 1962).

[45] 17 C.F.R. § 230.506 (1985).

[46] 17 C.F.R. §§ 230.251–230.264 (1985).

[47] 17 C.F.R. §§ 230.504 and 230.505 (1985).

[48] Securities Act of 1933, § 4(6); 15 U.S.C. § 77d(6) (1982).

[49] *See generally Blue Sky Laws 1985*, 31–43 (Practicing Law Institute, Corporate Law and Practice Course Handbook No. 473, 1985): James Mofsky, *The Expanding Definition of "Security" under the Blue Sky Laws*, 1 Sec. Reg. L. J. 217 (1973).

[50] *United Housing Foundation, Inc. v. Forman*, 421 U.S. 837 (1975).

[51] *See generally Blue Sky Law Rptr.* (CCH) (1984).

[52] Disclosure only states include Pennsylvania, New York, and New Jersey.

[53] Merit states include California, Colorado, Michigan, Ohio, Oregon, Texas, and Washington.

[54] See generally, H. Bloomenthall, C. Harvey, and S. Wing, *1986 Going Public Handbook* (Clarke Boardman Co., Ltd., 1986), 2-12–2-25.

[55] 15 U.S. Code §§ 11, 12(1), 12(2) (1982); Securities and Exchange Act of 1934, § 10(b); 15 U.S.C. § 77(k) (1982); Rule 10b-5.

[56] Securities Exchange Act of 1934, § 15; 15 U.S.C. § 78(o).

[57] American Medical Association, Sect. 4.04 *Current Opinions of the Judicial Council of the American Medical Association* (Chicago: American Medical Association, 1984), p. 14.

[58] Emphasis supplied.

[59] Fla. Stat. Ann. § 768.28 (West Supp. 1986).

[60] *North Broward Hospital District v. Eldred*, 466 So.2d 1210 (Fla. 4th DCA 1985), *review granted*, Case No. 67,002) (Fla. 1985).

[61] Okla. Const. art. X, § 15; Okla. Op. Att'y Gen. No. 81-120 (Oct. 29, 1981).

[62] Cal. Const. art. XVI, § 6; *California Housing Finance Agency v. Elliott*, 17 Cal.3d 575, 551 P.2d 1193, 131 Cal. Rptr. 361 (1976); *Mannheim v. Superior Court*, 3 Cal. 3d 678, 478 P.2d 17, 91 Cal. Rptr. 585 (1970); *County of Alameda v. Janssen*, 16 Cal.2d 276, 106 P.2d 11, 130 A.L.R. 1141 (1940).

[63] Cal. Const. art. XVI, § 6; *but see Board of Supervisors v. Dolan*, 45 Cal. App.3d 237, 119 Cal. Rptr. 347 (1975).

[64] *Public Utility Dist. No. 1 of Snohomish County v. Taxpayers of Snohomish County*, 78 Wash.2d 724, 479 P.2d 61 (1971).

[65] Cal. Const. art. XVI, § 6.

[66] *City of Miami Beach v. Berns*, 245 So.2d 38 (Fla. 1971).

[67] 42 C.F.R. § 416.40 (1985).

[68] Cal. Dept. of Health Services, *Licensing Procedure Memorandum No. 83-3* (June 7, 1983).

[69] *See e.g.*, Ill. Ann. Stat. ch. 111-1/2, § 157-8.4 (Smith-Hurd 1982).

[70] Cal. Health & Safety Code § 1204 (West Supp. 1986); Ohio Rev. Code Ann. § 1739.01.

[71] Conn. Admin. Code § 19a-77-200(B). Georgia regulations subjecting organizations advertised as "emergency treatment centers were recently held unconstitutional. *Primary Care Physicians Group, PC v. Ledbetter*, Civ. C 84-766A (N.D. Ga., Feb. 21, 1986).

[72] 42 C.F.R. §§ 416.20–416.150 (1985); see generally Hoffman & Phillips, "Developing Plan for Medicare Certification," *Medicenter Management* 3, no. 2 (February 1986), p. 27.

[73] It is currently the policy of Blue Cross of Michigan not to reimburse the facility charges of physician-owned ambulatory surgery centers. Telephone conference with Rudolph Difazio at Blue Cross of Michigan, April 4, 1986.

[74] 42 C.F.R. § 416.43 (1985).

[75] P. Starr, *The Social Transformation of American Medicine* (New York: Basic Books, 1982), pp. 1 and 204. (footnote omitted).

[76] *See e.g.*, Cal. Bus. & Prof. Code § 2286 (West Supp. 1986); Colo. Rev. Stat. § 12-36-117(m) (1981); Ky. Rev. Stat. § 311.595(10) (1980).

[77] *See e.g.*, *Garcia v. Texas Board of Medical Examiners*, 358 F. Supp. 1016 (W.D. Tex. 1973); *People v. United Medical Service, Inc.*, 362 Ill. 442, 200 N.E. 157 (1936).

[78] N.Y. Pub. Health Law § 2801-a (Consol. 1984); Wis. Stat. Ann. § 448.08(4) (West Supp. 1985).

[79] *Compare* Ohio Op. Att'y. Gen. (No. 82) 145 (Mar. 8, 1963) (corporate practice by non-profit corporations is illegal) *with* 37 Ore. Op. Att'y. Gen. (No. 7230) 963 (Oct. 28, 1975) (hospitals are exempt from corporate practice prohibition).

[80] Ohio Op. Att'y. Gen. (No. 82) 145, 147 (Mar. 8, 1963).

[81] Minn. Op. Att'y. Gen. (No. 92-B-11) 80 (Oct. 5, 1955).

[82] *See e.g.*, 55 Cal. Op. Att'y. Gen. (No. CV 71-207) 103 (Mar. 3, 1972) (percentage of net income contracts are illegal); Ohio Op. Att'y. Gen. (No. 3197) 622 (Aug. 10, 1962) (payment of salary to emergency room physician is corporate practice of medicine).

[83] *See e.g.*, *Blank v. Palo Alto-Stanford Hospital Center*, 234 Cal. App.2d 377, 44 Cal. Rptr. 572 (1965) (percentage of gross contracts are permissible).

[84] *See e.g.*, Ark. Stat. Ann. § 72-559 (1955) (dentistry); Ga. Code § 43-11-47 (1984) (dentistry); Me. Rev. Stat. Ann. tit. 32, § 2435 (1974) (optometry); N.H. Rev. Stat. Ann. § 327:27 (1951) (optometry); Ohio Rev. Code Ann. § 1701.03 (1955) (any learned profession); and S.C. Code Ann. § 40-51-210 (1960) (podiatry).

[85] Ohio Rev. Code Ann. § 4731.22(B)(13) (Baldwin Supp. 1986).

[86] Ohio Op. Att'y. Gen. (No. 3197) 622 (Aug. 10, 1962).

[87] 65 Cal. Op. Att'y. Gen. (No. 81-1004) 223 (1982).

[88] Joint Commission on Accreditation of Hospitals, *Ambulatory Health Care Standards Manual, 1986* (Chicago: Joint Commission on Accreditation of Hospitals, 1985).

[89] *Ambulatory Health Care Standards Manual, 1986.*

[90] Accreditation Association for Ambulatory Health Care, *Accreditation Handbook for Ambulatory Health Care 1985–86* (1985).

[91] *See e.g.*, "Accreditation Tips," *Ambulatory Care* 6, no. 3 (March 1986), p. 15.

[92] *See e.g.*, Punch, "Freestanding Centers Sections Accreditation," *Modern Healthcare* 15, no. 8 (April 12, 1985) p.73; Baldwin, "Private Groups Seek Status in Certifying Process," *Modern Healthcare* 15, no. 8 (April 12, 1985), p. 68.

[93] *See generally* Zaremski & Weibel, *There Is No Answer to the Medical Malpractice Crisis,* J. Legal Med. 6, no. 2 (June 1985), p. 265.

[94] Rhode Island rules.

[95] Conn. Admin. Reg. § 19-13-D55 (1975).

[96] 42 C.F.R. § 416.41 (1985).

[97] Cal. Bus. & Prof. Code § 654.1 (West Supp. 1986); see also Enrolled Bill Report on S.B. No. 340, Dept. of Consumer Affairs (Aug. 13, 1975).

[98] In early 1986, the California Legislature Committee on Health published a report entitled "Ownership Interests and Referrals by Healing Acts Practitioners," in connection with the committee's consideration of A.B. 1325, which would, if enacted, have made it a misdemeanor for specified healthcare provider to charge, bill, or refer a patient to any organization in which the licensee or his immediate family has any significant beneficial interest. The conclusion of this report is quite revealing:

> The issue of ownership and referral abuse is not peculiar to California. The advent of medicine as big business is rapidly changing both the form and structure of the delivery of health care throughout America. These changes are beginning to result in significant alterations in the economies and methods of practice of many health care license categories. AB 1325, in addressing major ethical and costly overutilization concerns, serves to bring attention to the severe competition and "turf wars" that health care providers and health care industries are

experiencing. It is unfortunate that for all the questions and concerns that AB 1325 raises, there are at this time few answers.

[99] Cal. Bus. & Prof. Code § 654.2 (West Supp. 1986); *see generally* 68 Cal. Op. Att'y. Gen. (No. 89-105) 140 (June 25, 1985).

[100] *See* 42 C.F.R. § 405.1633 (1985); Deficit Reduction Act of 1984, Pub. L. No. 98-369, § 2300, 98 Stat. 494 (codified at scattered sections of 42 U.S.C.).

[101] *See e.g.*, Cal. Bus. & Prof. Code § 4080.5 (West Supp. 1986) (prohibits the issuance of a pharmacy permit to a physician, a partnership in which a physician is a partner, or a corporation which is controlled by, or which 10 percent of the stock is owned by a physician or a partnership in which a physician is a partner); *see also* Pa. Stat. Ann. tit. 63, § 390-5(9)(1961) (physician may not have a controlling interest in a pharmacy); Colo. Admin. Code § 1.00.15 (1985) (physician ownership interest limited to 10 percent).

[102] Conn. CON ruling regarding Bettom Medical Management No. 83-540 (approved March 1984), in which the applicant agreed to prohibit ownership by physicians or members of families of physicians, "[i]n order to eliminate the fiscal incentive for unnecessary surgery."

[103] Mich. Op. Att'y. Gen. (No. 5498) (June 8, 1979).

[104] 55 Pa. Admin. Code § 1101.51(c)(5) (1984).

8

Tax Planning for Joint Ventures

Douglas M. Mancino, J.D.

INTRODUCTION

Physicians and hospitals willing to commit risk capital in joint ventures are entitled to a number of tax benefits, including the immediate deduction of certain costs and the rapid recovery of others. The primary tax objective in planning and implementing a joint venture will be the maximization of such benefits, thus reducing the total tax bill payable by the joint venture and its owners. However, planning to accomplish this objective must be considered within the context of the business objectives of the venturers because at some point the accomplishment of business planning objectives may outweigh the total maximization of any tax benefits involved. Further, the recently enacted Tax Reform Act of 1986 contains numerous provisions that directly or indirectly affect tax economics of hospital-physician joint ventures. These changes will focus greater attention on business economics of the joint venture and not just the available tax benefits.

If a joint venture and its participants are to maximize the tax benefits available to them, at least four results should be achieved. First, the tax economics of the joint venture should result in the deferral of the payment of taxes that otherwise would be due currently. This can be accomplished in a number of ways, such as by maximizing accelerated cost recovery deductions. Second, certain types of tax benefits can result in a permanent reduction of tax liabilities. For example, the maximization of investment tax credits will result in a permanent reduction of tax liability unless partially or wholly recaptured at a later date. Third, tax planning by tax-exempt hospitals and related tax-exempt organizations may result, if properly structured, in the realization of income that is totally exempt from taxation. Finally, tax-exempt hospitals must structure their participation in joint ventures in a manner that will avoid jeopardizing their tax-exempt status.

While optimal tax planning is and should be an objective of any hospital-physician joint venture, the rules are extraordinarily complex and in a continual state of change. Because of the propensity of the U.S. Congress in recent years to change federal tax laws on a regular basis, hospitals and physicians alike should be aware of this potential for change and should ensure that their plans not only take into account current tax rules, but also anticipate changes that are imminent.

The purpose of this chapter is to provide hospital executives and physicians with an overview of the principal federal income tax considerations likely to be involved in most joint ventures.[1]

CHOICE OF BUSINESS ENTITY

One of the first decisions confronting hospitals and physicians desiring to pool their capital or services in a joint venture is the selection of the appropriate form of business organization. There are many business and nontax reasons that motivate the selection of one form of joint venture over another; these are discussed in Chapter 7. However, it is seldom that the choice among the various forms of business organizations is compelled solely by nontax considerations.

Contractual Model

The contractual model joint venture is probably the simplest business form from a tax standpoint. Under this model, the hospital enters into a contract or lease with a physician or physician group. To the extent the hospital retains the ownership of the equipment or facilities used in the business of the joint venture, it is entitled to enjoy the tax benefits available to owners of capital assets; it also is subject to tax, unless otherwise exempt, on the net income produced under the contract or lease. Likewise, if the physicians are lessees or mere users of the equipment or facilities, generally they are not entitled to the tax benefits of capital asset ownership with certain limited exceptions.

Partnerships

A partnership is not a taxable entity. Instead, the partners are taxed directly on partnership income regardless of whether it is actually distributed to them. Similarly, partnership tax losses are passed through to the partners.[2]

In the case of partnership income, the effective rate of tax becomes a function of the tax brackets of the partners. In 1987, the tax rates for a married partner filing jointly will range from 11 percent to 38.5 percent of taxable income; in 1988 and future years, the rates will be 15 percent and 28 percent, with a special 5 percent rate adjustment for high-income persons. Corporate partners will be subject to a top corporate rate of 34 percent on their ordinary income and capital gain. If a tax-exempt organization (e.g., a not-for-profit hospital) is a partner and the income is not unrelated business taxable income, the effective rate of tax on that partner's share of income is 0 percent.

In the case of partnership losses, their tax effect will depend on each partner's other nonpartnership income, losses, and other tax items. Thus, if a medical office building partnership incurs a net loss for tax purposes, the value of that loss will be greater for the partner whose income from other sources places him in a higher marginal tax bracket, provided that the use of the losses is not limited by the passive loss limitation discussed below.

While, as a general matter, general partnerships and limited partnerships are treated alike, there are several significant tax differences that may affect the selection of a general partnership over a limited partnership and vice versa under appropriate circumstances.

Basis. Each partner has a basis in his or its interest in the partnership.[3] The partner's basis is used to determine gain or loss upon a taxable disposition of the partnership interest. The partner's basis also is used to limit the partner's share of partnership losses that a partner may deduct against other income.

A partner's basis generally is equal to the money or property the partner contributes or is obligated to contribute to the partnership, increased by the partner's share of income and decreased by the partner's share of losses. However, a partner's basis also may be increased if his share of liabilities is increased.[4]

If the partnership debt is recourse debt, that is, the lender has recourse against both partnership assets and the general partners themselves, the recourse debt will increase the basis of all general partners' interests in proportion to how they share gains. Thus, in a general partnership, each partner's basis is increased by a share of the recourse debt, while in a limited partnership only the general partner's basis is increased by recourse debt.[5]

If the partnership debt is nonrecourse, that is, it can be satisfied on default only by the asset securing it, the basis of all partners is increased by such nonrecourse debt in proportion to the amount of partnership losses they share. Thus, limited partners' basis is increased by their proportionate share of nonrecourse partnership debt.[6]

Characterization as Partnership. If a general partnership is formed pursuant to a state's equivalent to the Uniform Partnership Act, the general partnership will be treated as such for tax purposes. However, even if a limited partnership is formed pursuant to a state's equivalent of the Uniform Limited Partnership Act, a limited partnership may be recharacterized as an association taxable as a corporation if it has more than two of the following four corporation characteristics: continuity of life, centralized management, limited liability, and free transferability of interests.[7]

Corporations

Unlike partnerships, corporations are separate taxpaying entities. Income and losses derived by the corporation are taxable to or deductible by the corporation and cannot be passed through to the corporate shareholders, unless the corpora-

TABLE 8-1

	Corporate Shareholder	Individual Shareholder
Net income before taxes	$100,000	$100,000
Tax at corporate level	(22,250)	(22,250)
Net after-tax income	$ 77,750	$ 77,750
Tax on dividends received by individual in 28% tax bracket		$ 21,770
Tax on dividends received by corporation in 34% tax bracket	$ 5,287	
Effective combined tax rates	27.54%	44.02%
Effective rates if pass-through entity is used	22.25%	28.00%

tion qualifies for and elects treatment as an S corporation as discussed below. The tax rates on corporate taxable income beginning in 1987 are:

15 percent of first $50,000.
25 percent of next $25,000.
34 percent of all taxable income in excess of $75,000.[8]

Although shareholders are not taxed on corporate income, they are taxable on corporate distributions. Thus, for example, to the extent a corporation declares dividends out of its current or accumulated earnings and profits, such distributions generally will be taxable to its shareholders at the income tax rates generally applicable to each shareholder.

In many instances, a corporation may be a costly tax substitute for the partnership, due to the fact that maximum tax efficiency seldom can be achieved. Income earned through a corporate entity usually is subject to a double tax, since a corporation will pay a tax on the immediate realization of income and the shareholder ultimately will pay a second tax on the distribution of such income. Table 8-1 illustrates the effects of double taxation on corporate and individual shareholders.

The combined effective rate of double taxation will be a function of the marginal rate of tax paid by the corporation, and the marginal tax brackets of its shareholders. The character of the income realized at the corporate and shareholder levels either as capital gain or as ordinary income no longer is relevant under the Tax Reform Act of 1986 except during 1987 when the lower rates for individuals are being phased in.

S Corporations

The S corporation is a special type of corporation that combines most of the advantages under state law of doing business in corporate form with some of the federal income tax advantages of partnerships. To be eligible to elect to be subject to the provisions of Subchapter S of the Code,[9] a corporation may have only one class of stock and may have no more than 35 shareholders, all of whom must be individuals (other than nonresident aliens), estates, or certain special types of trusts. Once the corporation has been formed, all persons who are shareholders (and their spouses where shares are community property) at the time the election is made must execute a written consent to the S corporation election in order for the election to be effective.

Once a valid S corporation election has been made, an electing corporation will continue to be treated as an S corporation until the occurrence of an event that would cause the corporation to lose its status as an eligible corporation under the criteria discussed above (e.g., if the corporation acquired more than 35 shareholders or if a disqualified individual or entity became a shareholder) or until a voluntary revocation is filed with the Internal Revenue Service.

An S corporation is itself generally not subject to federal income taxation. Rather, items of income, gain, loss, deduction, or credit realized or incurred by an S corporation are allocated on a pro rata basis among its shareholders who are then obligated to take their respective allocable shares of such items into account in reporting their respective incomes and determining the amount of tax thereon. An S corporation is essentially a "pass-through" entity, very similar to a partnership. It is desirable for income tax purposes in that it avoids the "double taxation" that occurs when a regular corporation distributes earnings and profits, already taxed at the corporate level, to its shareholders, where such earnings and profits are again subject to tax as dividends (see Table 8–1).

However, whereas the shareholders of a regular corporation are taxed only to the extent that money or property is actually distributed to them to the extent of earnings and profits of the corporation (i.e., when dividends are paid), the shareholders of an S corporation are subject to tax on their allocable share of any income realized by the corporation in a given year regardless of whether any of such income is ever distributed to them. Accordingly, shareholders of an S corporation may incur a tax liability in a given year in excess of the amount of cash distributed to them in such year.

An S corporation may, under limited circumstances, incur a tax at the corporate level on certain capital gains where an S corporation election has not been in effect for all the corporation's taxable years or where the corporation has acquired property from another corporation in a nontaxable transaction.

A shareholder's pro rata share of each item of an S corporation's income, gain, loss, deduction, and credit is generally determined on a per share per day basis by assigning equal portions of such items to each day of the taxable year and then dividing the daily portions equally among all the shares outstanding on that day. Items of income, gain, loss, deduction, and credit passed through to the shareholders of an S corporation generally retain the same character in the hands of the shareholders that they had at the corporate level.

An S corporation shareholder may take his allocable share of losses and deductions into account in determining his tax liability only to the extent that such losses and deductions do not exceed the shareholder's adjusted basis in his stock plus his adjusted basis in any indebtedness owed by the corporation to the shareholder. An S corporation shareholder's ability to take corporate losses and deductions into account will also be limited by the amount the shareholder is "at risk" with respect to the corporation's activities.

An S corporation shareholder's adjusted stock basis determines the taxable character of distributions of money or property from the S corporation and the amount of gain realized upon a sale or exchange of the stock. Unlike a regular corporation, distributions of money or property by an S corporation generally will be tax free to the shareholder to the extent such distributions do not exceed the shareholder's adjusted stock basis; distributions in excess of adjusted stock basis will be taxable to the shareholder.

A shareholder's initial stock basis will be equal to the amount the shareholder paid for his shares. A shareholder will also have basis with respect to the amount of any debt the S corporation owes him. Stock basis will be increased by the amount of any additional capital contributions to the corporation and by the amount of the shareholder's allocable share of corporate income and decreased, but not below zero, by the amount of money or other property distributed to the shareholder and by the amount of the shareholder's allocable share of losses and deductions.

A shareholder's basis will not be increased as a result of any indebtedness incurred by the S corporation, regardless of any guarantees by the shareholder of such indebtedness, unless great care is used.

Selected Comparisons of Tax Advantages

Corporation versus Partnership. The determination of what entity should be used from a tax standpoint will depend on a number of factors. For example, if the joint venture is expected to generate substantial tax losses in its early years, a determination should be made as to whether those losses are better utilized as deductions against other income of the venture's owners on a current basis or deferred for use as deductions against future income of the joint venture itself. Consideration must be given to the impact of the passive loss limitation rules discussed below. If the deductions are best used in the early years and will not be limited by the at risk or the passive loss limitation rules, then the partnership form should be selected. On the other hand, if the losses will be more profitably used to offset other income generated by the joint venture itself, then the corporate form may be the preferred structure.

Similarly, if a joint venture is expected to generate substantial taxable income, the joint venturers must determine whether the income will be reinvested in the joint venture or distributed to its owners. If the income will be reinvested, then the corporate form may be preferred to the partnership. On the other hand, if the joint venture does not require substantial investment of capital from operations, then the partnership form may be the preferred joint venture entity.

Finally, since corporate owners, such as the hospital itself or an affiliate of the hospital, are likely to be involved in any joint venture, the impact of double taxation is substantially reduced if not eliminated with respect to the corporate owners because of the 80 percent dividends received deduction available to for-profit hospitals and the exclusion of dividends from taxation for tax-exempt hospitals (see Table 8–1) and the tax differences between a corporation and partnership are substantially reduced, although not limited entirely.

Regular Corporation versus S Corporation. If the joint venture is structured so that the corporate entity will be owned solely by individual shareholders, then the option of an S corporation will be available.

One of the most important factors in determining whether a corporation should elect to be treated as an S corporation is a comparison of the tax rates. The choice that produces the lowest tax under most circumstances will be the desirable one.

One of the factors to be considered in determining whether an S corporation election should be made is whether the earnings will be distributed currently. If earnings will be accumulated and either never distributed or distributed only on liquidation of the corporation, then an S corporation election may not be appropriate. If, on the other hand, all current earnings will be paid to the shareholders in the form of dividends or if there is no need for the retention of earnings, then an S corporation election may be preferable.

In addition, it is quite common for a new venture to operate at a loss during its early years of operation for a variety of reasons. The desirability of the S corporation election should also be considered when the venture anticipates one or more loss years. If a corporation does not elect S corporation status, it has a net operating loss carryback for the 3 preceding years, and if the loss is not fully utilized in those years it has a net operating loss carryforward for 15 years. If, however, the shareholders make the S corporation election, they may deduct the corporation's loss on their individual tax returns, subject to the S corporation limitations discussed earlier and the passive loss limitation rules enacted in the Tax Reform Act of 1986. In such circumstances, it may be advantageous for a corporation to elect to be treated as an S corporation in order to permit its shareholders to enjoy the current benefit from such losses. If, on the other hand, the joint venture is expected to break even and become profitable in a relatively short period of time and future earnings are expected to be accumulated for the business, then it may be undesirable to make the S corporation election because operating losses can be used and carried forward in future years to offset future income.

Of course, planning whether to make the S corporation election will also depend on the tax status of the individual shareholders. If the shareholders are in low tax brackets at the time the losses are incurred, but are likely to be in higher tax brackets in later years, it may be more advantageous to elect to be treated as a regular corporation.

Finally, one of the factors to be considered in determining whether a corporation should elect to be treated as an S corporation is the effect of applicable state income or franchise taxes. An S corporation election may not be recognized for state tax purposes and may result in additional cost which must be taken into account in deciding whether to make the election.

S Corporation versus Partnership. There are significant differences between the taxation of partners of a partnership and the taxation of shareholders of an S corporation. First, an S corporation allows much less flexibility than does a partnership with respect to variations in profit participation, liquidation preferences, and control among the owners of the business. This is largely due to the requirement that an S corporation can have only one class of stock outstanding. In addition, a change in the amount of shareholders' participation in profits may result in the imposition of taxes.

On the other hand, the partnership taxation rules make it possible to provide for different rights in particular partners or groups of partners and to enable a partner to have a larger or smaller share in profits than his proportionate investment. Further, some partners may have preferences over others on liquidation, and it is possible to either reduce or enlarge the percentage profit participation of a partner without such change constituting a taxable transaction. Finally, if debt will be incurred at the entity level, such debt generally will increase a partner's basis of his partnership interest, while there would be no basis increase in shares of an S corporation.

Observations

The tax advantages associated with the choice of entity need to be weighed very carefully by all parties to the venture. In some instances, the interests of corporate and individual joint venturers may be coincident. In other circumstances, however, the interests of individual and corporate venturers are likely to be adverse, such as where the corporate form may be preferable for a corporate venturer, whereas the partnership form may be preferable for individual venturers. It will be of paramount importance to reconcile these very important differences at an early stage of the negotiations because of their substantial economic implications.

OPERATIONAL TAX CONSIDERATIONS

There are numerous tax rules that will affect hospital-physician joint ventures. These all need to be considered in each joint venture in order to ensure that tax benefits are maximized. Two of the more significant rules, the accelerated cost recovery system and the at-risk rules, are considered below. In addition, some of the more significant rules enacted in the Tax Reform Act of 1986 are reviewed.

Cost Recovery Deductions

The "accelerated cost recovery system" (ACRS) permits the recovery of capital costs of acquiring or building certain depreciable property over eight statutory "recovery periods," which are unrelated to, and in some cases shorter than, the useful lives of the properties.[10] The cost recovery methods and periods are the same for both new and used "recovery property." Recovery property is defined as tangible property placed in service by the taxpayer after December 31, 1980, if the property is used in a trade or business or is held for the production of income. In addition, changes enacted by the Tax Reform Act of 1986 generally are applicable to property placed in service after December 31, 1986.

The recovery period for nonresidential real property, such as medical office buildings and their structural components, generally is 31.5 years. In addition, the joint venture will have to use the straight-line cost recovery method over such 31.5-year period.

Cost recovery deductions allowable for the taxable year in which nonresidential real property is placed in service will reflect only the months during such year that the property was in service or ready to be placed in service, while cost recovery deductions for the taxable year in which such property is disposed of will reflect only the months through disposition. Cost recovery deductions with respect to the first month in which nonresidential real property is placed in service will reflect cost recovery for only one half of the first month, regardless of the day of the month the property is placed in service.

The recovery periods for most types of tangible personal property used by joint ventures will be either three or five years, depending on the class life and type of property involved. It is typical for most of the tangible personal property purchased by a joint venture to be of a type eligible for a five-year recovery period. The cost of such property will be recovered using a prescribed accelerated method which will provide benefits approximating the 200 percent declining balance method for the early years of the recovery period and the straight-line method in later years.

If the taxable year in which three-year or five-year ACRS property is placed in service contains less than 12 months, cost recovery deductions allowable for such a taxable year will reflect only the portion of the percentage of such property's unadjusted basis otherwise recoverable in the first year property is placed in service which is allocable to the number of months and partial months in such taxable year. Also, if more than 40 percent of all property is placed in service by a joint venture during the last three months of a taxable year, a mid-quarter convention now applies.[11] Basically, the mid-quarter convention treats all property placed in service during any quarter of a taxable year as placed in service on the midpoint of such quarter. No cost recovery deductions with respect to three-year or five-year property are allowable for the taxable year in which a disposition (including a retirement) of such property occurs.

Lessees constructing buildings or improvements on leased property are also required to amortize the cost of such buildings or improvements over the normal recovery period, even if the lease term is shorter than the recovery period.[12]

Upon the disposition of recovery property, gain or loss will generally be recognized. All gain on the disposition of real and personal property of the joint venture will generally be taxed at the same rate.

"At Risk" Limitations

The shareholders of an S corporation and the individual partners of a partnership will be subject to the "at risk" rules with respect to any activity.[13] Thus, S corporation or partnership losses arising out of joint venture activities will be deductible to the extent the shareholders or partners have amounts at risk.

In the Tax Reform Act of 1986, the at risk rules were extended to the activity of holding real property, with an exception for qualified nonrecourse financing, which is secured by real property used in the activity. Under this rule, real estate joint ventures may obtain financing from an otherwise qualified lender who has an equity interest in the venture, provided that the terms of the financing are commercially reasonable and substantially similar to loans made by unrelated parties. Further, seller financing is not treated as qualified nonrecourse financing. These amendments became effective with respect to property acquired after December 31, 1986.

The amount at risk is limited to the amount of money and the adjusted basis of other property the taxpayer has contributed to the particular activity, income generated by the activity, the amount borrowed by the taxpayer and contributed to the activity to the extent the taxpayer is personally and primarily liable for such borrowed amounts, and the amount borrowed by the activity for use in the activity to the extent that the taxpayer is personally and primarily liable for such borrowed amounts, all as calculated at the end of the taxable year. The amount the taxpayer has at risk may not include any amount protected against loss through guarantees, stop-loss agreements, or other similar arrangements.

The holding of real property is generally considered to be an activity separate from other investment or business activities. Under the general rule, the amount for which the shareholder or partner will be deemed to be at risk will be computed separately for each activity of the joint venture. An allocation of income, deductions, and basis must be made among the activities constituting the holding of real property and other activities.

Any amount that is disallowed in any taxable year because of the at risk rules may be carried over to the next taxable year, but a taxpayer's at risk amount in subsequent taxable years with respect to the activity involved will be reduced by that portion of the loss which is allowed as a deduction. Recapture of previously allowed losses and the recognition of income is required when the taxpayer's amount at risk is reduced below zero. The amount recaptured is limited to the excess of loss amounts previously allowed in that activity over any amounts previously recaptured. If the shareholder's or partner's at risk basis is increased to a positive number, the amount disallowed can be utilized in later years to the extent of such increase.

The at risk rules may adversely affect physician investors if they borrow all or a portion of their capital contribution on a nonrecourse basis or are protected against loss of all or part of their investment in some manner, such as by guaranteed repurchase agreements.

THE TAX REFORM ACT OF 1986 AND JOINT VENTURES

The Tax Reform Act of 1986 (1986 Act) contained a number of provisions that have an effect on the structure and operations of hospital-physician joint ventures. As indicated earlier in this chapter, the lowering of the top individual rate from 50 percent to 38.5 percent in 1987 and to 28 percent in 1988 would decrease the overall value of tax losses. In addition, the 1986 Act extended the at-risk rules to the holding of real property, subject to certain limitations, expanded the scope of the investment interest limitation, increased the class lives of various types of tangible property potentially acquired by joint ventures, and repealed the net capital gains deduction for individuals. In addition, the 1986 Act contained a passive investment loss limitation and eliminated the use of the cash method of accounting for many hospital-physician joint ventures.

Taken together, the various changes contained in the 1986 Act require hospitals and physicians alike to plan their joint venture activities more carefully and to make sure that the joint venture activity itself will provide adequate economic returns that do not depend principally on the value of tax losses or other tax benefits.

A detailed analysis of the provisions of the 1986 Act as they affect hospital-physician joint ventures is beyond the scope of this chapter. However, three of the most significant provisions of the 1986 Act affecting hospital-physician joint ventures are described below.

Passive Investment Loss Limitation

Prior to the enactment of the 1986 Act, many hospital-physician joint ventures, such as medical office buildings and equipment leasing transactions, depended quite heavily on the individual physician investors' ability to claim the tax losses or investment credits available by reason of the activity of the joint venture against their other taxable income. The 1986 Act repealed the investment tax credit, while certain limited credits still remain available, such as the rehabilitation tax credit. However, one of the most significant provisions affecting hospital-physician joint ventures is the passive loss limitation contained in new Section 469 of the Internal Revenue Code.

Deductions from passive activities, to the extent that they exceed income from all such activities (exclusive of portfolio income), generally may not be deducted against other active income of a taxpayer. Thus, for example, if a limited partnership is structured to acquire and operate a medical office building, the tax losses generally may not be deductible against other active and portfolio income of the physician investor. Similarly, credits from passive activities generally are limited to the tax allocable to the passive activities. The suspended losses and credits are carried forward and treated as deductions and credits from passive activities in the next taxable year. When a taxpayer disposes of his entire interest in an activity, any remaining suspending losses incurred in connection with that activity will be allowed in full.

Passive activities for purposes of Section 469 are defined to include trade or business activities in which the taxpayer does not materially participate (e.g., a limited partnership activity) and rental activities, such as real estate and equipment leasing. Also, limited partners are conclusively deemed to be involved in a passive activity.

Section 469 generally applies to individuals, trusts, and personal service corporations. Certain closely held corporations are subject to a more limited rule under which passive losses and credits may not be applied to offset portfolio income.

Limitation on Use of Cash Method of Accounting

Most hospital-physician joint ventures utilize the cash method of accounting for tax purposes. Although accrual basis financial statements may be prepared for lenders and for other purposes, use of the cash method of accounting for tax purposes often provides an opportunity to defer the recognition of some income until subsequent taxable years.

The 1986 Act now prohibits the use of the cash method of accounting by any C corporation, partnerships that have a C corporation as a partner, and all tax shelters. Most joint ventures will be treated as tax shelters. Although certain organizations are excepted from the application of these rules, such as qualified personal services corporations or C corporations with average annual gross receipts of $5 million or less, most joint ventures are going to be required to utilize the accrual method of accounting. This requirement will, among other things, have the probable effect of accelerating the taxability of income derived from the provision of services to third parties on other than a cash basis. In addition, it will require more costly accounting due to the greater complexity required to account for income and expenses utilizing the accrual method of accounting.

Taxable Year Rules

Many joint ventures select fiscal years that provide an opportunity for the participants in the joint venture to defer the recognition of gain. The 1986 Act now requires that partnerships, S corporations, and personal service corporations use a taxable year that generally conforms to the taxable year of their owners. A partnership must use (in order of priority) the taxable year of the partners owning the majority of the partnership profits and capital, the taxable year of all of its principal partners, or the calendar year. An S corporation or a personal service corporation must use the calendar year. An exception is made for any partnership, S corporation, or personal service corporation that establishes to the satisfaction of the secretary of the Treasury a business purpose for having a different taxable year. The deferral of income to partners or shareholders for any period is not to be treated as a business purpose.

ALTERNATIVE DEPRECIATION SYSTEM

The Alternative Depreciation System is a comprehensive set of rules designed to reduce or eliminate the tax benefits associated with property leased to or otherwise used by tax-exempt organizations. In general, this system deals with three basic areas. First, the recovery periods for real and personal property classified as tax-exempt use property are greater than the recovery periods for all other real or personal property. Second, special rules identify criteria to be used to distinguish service and other contracts from leases of real or personal property. Finally, several rules are applicable to partnerships that have tax-exempt organizations as partners, to lessors of personal or real property to such partnerships, and to corporations with tax-exempt shareholders.

The Alternative Depreciation System will have a direct and significant impact on joint ventures that involve one or more tax-exempt hospitals (or related organizations) directly or through separate partnerships or subsidiaries.

Tax-Exempt Entity Defined

In order to be treated as tax-exempt use property, real or personal property must be leased to a tax-exempt entity. Consequently, the organizations that constitute tax-exempt entities are important.

A tax-exempt entity is defined generally as meaning the United States, any state or political subdivision thereof, any possession of the United States, or any agency or instrumentality of any of the foregoing, an organization which is exempt from federal income taxes and any foreign person or entity.[14] Thus, federal, state, local, and foreign governments, as well as tax-exempt and public hospitals, will be treated as tax-exempt entities for purposes of these provisions. In addition, certain partnerships and for-profit corporations with tax-exempt partners or shareholders will be treated as tax-exempt entities for purposes of these rules.

Tax-Exempt Use Property

The tax-exempt entity leasing rules divide property leased to tax-exempt organizations into two classes, nonresidential real property and tangible property other than nonresidential property.

Tangible Property Other than Nonresidential Real Property. That portion of any tangible property other than nonresidential property which is leased to tax-exempt organizations will be treated as tax-exempt use property. The cost recovery deductions for tax-exempt use personal property must be determined by using the straight-line method (without regard to salvage value) and by using a recovery period of 12 years if the property has no present class life or the present class life if the property has been assigned one. Under certain operating rules, the recovery period for tax-exempt use personal property must be at least 125 percent of the lease term, and improvements to property other than land are not treated as separate property.

Notwithstanding the breadth of their application, the rules applicable to tax-exempt use personal property are subject to numerous exceptions that act to mitigate their adverse impact.

First, property subject to a short-term lease to a tax-exempt organization will not be treated as tax-exempt use property. For purposes of this rule, a short-term lease is defined as any lease the term of which is less than three years and less than the greater of one year or 30 percent of the property's present class life. Property leased to a tax-exempt organization pursuant to a short-term lease will not be subject to the Alternative Depreciation System.

Second, any portion of personal property predominantly used by a tax-exempt organization in an unrelated trade or business will not be treated as tax-exempt use property.

Third, qualified technological equipment, when used by a tax-exempt organization pursuant to a lease with a term of five years or less, is not subject to the Alternative Depreciation System and thus can be depreciated under ACRS utilizing either a three-year or a five-year recovery period currently applicable to that property. However, if the qualified technological equipment is leased to a tax-exempt organization for a term of more than five years, including renewals, then the qualified technological equipment must be depreciated over a 12-year recovery period or the equipment's class life utilizing the straight-line method. Qualified technological equipment is defined to include any computer or peripheral equipment, any high-technology telephone station equipment installed on a customer's premises, and high-technology medical equipment.[15]

Of greatest significance in the joint venture context is the special treatment afforded to high-technology medical equipment. High-technology medical equipment is defined as "any electronic, electromechanical, or computer-based high-technology equipment used in the screening, monitoring, observation, diagnosis, or treatment of patients in a laboratory, medical, or hospital environment."[16] High-technology medical equipment may include CT scanners, nuclear magnetic resonance equipment, clinical chemistry analyzers, drug monitors, diagnostic ultrasound scanners, nuclear cameras, radiographic and fluoroscopic systems, holter monitors, and bedside monitors.[17]

Real Property. Real property will treated as tax-exempt use property if it is leased to a tax-exempt entity pursuant to a *disqualified lease.* Significantly, these rules will apply only to a property if the *portion* leased to the tax-exempt entity pursuant to a disqualified lease constitutes more than 35 percent of the property. The threshold percentage will be determined utilizing net rentable floor space, not including common areas.

In addition, even if the 35 percent threshold test is satisfied, a lease must also meet one of the following criteria in order to be treated as a disqualified lease.

1. *Part or all of the property must be financed by a tax-exempt obligation and the tax-exempt entity (or a related entity) must participate in such a financing.* This provision was designed to deal with the much publicized sale-leasebacks of municipal facilities financed with tax-exempt bonds.

Whether a tax-exempt entity will be treated as having participated in financing the acquisition of property with tax-exempt obligations will depend on all relevant circumstances. However, a tax-exempt organization will be treated as having participated in the financing if it issues the obligations and if it is reasonable to expect at the time of issuance that the organization will be a user of all or a portion of the property. The organization will also be treated as having participated in the financing if, prior to the financing, it commits itself to lease space in the building.

2. *There is a fixed or determinable purchase price, option, or sale option that involves the tax-exempt entity (or a related entity) or there is an equivalent of such an option.* An option or a put at fair market value at the time of exercise will not be treated as a fixed or determinable price option or put. Certain types of formulas also are permissible if the parties reasonably expect such formulas will produce a figure approximately equal to fair market value at the time of exercise. However, any provision that has the effect of passing on to the lessee or a related party the risk that the property's residual value will decrease will be treated as the equivalent of a fixed or determinable price option. Furthermore, the option need not be contained in the lease, and the option to buy or put stock in a corporation or an interest in a partnership which owns the property may be treated as an option to buy or put that property.

3. *The lease has a term of more than 20 years.* In determining a lease term, all options to renew will be taken into account and two or more successive leases that are a part of the same transaction with respect to the same property will be treated as one lease. However, options to renew at fair rental value determined at the time of renewal will not be taken into account.

4. *The lease occurs after a sale or other transfer of the property by, or lease of the property from, the tax-exempt entity (or a related entity) and such* *property has been used by such entity (or by a related entity) before such sale or lease.* This provision brings under its coverage all forms of transactions in which the tax-exempt organization directly or indirectly sells, leases, disposes of, or otherwise transfers property previously owned by it or a party related to it and which it subsequently uses. However, lease-backs within the first three months after the date such property is first used by the tax-exempt organization are not taken into account.

Treatment of Tax-Exempt Use of Real Property

If real property is treated as tax-exempt use real property, the deductions allowable for depreciation and amortization must be determined by using the straight-line method (without regard to salvage value) and by using a recovery period of 40 years. Furthermore, the recovery period may be not less than 125 percent of the lease term. Thus, for example, if the joint venture were to enter into a long-term lease of a medical office building with a limited partnership, and the lease term to the hospital were to exceed 32 years, the recovery period for the property owned by the partnership would exceed 40 years. The recovery period would be determined on the basis of the number of months in a year in which the property is placed in service.

Service Contract Rules

Prior to the enactment of the Tax Reform Act of 1984, a number of transactions were ostensibly structured as service agreements between the hospital and physicians' venture in order to permit the physicians to obtain the investment credits and depreciation deductions, while at the same time passing the benefits of such deductions through to the lessee hospital through lower costs. Consequently, a new definition of lease was established.[18] Basically, criteria are specified that will be used to determine whether an arrangement that purports to be something other than a lease should be treated as a lease for tax purposes.

In determining whether a particular arrangement is more properly treated as a lease, six factors are to be taken into consideration:

1. *Physical possession* of the property indicates that the relationship is a lease for tax purposes.

2. *Control of the property* also is indicative of a lease. The concept of control is quite broad and will be viewed as existing when the tax-exempt organization may dictate or has a contractual right to dictate the manner in which the property is operated, maintained, or improved. Nevertheless, control will not exist merely by reason of contractual provisions designed to enable the tax-exempt entity to monitor or ensure the service provider's compliance with performance, safety, or other general standards.

3. A contract that conveys a *significant possessory or economic interest* to a tax-exempt organization more clearly resembles a lease than a service contract. The existence of a possessory or economic interest in property will be established by facts that show (*a*) the property's use is likely to be dedicated to the tax-exempt organization for a substantial portion of its useful life, (*b*) the tax-exempt organization shares the risk that the property will decline in value, (*c*) the tax-exempt organization shares any appreciation in the value of the property, (*d*) the tax-exempt organization shares the savings from the property's operating cost, or (*e*) the tax-exempt organization bears the risk of damage to or loss of the property.

4. Generally, a service provider bears the risk of substantially diminished receipts or substantially increased expenditures if there is nonperformance under the contract. If the facts establish that the service provider *does not bear any risk of nonperformance,* that will be indicative of a lease. This means that take-or-pay or similar types of agreements will presumably be brought under the umbrella of this provision.

5. If the service provider *does not use the property concurrently* to provide significant services to entities unrelated to the service recipient, then a lease is indicated by the arrangement. The mere ability to provide such services to others does not appear to be relevant; rather, the test will be based on actual rather than potential use of the property.

6. Perhaps one of the most critical elements of the test is *whether the contract price substantially exceeds the rental value of the property* for the contract period. If it does, then a service contract will be indicated. However, if the total contract price does not substantially exceed the rental value of the property for the contract period, then this is likely to be a significant factor in establishing that the relationship is, in fact, a lease rather than a service contract.

If the total contract price reflects substantial costs that are attributable to items other than the use of the property subject to the contract, then the contract will more closely resemble a service contract. If the contract states charges for services separately from charges for the use of the property, a lease will be indicated.

In addition to these six factors, all other relevant facts and circumstances will be taken into account. Unfortunately, neither the presence nor absence of one or more of the factors will be determinative, and there is very little guidance in this area.

Special Rules Applicable to Partnerships and For Profit Subsidiaries

Additional rules apply to determine whether property owned by a partnership or a corporation that has both tax-exempt and nonexempt partners or shareholders will be treated as tax-exempt use property.

Property Owned by Partnerships. A portion of any property held by a partnership having both a tax-exempt and a nonexempt partner will be treated as tax-exempt use property where the partnership makes other than a "qualified allocation" to the tax-exempt partner. A qualified allocation is defined as an allocation to the tax exempt entity which:

>   (i) is consistent with such entity's being allocated the same distributive share of each item of income, gain, loss, deduction, credit, and basis and such share remains the same during the entire period the entity is a partner in the partnership, and
>   (ii) has substantial economic effect within the meaning of Section 704(b)(2).[19]

The first criterion imposes the requirement that the allocations of all tax items to the tax-exempt organization must be the same and remain the same during the entire period the entity is a partner. The second criterion makes it clear that the rules pertaining to the substantial economic effect test will apply. Further, even where an allocation does not have substantial economic effect, the general tests of Section 704(b) will be applicable, and as long as such requirements are satisfied this prong of the test will be met.[20]

In the event a partnership agreement provides for other than a qualified allocation, the tax-exempt entity's proportionate share of partnership property will be determined according to the larger of the entity's share of partnership income or gain. Moreover, the tax-exempt organization's proportionate share will be the largest share of income or gain that the organization has during the period that the entity is a partner in the partnership, if its share varies during such time period.

Significantly, the rules applicable to tax-exempt entity partners are only applied after first applying the general tax-exempt use property rules as previously described.[21] For example, if a tax-exempt organization leases 60 percent of the space in a building owned by a partnership having an exempt entity partner, 60 percent of the building will be tax-exempt use property and not eligible for ACRS deductions, but the eligibility of the remaining 40 percent for ACRS will be tested under the qualified allocation rules. However, the converse is not true: a tax-exempt partner need not have more than a 35 percent interest in the partnership in order for the rules to be applicable. Thus, it is possible for a tax-exempt organization to own a small percent interest and still trigger the application of these rules.

Property Leased to Partnerships. Anticipating that transactions might occur involving property leased to partnerships that have one or more tax-exempt organizations as partners, Section 168(h) contains the following provision:

>   In the case of any property which is leased to a partnership, the determination of whether any portion of such property is tax-exempt use property shall be made by treating each tax-exempt entity partner's proportionate share . . . of such property as being leased to such partner.[22]

Thus, in the case of real property, these rules would be applicable to real property only if a tax-exempt organization had more than a 35 percent interest in the partnership. This 35 percent rule would be determined on the basis of income or gain.

If there is no special allocation, then the 35 percent rule would be applicable. However, if there is a special allocation to the tax-exempt organization partner, then the rules previously described would use the highest allocation of income or gain to the tax-exempt organization for purposes of determining whether the 35 percent rule is satisfied.

In the case of personal property, these rules would be applicable to the extent of the participation by a tax-exempt organization as a partner in such partnership, however large or small.

With respect to personal property, the Code does not clearly indicate whether the nonexempt partners are entitled to a full percentage share of the investment credit equal to their percentage interest in the partnership or whether the investment credit must first be reduced and then allocated in accordance with the partnership agreement. The language of the statute appears to contemplate the former arrangement under an aggregate approach similar to that in Revenue Ruling 78-268.[23] This reading is supported by literally following the mandate of the Code by treating the property as if a proportionate share were leased directly to the partners. However, again it would be necessary to have a proper allocation of the credit in the partnership agreement in order to avoid further problems.

For Profit Subsidiaries. For profit business corporations partially or wholly owned by tax-exempt organizations will also be affected by the tax-exempt entity leasing rules. In general, a "tax-exempt controlled entity" will be treated as a tax-exempt entity for purposes of Section 168. A "tax-exempt controlled entity" is any corporation where 50 percent or more (in value) of the stock is held by one or more tax-exempt entities. In addition, a tax-exempt entity will be treated as actually holding stock which it holds through the application of attribution rules. Thus, a partially or wholly owned subsidiary of a hospital's for profit subsidiary may also be treated as a tax-exempt controlled entity.

If a tax-exempt controlled entity makes an irrevocable election, it will not be treated as a tax-exempt entity for purposes of Section 168. However, if such election is made, any gain recognized by the tax-exempt shareholder on any disposition of an interest in such corporation, such as on the sale of the stock, as well as any dividends or interest received or accrued by the tax-exempt shareholder from such corporation, will be treated as unrelated business taxable income for purposes of Section 511 of the Code.

The treatment of for profit corporations as tax-exempt entities has significance to joint ventures in two contexts. First, corporate joint ventures in which a tax-exempt hospital owns at least 50 percent of the stock will be treated as a tax-exempt entity with respect to real and personal property it leases from third parties. As a consequence, property owned by third parties and leased to such corporations may be subject to·the Alternative Depreciation System, as discussed earlier in this chapter. Second, if the corporation is a partner of a partnership, the rules pertaining to the treatment of property owned by or leased to a partnership with a tax-exempt organization as a partner will be applicable. Careful planning will be required to minimize the impact of these rules.

Joint Ventures and Tax-Exempt Status

Nonprofit hospitals enjoy exemption from federal income taxation under Section 501(a) of the Internal Revenue Code, typically because they qualify as charitable organizations described in Section 501(c)(3) of the Code. Section 501(c)(3) describes those entities as "organized and operated exclusively for . . . charitable, scientific . . . or educational purposes."

In order to obtain or maintain tax-exempt status under Section 501(c)(3), no part of a hospital's net earnings may inure in whole or in part to the benefit of any private shareholder or individual.[24] In addition, a hospital must be organized and operated to further a public purpose, and thus may not be organized or operated for the benefit of private interests such as designated individuals or persons directly or indirectly controlling the charitable hospital.[25]

When nonprofit hospitals become involved in joint ventures, the key concerns are twofold: The first is whether any of the financial or nonfinancial arrangements contemplated by the joint venture will result in the inurement of any portion of the nonprofit hospital's net earnings to the benefit of any private shareholder or individual. The second is whether the hospital's participation in the joint venture, regardless of its form, will confer a benefit upon private interests that is so substantial as to provide evidence that the hospital is operating for private benefit rather than for public purposes.

Inurement

The prohibition against inurement of net earnings is directed toward the conferral of financial or similar benefits upon insiders or other persons in control of a charitable organization other than as reasonable compensation for goods provided or services actually rendered. The inurement prohibition is closely related to the private benefit prohibition, since evidence that net earnings are inuring to the benefit of private shareholders or individuals also evidences that the organization is operated for private purposes rather than for public benefit. The prohibition against inurement of net earnings is likely to be of concern where the proposed joint venture involves the direct or indirect use or distribution of a hospital's assets through loans,[26] leases,[27] and compensation arrangements.[28]

For example, in a contractual joint venture the prohibition against inurement should not be violated if the hospital pays reasonable compensation for services actually rendered. However, if the physician (or physician group) is in a control position with respect to the hospital and is paid amounts in excess of what otherwise would be paid to unrelated physicians, inurement may exist. Another instance where the inurement prohibition could be violated involves the use of contingent compensation arrangements that are highly suspect by the IRS if the contingent compensation is based on a percentage of net earnings or net income.[29] For example, if a hospital contracts with a corporation controlled by members of its medical staff for utilization review or similar services to control its costs under the prospective payment system and such payments increase or decrease with the number of admissions, the hospital must be sure that the compensation paid for those services is not excessive in relation to the services performed.

In joint ventures organized and operated as partnerships, the prohibition against inurement can be of concern where, for example, the hospital leases ground to the partnership to construct a medical office building for nominal rent, or at rents substantially below market value, and with no further justification for such arrangement.[30] Another example might involve a provision in the partnership agreement for the allocation of excessive cost recovery deductions or cash flow by the nonprofit hospital to the physicians in a manner that results in excessive economic benefits being made available to physician limited partners.

Care also must be exercised in structuring joint ventures conducted through corporations. For example, in Revenue Ruling 67–5,[31] a charitable organization owned stock of a corporation as its principal asset. The corporation's shareholders voted to issue a new class of preferred stock, diluting the charitable organization's holdings. The charitable organization's trustees failed to vote against the issuance of the new preferred stock. The IRS held that the trustees failed to protect the interests of the charitable organization, thereby permitting excessive benefits to flow to private interests, and revoked the exemption. Similar types of problems may arise in the context of a corporate joint venture. Issues concerning the valuation of stock, corporate assets, stock options, going concern value or goodwill, the structure and amount of executive compensation, dividend policies, and the control of the corporation itself must be addressed in order to ensure that the participation by a hospital in a joint venture through a corporation co-owned with physicians or others does not jeopardize tax-exempt status.

Private Benefit

The requirement that a hospital must be operated for public purposes rather than for private benefit is but another way of requiring that it must be operated exclusively for exempt purposes. The difficulty in identifying where a private benefit problem exists in a joint venture is exemplified in the development of the IRS policy toward participation by charitable organizations in limited partnerships.

In 1975, the IRS dealt with the question of whether a corporation organized to provide low- and moderate-income housing on a nondiscriminatory basis through the use of a limited partnership qualified for tax-exempt status under Section 501(c)(3) of the Code.[32] The IRS concluded, among other things, that the participation in a limited partnership would make the corporation a direct participant in an arrangement for the sharing of net profits of an income-producing venture with private individuals or institutions of a noncharitable nature. Such participation, concluded the IRS, would be inherently incompatible with being operated exclusively for charitable purposes within the meaning of Section 501(c)(3) of the Code.

After considerable discussion within the IRS and challenges to this position in the courts, one of which was litigated to a successful conclusion,[33] the IRS reversed itself in 1983. In General Counsel Memorandum 39005 the IRS considered a fact situation involving an exempt organization that proposed to participate as one of several general partners in a limited partnership to be formed for the purpose of constructing, owning, and operating a federally assisted apartment complex for handicapped and elderly individuals of limited income. After reviewing various precedents, the IRS concluded that an exempt organization's participation in a partnership arrangement as a general partner should not automatically result in denial of Section 501(c)(3) status. Rather, the IRS stated that the partnership arrangement should be closely scrutinized to assure that the statutorily imposed obligations on the general partner do not conflict with the exempt organization's ability to pursue its charitable goals.

The IRS continues to apply a strict scrutiny standard. All joint venture relationships will be reviewed very carefully to determine the primary focus of the venture. If the primary focus is to further the private interests of the joint venturers, such as medical staff members, then tax-exempt status may be in jeopardy. If, on the other hand, it can be established that the primary purpose of the joint venture is to enable the charitable hospital to carry out its charitable mission more effectively, then tax-exempt status should not be in jeopardy.

The participation by a nonprofit hospital with private interests in an arm's-length transaction generally is permissible. However, the private benefit challenge is more frequently raised when the business relationship is with persons more closely linked to the charitable hospital, such as members of the medical staff, even though such persons are not "private shareholders or individuals" within the meaning of the inurement prohibition.[34] In advancing the interests of a charitable hospital in a case where private benefit may present a problem, the parties should provide as much definitive evidence as possible of the benefits accruing to the charitable hospital in the aggregate and establish some direct and substantial relationship between the benefits provided to the joint venture participants and the accomplishment of the charitable purposes of the hospital.

Use of Corporate Subsidiaries

A tax-exempt hospital or hospital system can conduct its various activities through wholly owned taxable subsidiaries.[35] However, when using taxable subsidiaries, it is important to bear in mind the general principle that an exempt organization cannot do indirectly through a taxable subsidiary what it cannot do directly itself if the subsidiary has no substantial independent business purpose. The IRS will scrutinize the activities of for-profit subsidiaries, particularly where there is a risk that the prohibitions against inurement or private benefit may be violated and that the for-profit subsidiary is being used primarily as a subterfuge to avoid direct involvement in such improper activities by the parent corporation or an affiliate.[36] If challenged, various activities conducted through for-profit subsidiaries may be imputed to the parent corporation when the circumstances surrounding the transaction are egregious or are in blatant disregard of established principles concerning inurement and private benefit.

Planning Concerns

In planning joint ventures the initial focus should be on whether or not the activities to be conducted by the joint venture serve a charitable purpose. If it can be established that the joint venture's activities would, if carried on directly by the hospital, further charitable purposes, the first hurdle will be overcome.

Next, contractual relationships between and among the venturers, including partnership agreements, corporate documents, leases, management contracts, or loans, must be examined to ensure that none of the arrangements will result separately or in the aggregate in inurement of any net earnings and that, taken as a whole, the arrangements evidence that the public purposes rather than private benefit are being served. This will require a finding, among other things, that the benefits to be received by the private investors (e.g., limited partners) are incidental to the public purposes served by the partnership and that the financial returns to be earned by investors are reasonable in light of the amount of their investment, its duration, and the degree of risk.

Special concerns arise when an operational joint venture such as an ambulatory surgery center (as distinguished from an investment joint venture such as an equipment leasing partnership) is involved. It can be expected that the IRS will scrutinize more closely the economic relationships among the parties as well as the economic performance of the business itself to ascertain whether the business conducted by the joint venture truly furthers a charitable purpose. Charge structures, policies with regard to indigent care, participation in the Medicare or Medicaid programs, free or below-cost community service programs, and similar factors will be scrutinized to ascertain whether a sufficiently broad segment of the community is likely to be benefited by the activity conducted by the joint venture.

Finally, consideration should be given to structuring agreements regardless of their form to include an expression of and a commitment to achieve values evidencing that the joint venture is designed to achieve a charitable purpose.

JOINT VENTURES AND THE UNRELATED BUSINESS INCOME TAX

Nonprofit hospitals, their general exemption from federal taxation notwithstanding, are subject to the regular corporate income tax on net income they derive from the regular conduct of unrelated trades of businesses.[37] However, certain types of income that are not debt financed are made expressly exempt from the unrelated business income tax. These types of income include dividends, interest, royalties, rents from real property, and gains from the sale of certain types of assets.[38]

The unrelated business income tax treatment of a nonprofit hospital involved in a joint venture will depend on the form that the joint venture takes, the nature of the activity engaged in by the joint venture, and other factors.

Contract Joint Ventures

The unrelated business income tax treatment of joint ventures conducted through contractual forms is complex and will depend on the specific activity involved, the types of goods, services, or facilities provided by the nonprofit hospital to the contractor (e.g., a physician under contract to operate an industrial medicine clinic), and other factors. If, however, the income received can be characterized as interest, rents from real property, royalties, or other forms of income specifically excluded from the definition of unrelated business taxable income, then the nonprofit hospital can avoid completely the taxation of net income it derives from the contractual joint venture.

If none of the exclusions from unrelated business income is available, then the nature of the relationship with the physician and the type of activity being conducted will have to be analyzed to ascertain whether the activity is being conducted primarily to accomplish a charitable purpose or whether it is being conducted primarily to generate net income. It is not enough to argue simply that the profits derived from the venture will be used by the nonprofit hospital to conduct its charitable activities.[39]

Corporate Joint Ventures

The unrelated business income tax treatment of joint ventures operated through separate corporations is relatively straightforward. The business corporation will be regarded as a separate entity for tax purposes, as discussed above. As a result, net income derived by the separate corporation will be subject to the regular corporate income taxes. It is of significance, however, to note that while the dividends paid to its tax-exempt shareholder by the separate corporation will not be deductible by it, such dividends will not be subject to a second tax in the hands of the nonprofit hospital (or its nonprofit parent) by reason of the exemption from taxation of dividends received by charitable organizations.[40]

Partnerships

If the joint venture is conducted through a general or limited partnership, the rules are even more complex and the variables affecting the tax treatment of the nonprofit hospital's distributive share of profits and losses will increase.

In general, the tax treatment of a nonprofit hospital's distributive share of profits, losses, gains, and so on from a partnership will be taxable at the partner level *only* when the activity of the partnership, if conducted directly by the hospital itself, would have been subjected to the unrelated business income tax.[41]

Thus, for example, if the primary activity of the partnership is the leasing of an office building that is not debt financed, then the distributive share of rental income received by a nonprofit hospital from the partnership would not be subject to the unrelated business income tax because the rental income, if received directly by the hospital itself, would have been exempt from the unrelated business income tax by reason of the exclusion of rentals from real property from taxation. A similar analysis would apply to dividend-producing securities held by a partnership, interest received by the partnership, and sales of qualifying assets by a partnership. On the other hand, if the business of the partnership is the sale or leasing of durable medical equipment to the general public, then the hospital's distributive share of net income would probably be taxable, because such an activity would likely be treated as unrelated trade or business.

A more difficult question arises when the partnership is operating an ambulatory surgery center or primary medical clinics. In those instances, the analysis will typically be made in two steps. The first step of the analysis will be to ascertain whether the primary purpose of the trade or business conducted by the partnership is to further a charitable purpose or whether it is being operated for commercial purposes. The primary concern of the IRS will be the fact that the involvement of third parties with the nonprofit hospital in the partnership suggests that the primary motivation of conducting the activity is commercial rather than charitable.

The second part of the analysis will revolve around the question of whether the actual operations of the partnership are being conducted in such a manner as to support the claim that the partnership operations are designed to accomplish a charitable purpose rather than a commercial purpose. Closely related to the first issue, this analysis will look at questions such as the accessibility of the partnership business to a broad segment of the community, for example, through the maintenance of a nondiscriminatory policy with regard to persons unable to pay. The exact nature of the criteria to be applied by the IRS will depend on the specific activity being conducted. Thus, specific factual information needs to be developed concerning operating policies and procedures sufficient to demonstrate that the business of the partnership is being conducted in the same manner as it would have been had the nonprofit hospital conducted the business directly rather than through the partnership.

CONCLUSION

Tax planning is an essential aspect of any hospital-physician joint venture. At a minimum, proper structuring of the timing and amount of tax benefits in a joint venture will have a significant impact on the economic performance of the joint venture and the after-tax returns to the participants. In addition, proper tax planning at the outset may avoid bad business or financial decisions that need to be restructured. Finally, tax-exempt joint venture participants need to be especially concerned about the impact of their participation in the joint venture on their tax-exempt status, as well as taking advantage of the opportunities to minimize the incidence of unrelated business income tax on their distributive shares of profits.

Notes

[1] This chapter is devoted solely to the federal income tax implications of hospital-physician joint ventures. No attempt has been made to discuss employment, state or local income, property, or sales taxes. Each of these taxes is, indeed, important and will require consideration in the context of the specific joint venture.

[2] Internal Revenue Code of 1986, § 701 (hereafter IRC); Treas. Reg. § 1.701-1.

[3] IRC §§ 722, 705.

[4] IRC § 752(a.)

[5] Treas. Reg. § 1.752-1(a).

[6] Treas. Reg. § 1.752-1(c).

[7] Treas. Reg. §§ 301.7701-2 and 301.7701-3.

[8] In the case of corporations with taxable income in excess of $100,000, the amount of tax determined under the regular rates is increased by the lesser of 5 percent of the amount in excess of $100,000 or $11,000. Thus, the benefit of graduated rates is fully phased out for corporations with more than $335,000 of taxable income. Corporate capital gains are taxed at a 28 percent rate.

[9] IRC §§ 1361–1378.

[10] IRC § 168, as amended by the Tax Reform Act of 1986.

[11] IRC § 168(d)(3).

[12] IRC § 168(i)(8).

[13] IRC § 465.

[14] IRC § 168(h)(2).

[15] The commissioner of the IRS is directed to propose regulations specifying additional categories of equipment which may be eligible for treatment as qualified technological equipment, although the commissioner is not expected to promulgate such regulations.

[16] IRC § 168 (i)(2).

[17] Temp. Reg. § 1.168(j)-1T, A-16.

[18] IRC §§ 7701 (e)(1) and (2).

[19] IRC § 168(h)(6)(B).

[20] Temp. Reg. § 1.168(j)-1T, A-23.

[21] See Temp. Reg. § 1.168(j)-1T, A-26.

[22] IRC § 168(h)(5)(A).

[23] 1978-2 C.B. 10.

[24] The term *private shareholder* or *individual* "refers to persons having a personal or private interest in the activities of the organization." Treas. Reg. § 1.501(a)-1(c).

[25] Treas. Reg. § 1.501(c)(3)-1(d)(ii).

[26] E.g., *Lowry Hospital Ass'n v. Comm'r*, 66 T.C. 850 (1976).

[27] E.g., *Harding Hospital v. United States*, 505 F.2d 1068 (6th Cir. 1974); Rev. Rul. 69-545, 1969-2 C.B. 119.

[28] E.g., *Mabee Petroleum Corp. v. United States*, 203 F.2d 872 (5th Cir. 1953); *Alive Fellowship of Harmonious Living v. Comm'r*, 47 T.C.M. 1134, 1143–44 (1984).

[29] The rationale for IRS challenges to percentage of net income arrangements is open to question where reasonable compensation clearly is involved and the contingent compensation arrangement is designed to accomplish an exempt purpose. See e.g., *People of God Community v. Comm'r*, 75 T.C. 127, 133 (1980); *World Family Corporation v. Comm'r*, 81 T.C. 958 (1983). Nevertheless, all contingent compensation arrangements should be structured carefully.

[30] *See e.g.*, Letter Ruling 8443125.

[31] 1967-1 C.B. 123.

[32] G.C.M. 36293 (1975).

[33] *Plumstead Theater Soc'y v. Comm'r*, 74 T.C. 1324, at 1334 n. 8 (1980), *aff'd*, 675 F.2d 244 (9th Cir. 1982).

[34] But *see* G.C.M. 39498 (Jan. 28, 1986).

[35] *See e.g.*, Letter Ruling 8435162, where the IRS stated:

There is no prohibition against a Section 501(c)(3) organization owning stock in a for-profit entity, so long as the for-profit entity operates separate and apart from the nonprofit organization, and the nonprofit organization continues to operate primarily for charitable purposes. The information submitted indicates that you and your subsidiary will be separately maintained, and common operating costs will be allocated, or charged to your subsidiary based on actual usage.

[36] *See Exempt Organizations Continuing Professional Education Technical Instruction Program for 1984*, at 23 (1984); *cf.* Rev. Rul. 67-5, 1967-1 C.B. 123.

[37] IRC § 511(a).

[38] IRC § 512(b).

[39] IRC § 513(a) Rev. Rul. 69-463, 1969-2 C.B. 131.

[40] IRC § 512(b)(1). For a discussion of the potential conflict of interest this creates, *see* D. M. Mancino, "Hospital-Physician Joint Ventures: Some Crucial Considerations," 65, no. 1 *Hospital Progress* (January 1984), pp. 30–35.

[41] IRC § 512(c). *See* Treas. Reg § 1.512(c)-1 for a description of the special rules applicable to partnerships; *see also Service Bolt & Nut Co. Profit Sharing Trust v. Comm'r*, 724 F.2d 519 (6th Cir. 1983).

9

Fraud and Abuse Implications of Joint Ventures

Cary M. Adams, J.D.

INTRODUCTION

A variety of federal and state laws seek to prohibit kickbacks and other payments made to induce or in exchange for patient referrals and other abusive practices. These laws must be carefully reviewed in any joint venture between hospitals and physicians. These laws, which are primarily criminal in nature, may apply to hospitals or their affiliates, freestanding facilities, physicians or other professionals, or the new entity created as a joint venture.

In any analysis of the possible application of antifraud and abuse laws to a joint venture, two fundamental and conflicting objectives must be identified. First, no matter how tempting an arrangement may be in terms of ensuring the steady volume of patient visits needed to maintain financial viability and professional quality of the joint venture, such arrangements should be avoided if they present a substantial risk of violating a criminal statute. The prospect of a criminal investigation, grand jury proceedings, indictment, plea bargaining in exchange for testimony by colleagues and partners, public trial, fine and imprisonment, not to mention adverse publicity, suspension of license, and exclusion from Medicare and Medicaid, should be effective deterrents. Second, competition is now as keen and dynamic in certain market segments and locations of the healthcare industry as in any other marketplace. An effective new means of attracting patient referrals can frequently spell rapid success for the innovator and failure for any competitor too slow or timid to respond in kind.

This tension between complying with the law and competing effectively is exacerbated immeasurably by vague and ambiguous statutory language and by inconsistent and evolving enforcement policy. Resolving this tension promptly and effectively can be one of the most important steps in structuring a successful joint venture. This chapter identifies and discusses many of these laws and attempts to chart a course for successfully steering hospital-physician joint ventures around and through the prohibitions and limitations contained in them.

MEDICARE AND MEDICAID ANTIFRAUD AND ABUSE LAWS

Chief among these laws are the Medicare and Medicaid antifraud and abuse statutes, which make it a federal felony to defraud the Medicare or Medicaid programs in a variety of ways, including offering, making, or receiving payments of any kind in exchange for, or to induce referrals of, Medicare or Medicaid patients. These statutes were adopted in response to various blatant fraudulent or abusive practices, such as filing false claims, which were perceived by Congress to have become widespread. Unfortunately, the statutory language is quite broad and can be read to have application in a variety of situations which have arisen in the more competitive decade of the 1980s, but which were never contemplated by Congress when the language was drafted. Because the statutes are criminal in nature, the only binding interpretations of them are made by the federal courts trying criminal cases brought by federal prosecutors. The number of cases decided and decisions published by the courts is quite limited and can be expected to grow only very slowly, with substantial time lags between the occurrence of an activity and its investigation, indictments, trials, and publication of decisions. For this reason, a great deal of joint venture activity of necessity will occur and is occurring based on sketchy and incomplete understanding of the controlling legal principles.

BASIC PROVISIONS

The Medicare and Medicaid antifraud and abuse statutes prohibit the knowing and willful filing of false claims for reimbursement or false information in a cost report. They also prohibit anyone from knowingly and willfully soliciting or receiving, or offering to pay or paying, any remuneration directly or indirectly, overtly or covertly, in cash or in kind, to induce or in return for a referral of a patient for services or items for which payment could be made under the Medicare or Medicaid programs. Violation of these provisions constitutes a felony and is punishable by five years imprisonment, a fine of up to $25,000, or both. The exact language of the law is important enough that it is quoted in full at the end of this chapter.

The statute has been amended several times, principally as follows: In 1972, Congress added the kickback and referral provisions;[1] in 1977, Congress elevated the crime from misdemeanor to felony status;[2] in 1980, Congress narrowed the crime slightly by adding the requirement that the activity, to be a violation, must be done knowingly and willfully.[3]

The legislative history illuminates the matters with which Congress was concerned. Medicare and Medicaid "fraud" involves an intentional misrepresentation or deception with the intention of receiving some unauthorized benefit. "Abuse" is less clearly defined and includes activities in which providers, practitioners, and suppliers of services operate in a manner inconsistent with sound, accepted medical or business practices, resulting in excessive and unreasonable costs, such as providing unnecessary health services or providing care in an unnecessarily costly manner.[4]

While these statutory provisions clearly prohibit the kind of blatant kickback arrangement that they were intended to deal with and that are dealt with by many state antikickback laws, the language is vague and overboard in various ways, thus creating uncertainty with respect to many other transactions not normally thought of as improper. One confusing area arises out of the exception for certain discounts discussed below. Is it to be inferred from the fact that certain very narrowly defined discounts are specifically excluded from the statute that all other discounts are illegal? This should not be the case, but the language of the statute does not clearly tell us the answer.

An interpretation issue that has received enormous attention, but that has still not been definitively resolved, is the question of waiver of copayments. Technically, the waiver of a Medicare copayment can be viewed as the payment of remuneration to induce the patient to select the provider offering to waive a self-referral. Early on, the Health Care Financing Administration (HCFA) identified such a practice as an example of a prohibited abuse. Enforcement of this provision has been sporadic and inconsistent. The Office of the Inspector General (OIG) of the Department of Health and Human Services has apparently referred numerous cases in which providers, including many prominent not-for-profit hospitals, were systematically waiving copayments and advertising their policy of doing so to the Criminal Division of the Department of Justice. In each of these cases the Department of Justice declined to prosecute. When asked by the OIG to state that it would not prosecute such matters so as to clarify the issue, Justice declined to do so, indicating that the waiver of copayments is a technical violation of a criminal statute and will continue to be analyzed on a case-by-case basis. The waiver issue is not directly implicated in structuring hospital-physician joint ventures (unless the joint venture decides to waive copayments), but it illustrates the inadequacy of the enforcement mechanism for establishing clear policy with respect to these laws.

EXCEPTIONS FOR DISCOUNTS AND EMPLOYEES

The statute carves out two exceptions to the prohibitions against kickbacks. Discounts are not proscribed if they meet two conditions set out in the statute. First, the reduction in price must be "properly disclosed," and then "appropriately reflected in the costs claimed or charges made." This language is clear enough when applied to a hospital or other institutional provider that is subject to cost reimbursement rules—it must not attempt to claim the undiscounted price as its cost, but it must instead reflect its discounted price as its cost in its records and as claimed on its cost report. What is not clear is the application of this language to physicians, laboratories, supply companies, and other providers that are not cost reimbursed. How are such entities and persons supposed to disclose and appropriately reflect such discounts in their charges? Must they disclose to a patient any discount received from any supplier where the discounted item is resold to the patient, or only certain discounts?

The statute also excepts amounts "paid by an employer to an employee (who has a bona fide employee relationship with such employer) for employment in the provision of covered items or services." This language should not be perceived as a means, through employment, of insulating from prosecution what would otherwise be inappropriate kickback arrangements. Instead, it seems intended to clarify that good faith salary and incentive compensation arrangements between employers and employees, where the employee as part of his job directs or refers patients to the employer, are not improper. Still the distinction is sometimes likely to be blurry.

INTERPRETING THE STATUTES

In interpreting vague statutes such as these, it is appropriate to focus on the underlying legislative intent. While vagueness may also constitute a defense to a criminal prosecution, for planning purposes it is much more helpful to understand the kinds of things that were intended to be proscribed and then plan to avoid those activities.

It seems probable that the underlying intent which prompted the legislation was to protect against transactions in which greed or a motive to obtain illicit profit would result in the delivery of medically unnecessary services, necessary services at higher than reasonable costs, detriment to the quality of healthcare services delivered, or other demonstrable harm to the Medicare or Medicaid programs or beneficiaries. It seems likely that OIG and Justice Department officials charged with enforcement also look for such examples of harm in reviewing payment and referral arrangements called to their attention. Novel payment and referral arrangements that do not cause any such harm are much less likely to justify criminal proceedings.

FRAUD AND ABUSE CONCERNS IN JOINT VENTURES

In considering the application of the Medicare and Medicaid antifraud and abuse statutes to joint ventures or to any kind of economic arrangement between hospitals and physicians, it is helpful to break the antireferral statute into three parts: (1) making or receiving a payment in whatever form, (2) in exchange for or to induce, (3) a referral of a Medicare or Medicaid patient. Any time that all three of these elements are present, the statute appears to be technically violated and there is substantial risk of legal problems arising. If any one of these three elements can be eliminated, then the technical violation should disappear. Thus, if there is no payment or no referral, there should be no violation.

Joint ventures sometimes present situations in which payments are made to providers and referrals are made in the opposite direction. In such cases, the question is whether the second element, that the payment is *in exchange for* or *to induce* the referral, is present. In the following examples, the inducement element seems present:

1. If payments (whether a distribution of profits of the joint venture or under separate contracts or leases between the provider and the joint venture) to provider/owners are directly related in whole or in part to the number of patients referred, there is a strong probability that the statute would be violated.
2. If participation in the joint venture were predicated on an express or implied agreement that the joint venture would be the exclusive point of referral for such services from the participating provider, then a violation of the statute is strongly indicated.
3. If either a minimum number of referrals or a specific percentage of the provider's .patients were required to be referred to the joint venture, then a violation of the statutes might be indicated.
4. If a provider's ownership interest in the joint venture is granted free or sold for a token price with the expectation of securing a stream of referrals from the physician in return, then a violation of the statutes might be indicated.

On the other hand, when a joint venture is established with the provider/owners contributing capital in exchange for their ownership interest, sharing in the profits and losses commensurate with their investments, and avoiding the problem payment arrangements as described above, there is substantially diminished risk that the arrangement will be found to violate the law. The basic issue here is whether the venture in its legal structure or in its actual operations will provide inappropriate incentives to any provider to refer patients to the joint venture.

The particular legal structure of the joint venture generally does not control the determination whether a fraud and abuse violation exists. Thus, stock ownership in a corporation versus a partnership interest in a general or limited partnership does not directly determine whether the arrangement is legal. One structure, however, is inherently more troublesome: the cooperative. Any time participation in the benefits of a cooperative is directly linked to the number of patients (or, for example, specimens in the case of a laboratory) referred to the cooperative—a frequent occurrence if patronage refunds or rebates are paid—

and Medicare or Medicaid patients are involved, a violation is risked unless the benefit takes the form of a discount which is disclosed and reflected in the charges made or costs claimed.

Generally, some comfort is taken in joint ventures where any financial benefit gained by the provider/investors is clearly and plainly a return on investment rather than a payment for referring patients. However, if, instead of or in addition to payments as a return on an investment, a referring provider also obtains fees for management services, consulting services, or training, the issue is whether the payments received for the additional services are in fact reasonable fees for those services and the services are themselves necessary and appropriate. Thus, for example, if a physician/investor in a joint venture, who refers some patients to the joint venture, is also asked to assist in training the employees of the joint venture and if the training is necessary, the fee reasonable and appropriate, there should be no area for concern. By contrast, if the training fee is paid monthly even though no training occurs after the first month or two or where no training ever occurs, the training arrangement is subject to be analyzed as a sham and the payment treated as intended to induce or pay for referrals.

In some cases, professional users of a referral facility or supplier are paid a consulting fee relating to the service provided to the user's patients. Again, if necessary and appropriate and the fee reasonable for the consulting services actually obtained, the payment should not be viewed as in exchange for or to induce referrals.

Fraud and abuse concerns also arise in connection with leases entered into between providers and other providers or entities in a position to refer patients. This situation can frequently arise in the joint venture setting. One obvious problem is leases that either calculate the rent as a percentage of the gross fees, net revenues, or net income from professional services and the lessor is in a position to refer patients, or those that determine the rent by multiplying some dollar value times the number of referrals. Such payments are directly related to the utilization of the facility or services and therefore would tend to induce more referrals. If such leases are used, it is important that rental payments approximate fair rental value. The government enforcement agencies are likely to be suspicious of lease payments that substantially deviate from fair rental value.

While reasonable value and avoiding any linkage with referrals provides substantial comfort, the area is not totally free from doubt. The problem is illustrated by a position taken and then withdrawn by HCFA in statements of policy relating to fees paid by durable medical equipment (DME) suppliers to respiratory therapists. In Intermediary Letter 84-9 HCFA made clear that it regarded finder's fees paid by DME suppliers to respiratory therapists for referring patients in need of home oxygen equipment to be a violation of the statute, and they clearly appear to be so. The Letter went further, however, and stated that in certain circumstances where respiratory therapists were paid a reasonable fee by the DME supplier for necessary services such as setting the equip-

ment up, instructing the patient in its use, and performing the monthly maintenance on it, these payments were also a violation. The Letter stated:

> The opportunity to generate a fee is itself a form of remuneration. The offer or
> receipt of such fee opportunities is illegal if intended to induce a patient referral.
> Thus, a supplier who induces patient referrals by offering therapists fee-generating
> opportunities is offering illegal remuneration, even if the therapist is paid no more
> than his or her usual fees.

This language caused a minor uproar in certain segments of the industry where
providers and/or suppliers, through referrals, provide each other the "opportunity to generate a fee." Seven months later, HCFA backed off from the strength
of this statement in Program Memo B-85-2 (April 1985), deleting the language
quoted above and explaining its action as follows:

> We have received a number of inquiries regarding the meaning of those sen-
> tences, and have concluded that they unduly prejudge the legality of certain referral
> arrangements which cannot be determined without consideration of the relevant
> factors and practice patterns described [below].

The Program Memo sets forth a number of additional factors that must be taken
into account in determining whether the opportunity to generate a fee is nonetheless an illegal payment in exchange for or to induce a referral. The factors
are not specifically relevant to the joint venture context, but in general they
seek to clarify whether the payments in fact are for necessary services and the
extent to which they appear to be intended to induce the referral as opposed to
compensating for needed services.

Although HCFA retreated somewhat in its April Memo, the U.S. Court of
Appeals for the Third Circuit in *United States* v. *Greber*,[5] at roughly the same
time decided an appeal by a physician convicted of Medicare fraud and abuse
in connection with interpretation fees paid by the defendant's cardiac monitoring laboratory to physicians referring their patients. The court rejected the defendant's argument that the payments could not be a violation of the statute
unless the "only purpose behind the fee was to improperly induce future services," finding instead that, "[i]f the payments were intended to induce the
physician to use [the laboratory's] services, the statute was violated, even if
the payments were also intended to compensate for professional services."

Some comfort can be taken from the fact that the situation presented in
United States v. *Greber* is very different from the typical joint venture: the
defendant was also convicted of routinely certifying that monitoring had occurred for substantially longer than was in fact the case, with intent to defraud
the Medicare program; the defendant had himself testified in another court proceeding that the purpose of the fee was to induce the referring physicians to
use his service; and the evidence also demonstrated that the defendant repeatedly ordered medically unnecessary services. Obviously, the good faith joint
venture will be structured and operated to avoid such patent misconduct. In
many cases, for example in joint ventured outpatient surgery centers, the hospital's medical staff or a smaller model of such a medical staff in freestanding

facilities will review for quality, medical necessity, and appropriate utilization. In certain kinds of joint ventures, Medicare and, frequently, Medicaid programs provide independent utilization review to guard against medically unnecessary procedures. In general, self-policing efforts for both quality assurance and utilization review will help to guard against fraud and abuse concerns in addition to their more obvious benefits of enhancing quality and cost-effectiveness.

The nagging doubt left by *United States* v. *Greber* and HCFA's policy memos for joint ventures is the suggestion that, regardless of medical necessity, quality, and reasonableness of fees with respect to all covered services, if a payment for whatever other legitimate purpose also is intended to or in fact induces referrals, it theoretically could be unlawful. Without an amendment to the statute by Congress,[6] there is no way to achieve total certainty in this area.

What can be done, and what is being done, is to ensure that none of the specific problem areas identified above appear either in the documents creating the joint venture or in the operation of the joint venture after it is created, and to take positive steps to ensure that payments made by the joint venture are exactly what they purport to be, that is, payments for services or payments as a return on investment, no more and no less. Such payments should also be fair and reasonable. For professional services, payments should be within a reasonable range, and for returns on investment, they should represent the results of a good faith business deal and its performance in the market. As mentioned above, self-imposed quality assurance and utilization review will also benefit.

Staff members at HCFA have made another informal suggestion for reducing the likelihood of prosecution under the antifraud and abuse provisions, namely, that the referrer of patients to the entity in which the referrer owns an interest should list several potential competitors, without highlighting or encouraging use of the entity in which the referrer holds an interest. It may not be feasible, however, for providers to list competitors in a market as equally available choices for the patient. This can arise where the physician will be performing a procedure at the facility referred to, but the physician does not have necessary privileges at competitive facilities or it is otherwise inconvenient or inconsistent with customary practice. Moreover, the quality of healthcare and its cost effectiveness can sometimes be enhanced if a physician consolidates his referrals at a single location, that is, to reduce travel time, ensure consistency in procedure, and facilitate his monitoring of healthcare delivery. Clearly, such factors mitigate against dispersal of referrals.

Even where it is contemplated that a physician will appropriately focus his practice on a particular facility, care should be taken in drafting any documents relating to the arrangement. It is one thing for a physician to refer his patients to a particular facility due to the appropriate concerns outlined above; it is another to make referrals because of a contractual obligation to do so. Specifically to be avoided should be commitments in written documents that a provider will refer all of his patients to the joint venture facility, a specified percentage, or a specified minimum. Moreover, such a commitment may be illegal even if unwritten. It will just be more difficult to uncover and prove.

Instead, the patient's freedom to choose among providers must be respected. It is therefore appropriate and possibly helpful to qualify any discussion of referrals with a written statement in the organizational documents or contracts that patients will be free to choose any facility that they desire.

Provisions that may be appropriate are those requiring, possibly as a prerequisite to investment, that joint venturers must be physicians in good standing, with an active practice in a particular specialty and geographical area, and possibly with active membership on the medical staff of the joint ventured facility or a related hospital. Such qualifications of investors must be analyzed carefully by legal counsel, not only from fraud and abuse, but from corporate, securities, and tax perspectives, to achieve an effective and legal result.

STATE ANTIKICKBACK AND RELATED LAWS

Joint ventures should also be analyzed in light of the laws in effect in the state or states in which the joint venture will be formed and operated. These laws vary substantially from state to state, and each state's particular rules must be taken into account. Moreover, there is a substantial amount of legislative activity in this area in many state legislatures such that the controlling rules may well change from year to year. In planning joint ventures, it is frequently prudent to consider the potential impact of likely changes to these rules under consideration by the state legislatures.

DIVERSITY OF STATE LAW PROVISIONS

While an exhaustive review of state law is beyond the scope of this chapter, a sampling of several state statutes will illustrate the diversity of statutory provisions. California law prohibits

> the offer, delivery, receipt or acceptance, by any person licensed under this division of any rebate, refund, commission, preference, patronage dividend, discount, or other consideration, whether in the form of money or otherwise, as compensation or inducement for referring patients, clients, or customers to any person, irrespective of any membership, proprietary interest or co-ownership in or with any person to whom such patients, clients or customers are referred.[7]

The same section, however, provides that it shall not be unlawful "solely because the licensee has a proprietary interest or co-ownership in a laboratory, pharmacy, clinic, or health care facility."

The California Attorney General has interpreted this statute as permitting physicians to refer patients to clinical laboratories in which they hold limited partnership interests, so long as the physician's return on investment is based "solely on capital contributed or another proportionate ownership interest that is not predicated per se on the number or value of the testing referrals the physician makes to it."[8] This statute and the results obtained under it closely parallel the Medicare and Medicaid fraud and abuse rules.

By contrast the similar statute in the state of Washington prohibits persons in the practice of medicine from receiving a "rebate, refund, commission, unearned discount or profit . . . in connection with the referral of patients."[9] It is significant that the Washington statute includes the word *profit* in the enumerated kinds of payments that are prohibited in addition to rebates on similar types of remuneration and also substitutes in the place of the requirement that there be an inducement or that the payment be in exchange for a referral, the much broader requirement that the payment merely be "in connection with" a referral. This statute has been interpreted by the Supreme Court of Washington as prohibiting an arrangement whereby a partnership of ophthalmologists owned the stock in a corporation that ran an optical dispensing business located in the same building with the ophthalmologists and to which the ophthalmologists referred their patients. The court concluded that "the accumulation of profits, increase in value of the common stock, growth in net worth, possible tax advantages, and right to a distribution of income" amounted to the prohibited rebate, refund, commission, unearned discount, or profit.[10]

Still another approach is reflected in the laws of the state of Michigan, which prohibit, among other things, "promotion for personal gain of an unnecessary drug, device, treatment, procedure, or service, or directing or requiring an individual to purchase or secure a drug, device, treatment, procedure, or service from another person, place, facility, or business in which the licensee has a financial interest."[11] This statute had originally contained a prohibition against kickbacks similar to the federal and California statutes. Like them, it was interpreted by the attorney general not to preclude referrals to facilities in which the physicians had an ownership interest and received back a return on that interest commensurate with investment.[12] The legislature responded to this attorney general's opinion by enacting the second portion of the statute quoted above, which was subsequently interpreted by the attorney general to prohibit referrals where there is a financial interest, regardless of whether the procedure for which the referral is made is medically necessary and regardless of any disclosure by the physicians.[13]

As discussed elsewhere in this book, states may have various other laws relating to disclosure of ownership interest, prohibitions on ownership in specific kinds of facilities, but not others, and other related provisions. The analysis of these other statutes read in conjunction with any antikickback statutes is an essential step in the joint venture structuring process.

Conflicts between State and Federal Laws

As the above sampling of state statutes indicates, while the state laws of many states parallel the federal law, it is not uncommon for state law to be either more or less restrictive than federal law. Where state law is more restrictive, any arrangement that will operate in the state must comply with that more restrictive state law, even if federal law would not prohibit it. Thus, an arrangement considered legal under federal law and the law of a neighboring state with less restrictive rules should not be implemented in a state with more restrictive rules without a careful analysis of the second state's rules.

Where a state statute is less restrictive than the federal law, the issue sometimes arises whether arrangements can be entered into with respect to patients other than Medicare and Medicaid patients. For example, certain states have no antikickback statute (although there are ethical constraints imposed by the medical profession that exist regardless of state law). A joint venture or other arrangement may be structured in such a state to permit payments in exchange for referrals without violating any state law and to avoid a federal violation by excluding federal program patients from the arrangement. There may be problems with such an approach and careful analysis is always required. For example, if Medicare and Medicaid patients are referred along with other patients but no rebate or fee is paid with respect to such patients, it is conceivable that the enforcement authorities would treat the other payments for non-Medicare patients as being in part designed to cover Medicare and Medicaid patients. Moreover, it is conceivable that a patient's freedom of choice right could be impinged upon by a policy that discriminated against Medicare and Medicaid patients in the manner in which they are treated or referred for treatment. These issues are complex and should always be dealt with carefully.

CONCLUSION

It is regrettable that so many unresolved issues relating to poorly worded antikickback statutes can delay and hamper the successful establishment of a viable joint venture between hospitals and physicians. At the federal level, legislative reform is being pursued. Proposals currently before Congress include the addition of elements to the crime of a showing that the practice caused some form of specified harm to the program. Such an amendment would make much easier the task of analyzing arrangements to determine their legality.

On a state level, it is frequently possible to secure the opinion of the state attorney general with respect to a particular arrangement. Depending on state law, these opinions are not likely to be binding on courts, but they are likely to be binding or carry great weight with state officials, including prosecutors who might be charged with enforcement of the underlying state statutes. Such opinions may have to be requested by specified state elected or appointed officials and can delay completion of the organization of a joint venture. On the other hand, they may provide substantial peace of mind to the participants and should be considered as an option whenever the antikickback issues are substantial.

Notes

[1] H. Rep. No. 92-231, 92d Cong., 2d Sess. 1972, *reprinted in* 1972 U.S. Code Cong. & Ad. News 5007.

[2] H. Rep. No. 95-393, 95th Cong., 1st Sess. 1977, *reprinted in* 1977 U.S. Code Cong. & Ad. News 3041.

[3] H. Rep. No. 96-1167, 96th Cong., 2nd Sess. 1980, *reprinted in* 1980 U.S. Code Cong. & Ad. News 5574.

[4] H. Rep. No. 95-393, 95th Cong., 1st Sess. 1977, *reprinted in* U.S. Code Cong, & Ad. News 3050; *see also* Medicare Carriers Manual, H.I.M.-14 § 11012.

[5] [1985 Transfer Binder] Medicare & Medicaid Guide (CCH) ¶ 34,596 (3d Cir. 1985).

[6] One proposal suggested by this author is that an element be added to the crime requiring the demonstration that the purpose or effect of the payment is to cause medically unnecessary services to be rendered, unreasonably high fees to be charged, or an adverse impact on the quality of care. C. Adams and S. Klein, "Medicare & Medicaid Anti-Fraud and Abuse Law: The Need for Legislative Change,"*Healthspan* 2 (January 1975), pp. 19 and 24.

[7] Cal. Bus. & Prof. Code § 650 (West 1986).

[8] 68 Op. Att'y Gen. of Calif. 28 (1985).

[9] Wash. Rev. Code § 19.68 (1974).

[10] *Day v. Inland Empire Optical,* 76 Wash.2d 407, 456 P.2d 1011 (1969).

[11] Mich. Stat. Ann. § 14.15 (1101) (Callaghan 1985).

[12] 1977–1978 Op. Att'y. Gen. Mich. 234 (1977).

[13] 1979–1980 Op. Att'y. Gen. Mich. 186 (1979).

REFERENCE

Medicare and Medicaid antifraud and abuse statutes, contained in §§ 1877 and 1909 of the Social Security Act read:

(a) Whoever—

    (1) knowingly and willfully makes or causes to be made any false statement or representation of a material fact in any application for any benefit or payment under this title,

    (2) at any time knowingly and willfully makes or causes to be made any false statement or representation of a material fact for use in determining rights to any such benefit or payment,

    (3) having knowledge of the occurrence of any event affecting (A) his initial or continued right to any such benefit or payment, or (B) the initial or continued right to any such benefit or payment of any other individual in whose behalf he has applied for or is receiving such benefit or payment conceals or fails to disclose such event with an intent fraudulently to secure such benefit or payment either in a greater amount or quantity than is due or when no such benefit or payment is authorized, or

    (4) having made application to receive any such benefit or payment for the use and benefit of another and having received it, knowingly and willfully converts such benefit or payment or any part thereof to a use other than for the use and benefit of such other person, shall (i) in the case of such a statement, representation, concealment, failure, or conversion by any person in connection with the furnishing (by that person) of items or

services for which payment is or may be made under this title, be guilty of a felony and upon conviction thereof fined not more than $25,000 or imprisoned for not more than five years or both, or (ii) in the case of such a statement, representation, concealment, failure, or conversion by any other person, be guilty of a misdemeanor and upon conviction thereof fined not more than $10,000 or imprisoned for not more than one year, or both.

(b) (1) Whoever knowingly and willfully solicits or receives any remuneration (including any kickback, bribe, or rebate) directly or indirectly, overtly or covertly, in cash or in kind—

   (A) in return for referring an individual to a person for the furnishing or arranging for the furnishing of any item or service for which payment may be made in whole or in part under this subchapter, or

   (B) in return for purchasing, leasing, ordering, or arranging for or recommending purchasing, leasing, or ordering any good, facility, service, or item for which payment may be made in whole or in part under this subchapter, shall be guilty of a felony and upon conviction thereof, shall be fined not more than $25,000 or imprisoned for not more than five years, or both.

(2) Whoever knowingly and willfully offers or pays any remuneration (including any kickback, bribe, or rebate) directly or indirectly, overtly or covertly, in cash or in kind to any person to induce such person—

   (A) to refer an individual to a person for the furnishing or arranging for the furnishing of any item or service for which payment may be made in whole or in part under this subchapter, or

   (B) to purchase, lease, order, or arrange for or recommend purchasing, leasing or ordering any good, facility, service, or item for which payment may be made in whole or in part under this subchapter, shall be guilty of a felony and upon conviction thereof, shall be fined not more than $25,000 or imprisoned for not more than five years, or both.

(3) Paragraphs (1) and (2) shall not apply to—

   (A) a discount or other reduction in price obtained by a provider of services or other entity under this title if the reduction in price is properly disclosed and appropriately reflected in the costs claimed or charges made by the provider or entity under this title; and

   (B) any amount paid by an employer to an employee (who has a bona fide employment relationship with such employer) for employment in the provision of covered items or services.

(c) Whoever knowingly and willfully makes or causes to be made, or induces or seeks to induce the making of, any false statement or representation of a material fact with respect to the conditions or operation of any institution or facility in order that such institution or facility may qualify (either upon initial certification or upon recertification) as a hospital, skilled nursing facility, or home health agency (as those terms are defined in section 1861), shall be guilty of a felony and upon conviction thereof shall be fined not more than $25,000 or imprisoned for not more than five years, or both.

(d) Whoever accepts assignments described in section 1842(b)(3)(B)(ii) or agrees to be a participating physician or supplier under section 1842(h)(1) and knowingly, willfully, and repeatedly violates the term of such assignments, shall be guilty of a misdemeanor and upon conviction thereof shall be fined not more than $2,000 or imprisoned for not more than six months, or both.

10

Antitrust Planning for Joint Ventures

Douglas M. Mancino, J.D.

INTRODUCTION

For more than seven decades, the healthcare industry was largely immune from regulation under the federal and state antitrust laws. Beginning with the elimination of the learned professions exemption in 1975, however, the U.S. Supreme Court has removed most barriers to the scrutiny of activities within the healthcare industry under the federal antitrust laws.[1]

The establishment of joint ventures between hospitals and physicians necessarily presumes varying degrees of cooperation, collaboration, and asset exchange. In some cases, hospitals and physicians form a joint venture to enter new geographic or product markets. In others, hospitals and physicians use a joint venture to enter a geographic or product market in which one of the venturers is already active. Whether vertical, horizontal, or conglomerate relationships are contemplated,[2] joint ventures can have several anticompetitive effects, including reducing potential competition, eliminating actual competition, foreclosing competition at either the supplier or customer level, and creating anticompetitive collateral restraints. Consequently, federal and state antitrust laws must be carefully considered in connection with the formation and operation of joint ventures.

A comprehensive review of the application of federal and state antitrust laws to hospital-physician joint ventures is beyond the scope of this chapter. Rather, what follows is a brief overview of some of the essential antitrust rules and how such rules may apply to hospital-physician joint ventures.

OVERVIEW OF FEDERAL ANTITRUST LAWS

The basic objective of the federal antitrust laws is to eliminate practices that interfere with free competition. The laws are designed to promote a vigorous and competitive economy in which each business has a full opportunity to compete on the basis of price, quality, and service, thus affording the public a meaningful choice among vendors.

The four principal antitrust laws that may have an effect on joint ventures are the Sherman Act, the Clayton Act, the Robinson-Patman Act, and the Federal Trade Commission Act. While each law contains specific prohibitions, the laws generally express the philosophy that a free market—in which the laws of supply and demand operate to determine price, volume of production, sources of supply, and channels of distribution—should be protected. One overriding concern is that each business entity makes its own independent decisions concerning prices, methods of distribution, the volume of production, product design, and similar matters.

Sherman Act Section 1

Section 1 of the Sherman Act prohibits all contracts, combinations, and conspiracies that restrain trade in interstate commerce.[3] In order to establish a Section 1 violation, a plaintiff must first establish the existence of a contract, combination, or conspiracy, which requires that two or more distinct and unrelated entities be involved.[4] In most joint venture contexts, the hospital and participating physicians will be regarded as separate entities. A hospital or a physician and the separate joint venture entity created by them will also be viewed as separate entities.[5]

Second, the plaintiff must show that the joint venture's actions relate to trade or commerce "among the several States." This requirement is satisfied if the challenged conduct is in interstate commerce. It may also be satisfied by a purely intrastate activity that has a substantial and adverse effect on interstate commerce.[6]

Finally, a plaintiff must establish that the joint venture itself or its method of operation restrains trade. Recognizing that *every* contract or agreement "restrains trade," the U.S. Supreme Court basically uses a "rule of reason" analysis to determine whether a contract, combination, or conspiracy *unreasonably* restrains trade in the relevant geographic and product markets.[7]

While most agreements and practices are analyzed under the "rule of reason," the Supreme Court has held certain types of agreements and practices to be so inimical to competition that they will be conclusively presumed to be unreasonable, and therefore found illegal, without elaborate inquiry as to the precise harm they cause or the business justifications for their use. The activities and practices that are presumptive or *per se* violations of Section 1 of the Sherman Act are (1) horizontal and vertical price-fixing, (2) horizontal divisions of markets, (3) certain group boycotts (concerted refusals to deal), and (4) certain tying arrangements. It has been argued that the healthcare industry should be treated differently when alleged per se violations are involved because the judiciary has had little experience in the healthcare industry, but the Supreme Court has rejected that argument.[8]

Sherman Act Section 2

Section 2 of the Sherman Act prohibits monopolizations, attempts to monopolize, and conspiracies to monopolize.[9] While a monopoly in and of itself is not illegal if it results from "superior skill, foresight and industry," or if it is "thrust upon" a business, conduct designed or intended to monopolize the relevant market is illegal.

Clayton Act Section 7

Section 7 of the Clayton Act prohibits any person engaged in commerce from directly or indirectly acquiring the stock or assets of another organization also engaged in commerce "where in any line of commerce in any section of the country, the effect of such acquisition may be substantially to lessen competition, or to tend to create a monopoly."[10]

While Section 7 is normally used to challenge mergers and asset acquisitions, Section 7 can also be used to block certain types of joint ventures before they become operational or engage in prohibited practices.

Robinson-Patman Act

Section 2 of the Clayton Act, which is popularly known as the Robinson-Patman Act, generally prohibits vendors and other sellers of commodities from discriminating among purchasers of commodities of like grade and quality.[11] While there are several defenses that may exempt otherwise discriminatory transactions, such as that price discrimination was intended to meet competition, the most significant exemption affecting healthcare organizations is the Nonprofit Institutions Act.[12] The Nonprofit Institutions Act exempts from the price discrimination prohibitions of the Robinson-Patman Act purchases of commodities by not-for-profit hospitals and other charitable organizations for their "own use."

Federal Trade Commission Act Section 5

Section 5 of the Federal Trade Commission Act generally prohibits use of unfair methods of competition and unfair deceptive acts or practices.[13] Section 5 prohibits all Sherman Act and Clayton Act violations, as well as other restraints of trade contrary to the policy or spirit of those laws.[14] Although not discussed further in this chapter, Section 5 of the Federal Trade Commission Act has been applied to joint ventures.[15]

Penalties

Penalties for violations of the federal antitrust laws can be very severe, including prison sentences for the corporate managers guilty of the violation, individual fines of up to $100,000 for each criminal offense and corporate fines of up to $1 million for each criminal offense. Even if a violation is not sufficiently willful to warrant criminal prosecution, injunctions or consent decrees may be imposed that will limit the future freedom of a joint venture or its participants. Moreover, private parties injured by violations of the antitrust laws can recover three times the amount of the damages they suffer plus reasonable attorneys fees. In certain circumstances, damages may be recovered for many years, particularly where the violation is a continuing one.

POTENTIAL CHALLENGES TO JOINT VENTURE FORMATION

The formation of a joint venture may be subject to challenge under Section 7 of the Clayton Act or under Sections 1 or 2 of the Sherman Act.

A joint venture may be challenged under Section 7 of the Clayton Act if it involves the acquisition of shares or assets in another enterprise. Section 7 would condemn a joint venture where "the effect of such [joint venture] may be substantially to lessen competition, or to tend to create a monopoly." [16] Section 7 is designed to be applied prospectively, that is, "to arrest apprehended consequences before those relationships could work their evil." [17] Thus, Section 7 can be used to challenge a joint venture *before* a violation of Section 1 or 2 of the Sherman Act occurs.

In *United States* v. *Penn-Olin Chemical Company*, the Supreme Court dealt with a challenge under Section 7 of the Clayton Act to a corporate joint venture formed to create a new competitive unit. [18] The Court stated that a merger analysis should apply to joint ventures. Once it is determined that the joint venturers are potential competitors in the joint venture's market, several criteria must then be taken into account in assessing whether the formation of a joint venture between actual or potential competitors will result in a substantial lessening of competition. The criteria identified by the Supreme Court are as follows:

> [T]he number and power of the competitors in the relevant market; the background of their growth; the power of the joint venturers; the relationship of their lines of commerce; the competition existing between them and the power of each in dealing with the competitors of the other; the setting in which the joint venture was created; the reasons and necessities for its existence; the joint venture's line of commerce and the relationship thereof to that of its parents; the adaptability of its line of commerce to noncompetitive practices; the potential power of the joint venture in the relevant market; an appraisal of what the competition in the relevant market would have been if one of the joint venturers had entered it alone instead of through [the joint venture]; the effect, in the event of this occurrence, of the other joint venturer's potential competition; and other such factors as might indicate potential risk to competition in the relevant market. In weighing these factors, the court should remember that the mandate of the Congress is in terms of the probability of a lessening of substantial competition, not in terms of tangible present restraint." [19]

In addition to being challenged under Section 7 of the Clayton Act, early case law analyzing joint ventures suggested that all joint ventures between horizontal competitors might violate Section 1 of the Sherman Act because such ventures always involve a division of markets, which is a per se violation of Section 1.[20] In recent years, however, the courts generally have applied a rule of reason analysis to joint ventures.[21] While the formation of joint ventures generally will be considered under a rule of reason analysis, the operating practices and collateral restraints associated with the joint venture will be subject to a separate analysis, as discussed below.

Section 2 of the Sherman Act supplements Section 1 by prohibiting any person or any group of persons from monopolizing or attempting to monopolize a market. Monopoly power is generally defined as the power to fix or control prices or to exclude or control competition.[22] It is conceivable that some types of hospital-physician joint ventures, such as health maintenance organizations, could be challenged as combinations or conspiracies to monopolize when the market share of the joint venture is significant. The risk of a Section 2 challenge will depend on the relevant geographic and product markets involved and the degree of power the proposed joint venture will exercise over price or competition.

ANTITRUST ISSUES AFFECTING JOINT VENTURE OPERATIONS

The most common violations of the antitrust laws are those resulting from concerted or collusive activities by two or more parties. Agreements or understandings between the joint venture and its hospital or physician owners relating to any competitive factor such as price, terms of sale, amount of production, or the selection of customers or suppliers are prohibited in most situations. Such agreements need not be formal contracts and seldom are. In fact, the antitrust laws can be applied to mutual understandings even where there is no formal commitment by either party. Evidence of an illegal agreement is usually circumstantial, consisting of a compilation of different facts pointing to a common course of action by the alleged conspirators appearing to result from a common understanding. Consequently, it is important not only to act within the law, but also to avoid actions or a course of conduct that gives the appearance of collusion.

Per Se Violations

As previously noted, certain types of agreements between actual or potential competitors are deemed so inimical to competition that they are always illegal, no matter how reasonable they may appear or how slight their effect on competition. To establish an antitrust violation, the antitrust authorities and private parties need only prove—and only by circumstantial evidence—that such an agreement existed. Moreover, such agreements are the most likely candidates for criminal prosecution. The main categories of these per se offenses involve anticompetitive agreements or collusion between competitors, and these arguments are the most frequent targets of enforcement action and challenges by third parties.

Horizontal and Vertical Agreements Relating to Price. Agreements between competitors or between a producer and a supplier relating in any way to price, even agreements which may only indirectly affect price, are illegal under Section 1 of the Sherman Act. Prohibited agreements include not only the obvious—price-fixing—but also the taking of any collusive action which stabilizes prices, whether the intent is to set a maximum or a minimum price, or which interferes with a competitor's freedom to make pricing changes independently. In fact, agreements between competitors on terms of sale, standardization of costs, discount policy, bidding formulas, and similar matters may affect price competition and thus are routinely attacked as price-fixing.

In the hospital and medical fields, numerous practices have been condemned as illegal price-fixing, such as the establishment of relative value scales and maximum fee schedules. Nonetheless, price-fixing is merely a way of describing certain categories of business behavior to which the *per se* rule has been held applicable. Hospitals and physicians literally will be price-fixing when they form a joint venture to sell goods or services, but this will not necessarily be a *per se* violation of the Sherman Act.[23] As the Supreme Court has noted: "Joint ventures and other cooperative arrangements are also not usually unlawful, at least not as price-fixing, where the agreement on price is necessary to market the product at all."[24]

In *Arizona* v. *Maricopa County Medical Society*, the Supreme Court held that two foundations for medical care were engaged in illegal price-fixing because the participating physicians, through the foundations, established prices.[25] However, the Supreme Court offered the following example of a joint venture arrangement among physicians that would not involve price-fixing:

> The foundations for [medical care] are not analogous to partnerships or other joint arrangements in which persons who would otherwise be competitors pool their capital and share the risks of loss as well as the opportunities for profit. In such joint ventures, the partnership is regarded as a single firm competing with other sellers in the market. . . . If a clinic offered complete medical coverage for a flat fee, the cooperating doctors would have the type of partnership arrangement in which a price-fixing agreement among the doctors would be perfectly proper.[26]

Thus, in order for a hospital-physician joint venture to escape from the application of the per se rule against price-fixing, there must be economic integration—a combination or pooling of productive assets or a sharing of economic risks and benefits. Generally, this will require all of the venturers to make meaningful contributions of capital to the joint venture or to share risks of loss as well as opportunities for profit that might result from the joint venture's operations. In *Maricopa,* the physician members of the foundations for medical care did not pool their assets, nor did they share the prospects of any economic risks or benefits from their joint enterprise.

Even if the relationship between the hospital and physicians is itself treated as a joint venture, the joint venture will be a separate entity and can conspire to fix prices with its owners or with others. Suppose, for example, that a hospital and members of its medical staff form a partnership to own and operate a freestanding ambulatory surgery center. The establishment of a fee schedule for the surgery center's services will not constitute price-fixing. If, however, the hospital agrees expressly or implicitly, to charge the same or more than the center for identical procedures performed in the hospital's outpatient surgery department, the hospital and the joint venture may be engaged in horizontal price-fixing.

Another potential problem area involves the setting of professional fees by the joint venture and its physician investors. Suppose, for example, that a hospital and a group of primary care physicians form a corporation to establish and operate a network of primary or urgent care centers. If the joint venture enters into contracts with the physicians' separate professional corporations for professional services and the contract requires the joint venture and the professional corporation to agree on the fee schedule to be used by the professional corporations, such an agreement could be challenged as vertical price-fixing or resale price maintenance.

Horizontal Market Allocations. Horizontal allocations of markets or services have been held to be per se violations of Section 1 of the Sherman Act because market or service divisions prevent open competition by persons who normally would be competing among themselves. In the joint venture context, this type of violation can arise when a hospital and the joint venture of which it is an owner agree upon the products or services each will separately offer. For example, if a hospital and members of its medical staff form a joint venture to own and operate a freestanding ambulatory surgery center, the hospital and the joint venture could not agree that the hospital would close its outpatient surgery department without the action being subject to challenge as a per se division of service markets. Even if it were not a per se illegal restraint of trade, an analysis of the action would be required under the rule of reason to determine its anticompetitive effects.

A territorial allocation of markets might occur if a hospital and its primary care physician jointly develop a network of primary care centers. If the hospital and the physicians are not partially integrated into a true joint venture, an agreement to allocate territory among themselves on an exclusive basis could be challenged as a per se division of markets, particularly if such conduct were coupled with the establishment of fee schedules.[27]

Group Boycotts and Concerted Refusals to Deal. A refusal to deal is perfectly legal if made independently under Section 1 of the Sherman Act. However, any refusal to deal with either a customer or supplier (such as an insurance company, another hospital, or another physician) which results from an understanding or agreement with another party may violate Section 1 of the Sherman Act under the rule of reason or under the per se rule.

In a conventional group boycott or refusal to deal, horizontal competitors (e.g., a group of physicians) seek to protect themselves from competitors or would-be competitors (e.g., nongroup physicians) by taking concerted action aimed at depriving the excluded competitors of some type of business relationship (such as medical staff membership) they require in order to compete effectively.

In *Northwest Wholesale Stationers, Inc.* v. *Pacific Stationary and Printing Co.*, the Supreme Court made it clear that not all group boycotts are per se illegal under Section 1.[28] It identified three circumstances in which the per se approach would be appropriate:

1. The boycott cuts off access to a supply, facility, or market necessary to enable the boycotted firm to compete.
2. The boycotting firms possess a dominant position in the relevant market.
3. The boycott is not justified by a plausible argument that it is intended to enhance overall efficiency and make the market more competitive.

Further, the Court stated:

A plaintiff seeking application of the *per se* rule must present a threshold case that the challenged activity falls into a category likely to have predominantly anticompetitive effects. The mere allegation of a concerted refusal to deal does not suffice because not all concerted refusals to deal are predominantly anticompetitive. Absent a showing of one or more of the above circumstances, the courts will apply a rule of reason analysis.[29]

In hospital-physician joint ventures, allegations of a group boycott or a concerted refusal to deal can be made in several instances. For example, in a joint venture to establish and operate a freestanding surgery center, if the hospital and investor-physicians decide to exclude noninvestor surgeons from obtaining privileges at the surgery center, that refusal could be alleged to be a group boycott or concerted refusal to deal. Similarly, such an allegation could be made if the hospital declines to grant new surgical privileges at the hospital at the insistence of medical staff members who are investors in a surgery center joint venture.

Tying Arrangements. A tying arrangement has been defined as "an agreement by a party to sell one product but only on the condition that the buyer also purchases a different (or tied) product, or at least agrees that he will not purchase that product from any other supplier."[30] In order for a tying arrangement to be treated as a per se violation of Section 1 of the Sherman Act, the tying arrangement must exhibit four characteristics:

1. Two separate products, the tying product and the tied product.
2. Sufficient market power in the tying market to coerce purchase of the tied product.
3. Involvement of a not insubstantial amount of interstate commerce in the tied market.
4. Anticompetitive effects in the tied market.[31]

In *Hyde* v. *Jefferson Parish Hospital District No. 2*, an anesthesiologist was denied staff privileges at a New Orleans hospital because that hospital had an exclusive contract with a professional medical corporation for the provision of anesthesia services.[32] The anesthesiologist sued the hospital alleging that the exclusive contract constituted a per se illegal tying arrangement.

The Supreme Court found that two products were involved because the users of the hospital's operating rooms (the tying product) were also compelled to purchase the hospital's chosen anesthesia service (the tied product). The Court concluded, however, that the exclusive contract did not constitute a per se violation of Section 1 because the hospital did not have sufficient market power.

In the joint venture context, tying allegations are most likely to arise when exclusive contracts are involved. For example, if a joint venture is formed to establish a lithotripsy center, the exclusion of a urologist from participation may be challenged, particularly if the center has a substantial market share either because of economic conditions or because certificate of need laws have limited the number of lithotripters in the relevant geographic market. Similarly, an exclusive referral agreement with a home health agency or durable medical equipment supplier jointly owned by a hospital and physicians could be challenged as an illegal tying arrangement.

Nonprice Predation

Nonprice predation is strategic behavior designed to increase a competitor's costs, and it can be challenged as a violation of Section 2 of the Sherman Act.

In the joint venture context, nonprice predation could arise, for example, if the joint venture determines to oppose all applicants for a certificate of need to establish a competing facility or service, such as a new surgery center or a new home health agency. In such a case, the potential competitor would face increased costs and delays and may in fact be deterred or prevented from entering the market. However, opposition to applications for certificates of need, even if it intended to eliminate unwanted competition, would generally be exempt from antitrust challenge. The *Noerr-Pennington* doctrine generally protects efforts to solicit government action, even where those efforts are motivated by anticompetitive intent.[33] Nevertheless, there may be situations that on their face appear protected under *Noerr-Pennington*, but on closer inspection are not,[34] because the attempts to seek government action are so frivolous or harassing in nature that the courts may conclude that those attempts were a "sham" to disguise anticompetition objectives.

Vertical Market Allocations

Vertical market allocations—such as geographical limitations placed by a manufacturer on its dealers or by a franchisor on its franchisees—are analyzed under the rule of reason. The test is whether, in the context of the particular industry, "the restraint imposed is such as merely regulates and perhaps thereby promotes competition or whether it is such as may suppress or even destroy competition."[35]

In the joint venture context, a vertical allocation of markets might be made between a hospital franchisor of primary care centers and its franchisee physicians, where the franchisor places a territorial restriction on the franchisee. Generally, such territorial restrictions have been sustained because their pro-competitive effects outweigh their anticompetitive effects. However, if physicians own a portion of the franchisor, care must be used to avoid having the joint venture itself treated as a sham, intended merely as a facade for horizontally allocating markets.[36]

Collateral Restraints

When hospitals and physicians form a joint venture, they frequently desire to impose restraints on other types of activities in which the venturers can engage independent of, or in addition to, the business of the joint venture. If these collateral restraints are reasonably related to the conduct of the business of the joint venture, they generally should be permissible under Section 1 of the Sherman Act. In general, covenants not to disclose confidential information, reasonable noncompetition covenants, and rights of first refusal in derivative activities generally are permissible. For example, if a joint venture is formed to purchase and operate a CT scanner in an outpatient setting, it should be permissible to require the venturers to present an opportunity to establish a magnetic resonance imaging center to the venture before pursuing that project independent of the joint venture.

However, not all collateral restraints will be immune from challenge. For example, a restraint on participation in other joint ventures of a similar kind will be subjected to closer scrutiny. Moreover, restraints that bear no relationship to the venture at all will be subject to challenge. These latter types of restraints may include agreements to share confidential cost and price information concerning products or services unrelated to the joint venture, as well as commitments to forgo other services.[37]

Spillover Collusion

Even if the joint venture itself does not violate the federal antitrust laws, care must be taken to ensure that the joint venture does not result in the spillover of its activities into other markets. This risk has been identified in Section 1 cases as well as in Section 7 cases. While the courts have repeatedly recognized that joint ventures have the potential for achieving efficiency and intensifying competition, they have also recognized that joint ventures have the potential for facilitating collusion among the venturers in formal as well as informal ways, especially with respect to pricing information. By participating in a joint venture, for example, the partners may obtain information about each other that they could use in other aspects of their separate operations or businesses. In a joint venture formed by two horizontal competitors, particularly in a highly concentrated market where one of the partners has a significant market share, another partner may forgo other competitive advantages in order to increase the effectiveness of the joint venture.

Consequently, even when a joint venture is not inherently anticompetitive and there are no overt contractual restraints on competition among the partners and the joint venture, the partners must be particularly careful in their future dealings in order to avoid acting jointly, or appearing to act jointly, with regard to their separate business decisions.

Price Discrimination Laws

The Robinson-Patman Act generally prohibits a seller from charging different prices to different customers where the effect is to injure either a competitor of the seller, the disfavored competitor of the customer, or even the disfavored customer of the seller's customer. However, price discrimination is permissible when the seller in good faith meets the equally low price of a competitor or when the lower price is commensurate with the cost savings attributable to the larger-volume purchaser. Additionally, the Robinson-Patman Act prohibits the granting of merchandizing allowances or services that are not available to all competing customers on equal terms. In the joint venture context, Robinson-Patman Act problems are most likely to arise when a not-for-profit hospital purchases supplies, equipment, or pharmaceuticals from a vendor and attempts to resell such supplies, at cost or at a mark-up, to the joint venture of which it is a partner.[38]

The Nonprofit Institutions Act exempts from Robinson-Patman Act coverage purchases by nonprofit hospitals and other charitable institutions *for their own use*. Thus, purchases of equipment, supplies, pharmaceuticals, and so on by a charitable hospital for its "own use" are exempt from coverage under the Robinson-Patman Act. However, the key issue in the joint venture context is whether resales to the joint venture are for the hospital's own use, such as resales of drugs or supplies to a home health agency, nursing home, or ambulatory surgery center joint venture or purchases of durable medical equipment by a hospital for resale to a DME joint venture with physicians.

In *Abbott Laboratories, Inc.* v. *Portland Retail Druggists Association,* the Supreme Court discussed what sales of drugs by nonprofit hospitals are for their own use.[39] The general standard set forth by the Court was that a hospital's own use "is what reasonably may be regarded as used by the hospital in the sense that such use is a part of and promotes the hospital's intended institutional operation in the care of patients who are its patients."[40] This concept was recently extended to the Kaiser Foundation Health Plan's distribution of drugs to its members, regardless of whether the members were in the hospital.[41]

Thus, resales of drugs and other goods, equipment, and supplies by a hospital to a joint venture of which it is a partner or shareholder may raise serious problems under the Robinson-Patman Act. In short, the exemption may be inapplicable if it would not have immunized purchases by the joint venture directly from the vendor.

STATE ANTITRUST LAWS

Every state has enacted antitrust laws, and most have enacted other laws that limit or proscribe activities that constitute restraints of trade and other anticompetitive practices. In most states, the attorney general is the primary or exclusive public enforcer of these laws, although in an increasing number of states local district attorneys have authority to prosecute violations that occur in their jurisdiction.

Joint venture activity must also be analyzed under the various state laws. In many instances, practices that do not violate the Sherman Act or the Clayton Act will also not violate state antitrust laws. However, some practices permitted by federal law may nonetheless violate state law.

CONCLUSION

The review of antitrust considerations affecting joint ventures in the chapter is, as previously indicated, not intended to be comprehensive. In many instances, the ultimate test for the legality of a joint venture will turn on whether the venture is intended to create a new competitor in the market or whether the restraints associated with the formation and operation of the venture are themselves its primary purpose. As a general rule, however, restraints associated with the joint venture that are reasonably necessary to legitimate business transactions will not lead to a finding of illegality.

In this regard, the antitrust analysis of joint ventures by enforcement agencies and the courts is becoming more sophisticated. The Justice Department has recognized that joint ventures will be viewed in a generally favorable light, in recognition of their importance to business efficiency and innovation.[42]

As the courts begin to explore the application of antitrust laws to various types of hospital-physician joint ventures, further guidance and, it is hoped, comfort will become available to physicians and hospitals who currently believe that they may be entering dangerous uncharted waters. It is safe to predict that without the motive or design specifically to restrain competition, most joint ventures in the healthcare field should survive antitrust scrutiny.

Hospitals and physicians need to plan in advance for their joint venture activities and monitor their continuing operations to ensure continued compliance. This is an area where the advice of competent antitrust counsel is indispensable. In many cases, it also will be advisable for the venturers to put in place an antitrust compliance program. In others, it may be necessary to rely on the Justice Department's business review letter process or the Federal Trade Commission's advisory opinion letter process if the venturers are concerned about the antitrust treatment of a specific joint venture or practice.[43]

Notes

[1] The seminal federal antitrust decisions of the U.S. Supreme Court affecting the healthcare industry include *Goldfarb v. Virginia*, 421 U.S. 773 (1975) (holding that professions are subject to the antitrust laws); *Hospital Building Co. v. Trustees of the Rex Hospital*, 425 U.S. 738 (1976) (finding sufficient impact on interstate commerce); *Bates v. State Bar of Arizona*, 433 U.S. 350 (1977) (limiting the state action exemption as it applies to professions). In addition, the states have generally followed the lead of the federal courts, particularly when the state antitrust laws parallel the federal laws. *See generally* M. Thompson, *Antitrust and the Health Care Provider* (Rockville, Md: Aspen Systems Corp. 1979).

[2] A horizontal joint venture typically involves two competitors in the same business who create a joint venture to assume control of some present portion of their existing competitive operations or create a joint venture to enter a new geographic market. A vertical joint venture typically involves the creation of a joint venture by hospitals and physicians to enter into a new business, but one which is vertically connected with the present operations of the venturers. An example of a vertical joint venture is a diagnostic center. Some joint ventures may be both vertical and horizontal. Finally, some joint ventures may be conglomerate joint ventures; that is, the venturers and the venture neither produce the same product or service nor are they in a buyer-seller relationship.

[3] 15 U.S.C. § 1.

[4] *See e.g.*, *Copperweld Corp. v. Independence Tube Corp.*, 467 U.S. 752 (1984), which held that a parent and its wholly owned subsidiary must be viewed as a single enterprise for purposes of Section 1 of the Sherman Act.

[5] *See e.g.*, *Weiss v. York Hospital*, 745 F.2d 786 (3rd Cir. 1984), *cert. denied*, 105 S.Ct. 1777 (1985).

[6] *See generally McLain v. Real Estate Board of New Orleans, Inc.*, 444 U.S. 232 (1980); *compare Stone v. William Beaumont Hospital*, 782 F.2d 609, 613 (6th Cir. 1986), *with Cardio-Medical Associates v. Crozer-Chester Medical Center*, 721 F.2d 68, 74 (3rd Cir. 1983).

[7] Justice Brandeis provided the classic statement of the rule of reason in *Board of Trade of City of Chicago v. United States*, 246 U.S. 231, 238 (1918):

> The true test of legality is whether the restraint imposed is such as merely regulates and perhaps thereby promotes competition or whether it is such as may suppress or even destroy competition. To determine that question the court must ordinarily consider the facts peculiar to the business to which the restraint is applied; its condition before and after the restraint was imposed; the nature of the restraint and its effect, actual or probable. The history of the restraint, the evil believed to exist, the reason for adopting the particular remedy, the purpose or end sought to be attained, are all relevant facts. This is not because a good intention will save an otherwise objectionable regulation or the reverse; but because knowledge of intent may help the court to interpret facts and to predict consequences.

[8] *Arizona v. Maricopa County Medical Society*, 457 U.S. 332, 349 (1982).

[9] 15 U.S.C. § 2.

[10] 15 U.S.C. § 18.

[11] 15 U.S.C. § 13.

[12] 15 U.S.C. § 13c.

[13] 15 U.S.C. § 45.

[14] *See e.g., Federal Trade Commission v. Indiana Federation of Dentists,* 106 S.Ct. 2009, 2016 (1986). ("The standard of 'unfairness' under the FTC act is, by necessity, an elusive one, encompassing not only practices that violate the Sherman Act and the other antitrust laws [citation omitted], but also practices that the Commission determines are against public policy for other reasons.").

[15] *See e.g., Continental Oil Co.,* 3 CCH Trade Reg. Rep. at 25,743 (FTC Consent Order, Nov. 21, 1967).

[16] 15 U.S.C. § 18.

[17] *United States v. Penn-Olin Chemical Co.,* 378 U.S. 158 (1964).

[18] 378 U.S. 158 (1964).

[19] 378 U.S. at 177.

[20] *United States v. Penn-Olin Chemical Co.,* 378 U.S. 158, 18–81 (1964) (dissent of Mr. Justice Douglas).

[21] *Broadcast Music, Inc. v. Columbia Broadcasting System, Inc.,* 441 U.S. 1 (1979); *National Collegiate Athletic Ass'n v. Board of Regents of University of Oklahoma,* 468 U.S. 85 (1984).

[22] *United States v. E. I. du Pont de Nemours & Co.,* 351 U.S. 377, 391 (1956).

[23] *Broadcast Music, Inc. v. Columbia Broadcasting System, Inc.,* 441 U.S. 1, 9 (1979). ("When two partners price the goods or services, they literally are price-fixing, but they are not *per se* in violation of the Sherman Act.")

[24] Ibid., p. 23.

[25] 457 U.S. 332 (1982).

[26] Ibid., pp. 356–57.

[27] *United States v. Sealy Inc.,* 388 U.S. 350, 355 (1967).

[28] 105 S. Ct. 2613 (1985).

[29] 105 S. Ct. at 2621.

[30] *Northern Pac. Ry. Co. v. United States,* 356 U.S. 1, 5–6 (1958) (footnote omitted).

[31] *E.g., Konik v. Champlain Valley Physicians Hospital Medical Center,* 561 F. Supp. 700, 713 (N.D. N.Y. 1983), *aff'd.* 733 F.2d 1007 (2d Cir. 1984).

[32] 466 U.S. 2 (1984).

[33] *See e.g., Garst v. Soco, Inc. (dba Mountain View General Hospital),* [1985 Trade Cases] Commerce Clearing House ¶ 66,838 (U.S. Dist. Ct., E.D. Ark., Jan. 9, 1985) (suit challenging a hospital and its doctor owners' opposition to a birthing center certificate of need).

[34] See generally Remarks of Terry Calvani, FTC Commissioner, prepared for delivery to the Antitrust Law Section of the American Bar Association (July 9, 1985), reprinted at [1985 Trade Cases] Commerce Clearing House ¶ 50,475.

[35] *Board of Trade of City of Chicago v. United States,* 246 U.S. 231, 238 (1918); *Continental T.V., Inc. v. GTE Sylvania, Inc., 433 U.S. 36 (1979).*

[36] *See e.g., United States v. Sealy, Inc.,* 388 U.S. 350, 354 (1967).

[37] *See e.g., Yamaha Motor Co., Ltd. v. FTC,* 657 F.2d 971 (8th Cir. 1981), *cert. denied,* 456 U.S. 915 (1982).

[38] For an excellent discussion of the legal implications of pharmaceuticals resales, see American Hospital Association, *Legal Memorandum Re Legal Implications of Hospital Resale of Pharmaceuticals,* April 1984.

[39] 425 U.S. 1 (1976).

[40] Ibid., p. 14.

[41] *De Modena v. Kaiser Foundation Health Plan;* 743 F.2d 1388 (9th Cir. 1984), *cert. denied,* 105 S. Ct. 1230 (1985).

[42] See, generally, remarks of J. Paul McGrath, Assistant Attorney General, Antitrust Division,

delivered at 18th Annual New England Antitrust Conference, November 2, 1984, reprinted at [1985 Trade Cases] Commerce Clearing House ¶ 50,470.

[43] The Justice Department will on request, review proposed business conduct and state its enforcement intentions in business review letters. See 28 C.F.R. § 50.6 (1985). In addition, the Federal Trade Commission will, on request, issue formal and informal advisory opinions. See 16 C.F.R. §§ 1.1–1.4 (1986).

IV

FEASIBILITY, FINANCE, AND OPERATIONS

11

Market Analysis for Joint Ventures

Douglas D. Gregory, Ph.D.

INTRODUCTION

Hospitals pursue joint ventures with their medical staffs for many reasons, including management's desire to build closer relationships with key medical staff members, recruitment or retention of physicians, recognition that the hospital may lose all or part of significant outpatient services if physicians develop the venture on their own, anticipation of increased hospital admissions as a result of joint hospital-medical staff participation in the project, and development of new sources of revenue or capital financing.

Physicians' interests in joint ventures, on the other hand, are primarily economic since they usually invest their personal capital in the business. Clearly, then, it is possible that expectations and motivations may differ between hospital and physician participants in such transactions. Since partners in joint ventures bear significant litigation risk for each other's performance relative to the business plan, the consequences of not meeting medical staff financial expectations for the new business are disturbing at best.

Hospitals, therefore, must carefully evaluate the business economics of ventures involving physician participation since the risks from failure to achieve economic objectives are heightened in this case. The joint venture option ought to be conceptualized as an entry strategy which may confer competitive advantage for the business as well as a source of equity financing. By focusing on economic and market factors, the venture stands a better chance of succeeding, and the risks of deteriorating relationships between the hospital and its medical staff following a bad business relationship are minimized.

This chapter discusses market analysis of new ventures building on an earlier framework.[1] Market planning for new business ventures may be conceptualized as a six-step process:

- Define the business concept.
- Segment and size the market.
- Determine the market's attractiveness.
- Analyze the business's internal economics.
- Assess success requirements.
- Determine joint venture economics.

BUSINESS CONCEPT

The business concept defines the rationale for the new venture. It may be thought of as the basis for exchange between buyers and the seller. The concept must embody sufficient value for the providers' products or services to be continuously offered. Sometimes potential joint venture concepts fail simply because there is not sufficient value for the participants.

For example, the developers of a comprehensive freestanding diagnostic imaging center wanted to offer participation to referring primary care physicians. The developers invested considerable time and expense in creating a private placement memorandum involving participation in the real estate which housed the center. The potential rewards were not sufficient to attract any primary care physician investors, however, and the project was therefore vulnerable to competitors able to secure participation by referring physicians.

The venture must also entail distinctive perceived value for potential customers.[2] If the concept is new, it must be differentiated from existing product/service offerings so that either incremental value is created for users or a protected market position is established for the provider. For example, urgent care centers which offer primary care appointments and HMO access may differentiate themselves from centers specializing in episodic care. Many home healthcare and durable medical equipment businesses are being developed by hospitals based on their access to discharge planners. Since the service in most instances is already available in the market, the business concept entails coupling these services with the in-hospital, discharge planning process. Whether or not this concept makes any sense depends on the economics, market structure, and hospital's effectiveness in controlling referrals through discharge planners.

SEGMENT/SIZE MARKET

Market strategy begins with segmentation of the market based on the differential probability of using the service or on price realization differences among different payers.[3] Figure 11–1, for example, segments the market for a minor

FIGURE 11-1 Market Segmentation

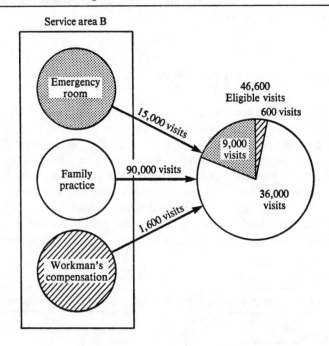

emergency center into three pieces: nonurgent business that normally would have gone to a hospital emergency room, primary care business destined for physician offices, and employer-related business such as workers' compensation.

The size of the segments determines both the business's ultimate potential and the relative importance of marketing targets. The key to success in the minor emergency market depicted in Figure 11-1 is clearly to penetrate the office-based business of primary care physicians in the area.

Figure 11-2 maps the potential market into demand in visits per day based on market penetration of minor emergency centers in the area (43 percent of

FIGURE 11-2 Demand

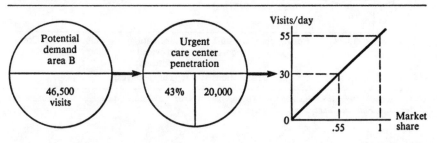

the market) and the market share captured by the business under study. Whether this market should be entered depends on the attractiveness of the market and the economics of the business.

MARKET ATTRACTIVENESS

Market attractiveness may be measured along many dimensions depending on the situation. Existing firm profitability, customer satisfaction, growth, entry barriers, competitive structure, competitor initiative, and buyer and supplier power combine to shape the market's attractiveness for a new entrant.[4]

Figure 11–3 presents data from a population survey conducted in the area targeted for placement of an urgent care center. Potential consumers were dissatisfied with the cost and wait associated with emergency services in the area and were correspondingly interested in using the new urgent care center. Table 11–1 demonstrates consumers' differential dissatisfaction with access to office-

FIGURE 11–3 Rating of Emergency Room Care by Intent to Use Urgent Care

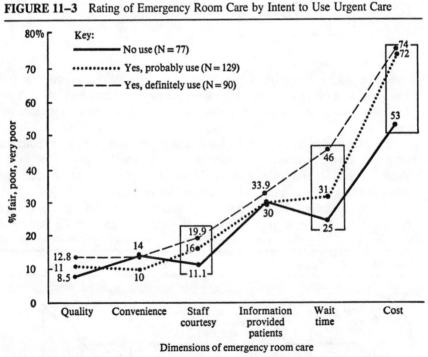

SOURCE: Reproduced from Douglas Gregory and Kenneth Kaufman, "Managing Diversification Risk," *Healthcare Financial Management,* December 1983.

TABLE 11–1 Urgent Care Screen

	A (N = 100)	B (N = 113)	C (N = 101)
Percent travel more than three miles for emergency care	20%	46%	42%
Percent unable to see a doctor when need to	15	20	15
Percent who do not have doctor	24	12	20
Percent with doctor more than five miles away	23	43	26
Percent dissatisfied with time it takes to see their doctor for urgent care	8	16	6
Percent use urgent care center	69	79	77

based physicians in Area B, one of three areas investigated for the center. Based on these findings, it appears that a market exists for minor emergency or urgent care services in Area B.

What about the industry structure? Profitability varies widely in this business—some major chains have experienced bankruptcy during the last few years. Moreover, the target business segment is in competition with primary care physician office practice, a mature market in most locations with little prospects for growth. Finally, there are no barriers to entry, which suggests that competitive conditions in any geographic market will change rapidly. If a new firm is initially successful in such markets, competitors will be attracted to the market, resulting in excess capacity and anemic returns. In such markets, careful attention must be paid to differentiation strategies and internal economics.

INTERNAL ECONOMICS

Figure 11–4 summarizes the cost structure of a new center. Break-even occurs at about 25 visits per day, and the center generates a 3 percent margin at 30 visits per day. In most cases resource consumption and associated cost structures differ across product segments requiring more detailed cost modeling to determine differential profitability by product-market segment.

Cost determinants for such centers include site location, configuration/layout, and operational considerations. Most costs are fixed due to the need to provide standby capacity for unscheduled visits; volume is therefore the key cost driver. Marketing strategy is consequently the paramount concern for a successful project.

FIGURE 11–4 Cost Structure

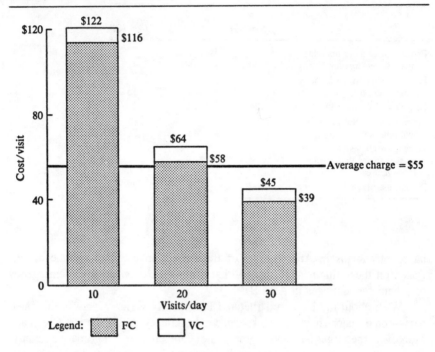

KEY SUCCESS REQUIREMENTS

Marketing strategy is derived from detailed understanding of the competitive economics of the business and the market requirements for competitive advantage. Competitor economics can be modeled from prospectuses and other published documents, as well as competitor interviews. Competitors' initiatives and strategies should be carefully profiled and analyzed to discover vulnerability, likely reactions to market entry, goals, and segments served. These data are synthesized into a clear set of requirements for success in the new business.

One source of data on competitors and market success requirements is the consumer focus group. Many insights into competitors' strengths and weaknesses may be gained from this technique. For example, consider the following quotes from a focus group concerning two competitive urgent care centers.

> I wouldn't go to either clinic for anything serious; they couldn't even take a white blood count and . . . missed my grandfather's acute appendicitis. . . . The emergency room has back-up equipment.

> I would go to an emergency room out of habit. . . . I don't like to try anything new when it comes to my health.

Clinic B is unstable. . . . I would worry if they are going to be there tomorrow. . . . I wouldn't go to an unstable place.

I'd rather go to my doctor's office for minor problems unless the wait is too long.

Why would a good doctor take this type of job. . . ? If he was any good, he'd be in private practice.

The building is important. . . . I'm looking for a corporation, not a doctor. . . . They need to design for the consumer. . . . You're choosing a company, not a doctor.

I like the word *family* in the name.

Hospital sponsorship would add credibility.

Insurance is a problem at A.

Clearly, among those consumers willing to use this type of service, stability, quality, and sponsorship are key concerns. Facility image is also important. Wait time, cost, and courtesy are other sources of dissatisfaction revealed by the survey which must be addressed by the new business.

Analysis of competitor economics might focus on scale advantages available to multisite players versus solo operations. If advertising and sales are success requirements, then significant economic advantage may accrue to multisite operators. An aggressive market coverage and promotion/sales-oriented strategy may be successful in fragmented markets with relatively undeveloped marketing approaches.

JOINT VENTURE ECONOMICS

Physician participation in the business may be a success requirement for many health-related ventures. The relative economic benefits to potential participants should be delineated before serious discussions begin.

Table 11–2 summarizes a hypothetical limited partnership for an urgent care center with the hospital and a professional medical corporation as general partners and 10 limited partners. The $400,000 capital requirement is contributed one half by the general partners and one half by the limited partners. The business is assumed to be sold after five years, and the limited partners would earn about 24 percent on their investment, including cash distributions and tax benefits which assume the limited partners are in 50 percent tax brackets.

Table 11–3 presents a general partnership structure in which 50 percent of the investment is financed with a bank loan or other source of debt financing. By trading on equity the venture's return on equity is increased to about 32 percent, and its risk is increased commensurately.

TABLE 11–2 Urgent Care Center Pro Forma—Equity Financing

	Year 1	Year 2	Year 3	Year 4	Year 5	
Visits	10,158	11,000	11,000	11,000	11,000	
Net revenue	$507,900	$572,000	$594,800	$618,675	$643,422	
Operating cost						
FC	$400,000	$385,000	$400,400	$416,416	$433,073	
VC	50,790	57,200	59,488	61,868	64,342	
OCF*	57,100	129,800	134,992	140,392	146,007	$584,029
Depreciation	46,000	46,750	46,750	46,750	46,750	
Income	11,110	83,050	88,242	93,642	99,257	
ITC	32,500					
Tax owed	5,500	41,525	44,121	46,821	49,629	46,007
Incremental						
net worth	84,055	88,275	90,571	93,571	96,379	538,022
ROE	24%					
Real estate	$ 75,000					
Building	225,000					
Equipment	100,000					
Venture structure						
Hospital	$100,000					
P.C.	100,000					
Ltd. partners						
(10 LPs @						
$20,000)	200,000					

Annual Increments to Limited Partnership

Start	Year 1	Year 2	Year 3	Year 4	Year 5	Liquidate
$20,000	$4,203	$4,414	$4,544	$4,679	$4,819	$26,901
ROE	24%					

Assumptions: All cash distributed in proportion to investment, 50 percent tax bracket, and 4 percent inflation.

*Depreciation excluded.

TABLE 11–3 Urgent Care Center Pro Forma—Debt Financing

	Year 1	Year 2	Year 3	Year 4	Year 5	
Visits	10,158	11,000	11,000	11,000	11,000	
Net revenue	$507,900	$572,000	$594,800	$618,675	$643,422	
Operating cost						
FC	$400,000	$385,000	$400,400	$416,416	$433,073	
VC	50,790	57,200	59,488	61,868	64,342	
OCF*	57,100	129,800	134,992	140,392	146,007	$584,029
Depreciation	46,000	46,750	46,750	46,750	46,750	
Interest	22,000	18,500	14,500	10,200	5,400	
Principal	32,000	35,700	39,300	44,000	49,000	
Income	(10,800)	64,550	73,742	83,442	93,857	
Cash flow	3,110	75,600	81,192	81,192	91,607	
ITC	32,500					
Tax owed	(5,445)	32,275	36,871	41,721	46,929	46,007

TABLE 11–13 *(concluded)*

	Year 1	Year 2	Year 3	Year 4	Year 5	
Incremental net worth	41,055	43,325	44,321	44,471	44,679	538,022
IRR	32%					
Real estate	$ 75,000					
Building	225,000					
Equipment	100,000					
Venture structure						
Hospital	$100,000					
P.C.	100,000					
Bank (five-year loan at 11%)	200,000					

Assumptions: All cash distributed in proportion to investment, 50 percent tax bracket, and 4 percent inflation.
*Depreciation excluded.

CONCLUSION

A six-step process for viewing and evaluating joint business ventures has been outlined in this chapter. Not only does this process lead to assessment of the potential risks and returns of new ventures, but it is also constructive in developing marketing strategy and the business plan for the project. It is instructive to view private placement memoranda for joint ventures between hospitals and physicians from this perspective. Many such documents amount to little more than pro formas with critical assumptions hidden in notes with such pithy analyses as "follows from management's best judgment." Pro formas are the last and easiest part of effective business planning.

Notes

[1] Douglas Gregory and Kenneth Kauffman, "Managing Diversification Risk," *Healthcare Financial Management* 37, no. 12 (December 1983), pp. 30–34.

[2] John A. Welsh and Jerry F. White, *The Entrepreneur's Master Planning Guide: How to Launch a Successful Business* (Englewood Cliffs, N.J.: Prentice-Hall, 1983), p. 78.

[3] Douglas Klegon, Douglas Gregory, and Paul Kingstrom, "Planning for Ambulatory Care Delivery Systems: A Market Segment Approach," *Health Care Management Review* 7, no. 1 (Winter 1982), p. 35.

[4] See Michael Porter, *Competitive Strategy* (New York: MacMillan, 1980), chap. 3, for a framework for analyzing market and competitive structures.

12

Financing Joint Ventures

Richard A. Baehr, M.A., M.S.

INTRODUCTION

As a result of the recent dramatic changes in the reimbursement climate and delivery system for healthcare in America, there has been substantial interest on the part of both hospitals and physicians in establishing joint ventures between the two groups. Many of the joint ventures have financed alternative delivery systems (ambulatory surgery centers, urgent care centers, diagnostic centers, home healthcare, health maintenance organizations) and new capital programs for the hospital (cardiac cath labs, magnetic resonance imaging).

The financing of hospital-physician joint ventures has taken several paths different from the traditional capital financing approaches that have been adopted for hospital projects. This is in large part attributable to the nature of the participants (typically a tax-exempt hospital and taxable independent physicians), the start-up character of many of the projects (and associated high degree of risk), and the amount of financing required.

This chapter examines several aspects of financing hospital-physician joint ventures. These include the financial planning process, screening financial alternatives, surveying alternative sources of funds, and developing a business plan to support the proposed financing. As a result of the rapid innovation in financing techniques for joint ventures, it is clear that no one best approach has been developed. This chapter is intended to serve as an introduction to the variety of options that currently are available.

THE FINANCIAL PLANNING PROCESS

The decision to pursue a hospital-physician joint venture is a separate decision from the selection of a financing technique for the project. Figure 12–1 displays schematically the joint venture evaluation process. While a financing methodology must be assumed in the preliminary assessment of interest and in the pro formas contained in a preliminary feasibility study, a technique need

FIGURE 12–1 Joint Venture Evaluation Process

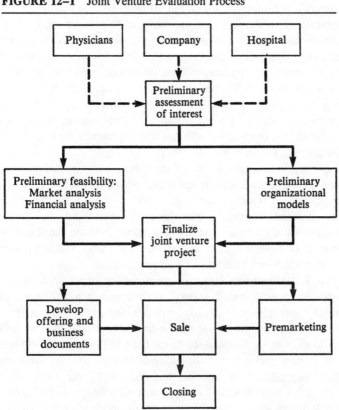

not be selected until agreement is reached to proceed with a joint venture project.

Most significantly, the availability of a particularly attractive financing technique and the interest in joint venturing should not take precedence over a determination of the wisdom of proceeding with a project. Joint venture projects should, to the greatest extent possible, be consistent with a hospital's strategic objectives. Hence, identifying the right projects (assuming a hospital has the luxury of time to decide) is the most important step in the planning process. Establishment of a joint venture structure, selection of a financing package, and making decisions requiring an analysis that is often more complex than the evaluation undertaken in the pure planning phase must await the results of this strategic screening process.

Unfortunately, many hospital executives and boards are rushed into agreeing to joint venture the development of a new service by insistent pressure from the hospital's physicians (many of whom are being solicited for joint venture activities by third-party entrepreneurs). Such projects will probably suffer higher failure rates and result in more ill will among the parties than those created as a result of a systematic planning process at the hospital.

Most healthcare joint venture projects are designed to achieve one or more of three major objectives. The first objective is to bring needed management expertise or marketing resources to the project that does not exist on the staff of the project's conceptualizer (the hospital, the physicians, or an independent third party). Physicians or entrepreneurs may want to bring hospitals into various alternative delivery projects to achieve greater market name recognition and prestige. Similarly, hospitals planning particular joint ventures may want the services of a syndicator or operator who has had experience packaging and managing related projects in the field.

A second objective is to increase market share for a service or freeze out competitors from entering a market. A hospital that allows physicians to invest in new imaging equipment is counting on increased referrals for this service and the spillover effect on volumes in other hospital departments. A hospital that develops a series of urgent care centers may want physician participation in the joint venture to co-opt the doctors and prevent them from affiliating with any other group with intentions to establish a similar center.

A third objective, and one that may take on increasing importance as capital cost reimbursement regulations are revised, is for hospitals to shift some of the financing burden and new project risk to physicians and outside parties. The proposals being discussed for replacing the capital cost pass-through will provide the same incentives for hospitals to be cautious in their use of debt and in the investment in new services and technologies that prospective payment system (PPS) have engendered on the operating side. Joint venture projects with significant financial participation by physicians offer hospitals the opportunity to continue to move ahead and compete without overloading the balance sheet with new debt. Significantly, many joint venture projects can be structured so that they represent more attractive investment opportunities for the physicians than other nonhealthcare partnerships or stock deals that may be presented by brokers. A limited partnership joint venture project, for example, can be put together with almost all of the invested funds reserved for project use instead of one third or more of the funds winding up in the hands of syndicators. In addition, physicians have the opportunity to influence directly the success of their investment by their referral activities, whereas real estate, oil, gas, and stock investments are passive in nature.

These reasons for joint venturing, along with those discussed in Chapter 3, need to be considered before evaluating the sources of financing available for a project.

SCREENING FINANCIAL ALTERNATIVES

Several basic screens or considerations need to be applied in selecting among the financing alternatives available for joint venture projects.

Amount of Capital

The amount of financing required is most critical. Many projects will require both debt and equity sources (partner contributions or stock sales). A hospital needs to gauge the availability of equity funds for a project and the ability to leverage that equity with debt funds for the difference. Hence, if debt financing is available for 80 percent of the project cost for a magnetic resonance imaging system (cost about $2 million), then $400,000 of equity capital must be raised from the joint venture participants. If the hospital expects physicians to provide 80 percent of the equity capital, then $320,000 needs to come from this source.

Size of Investment

The size of the medical staff and the size of investments individual physicians may be willing to make will determine the specific plan for selling the interests. For example, some physicians may be able to invest only a few thousand dollars, while others may not be interested in any investment requiring less than $10,000 to $15,000. A limited partnership that offers units at $5,000 each could accommodate both kinds of physicians, with the larger investors buying multiple partnership interests.

Term of Financing

Another major factor is the term of the financings. If the expected payback for the venture is 5 to 10 years, investors will be concerned with the liquidity of the investment (its "cash-in" ability). As an example, corporate stock investments, even in privately held corporations, generally offer more liquidity than limited partnership investments, which frequently have no trading market.

If debt financing is a major element of a financing package, the time the debt will need to be outstanding will have important bearing on the selection of a financing source. Most lenders prefer projects with intermediate terms rather than 20- to 30-year commitments to protect against long-term interest rate fluctuations. If a new project's forecasted cash flow does not permit rapid amortization of the outstanding debt, then the joint venture participants may have to offer a combination debt/equity package to the lender involving convertible debt, options, or warrants to make the loan more attractive.

Control

Hospitals in particular are concerned about the ownership and control of a joint venture project. Some financing methods, such as limited partnerships, allow a general partner with a minority financial interest to have complete autonomy in all operational aspects of the project. Certain equity participations such as venture capital, however, usually require board representation and significant input in management direction of an enterprise for the venture capitalist.

Timing and Costs

Another factor concerns the time required to put a deal together and the front-end financing costs associated with that method of financing. When deals are brought to a hospital by a physician group or by a syndicator, there is often real time pressure on the institution to make the decision on moving ahead, select a financing source, and put the deal together. Financing methodologies that are complex and time-consuming will be of less interest in this environment than transactions that are easily understood and can be concluded rapidly.

In addition, certain financing techniques involve substantial front-end fees (e.g., initial public offerings of stock, syndicator involvement in a limited partnership), and this could threaten the rate of return required to make the investment attractive to investors. Some methods of financing involve annual fees as well, though these are usually not significant enough to affect the selection decision.

Evaluation of Process

No one financing method will be perfect. Joint venture participants need to evaluate the adequacy and appropriateness of a particular financing technique by weighing the importance of the individual screens against achievement of the objectives of a particular project. If short-term tax considerations are very important to physician investors, then a limited partnership structure with a lower projected long-term rate of return may be superior to a corporate stock offering with a higher long-term potential rate of return. If a large number of physician participants in a venture are considered important for referral purposes for a new service, for creation of a physician hospital organization (a PHO), or for a medical staff hospital organization (a MeSH), then a stock corporation may be more suitable than a limited partnership offering restricted to 35 or fewer investors.

SURVEYING ALTERNATIVE SOURCES OF FUNDS

Debt Financing

Most hospital-physician joint ventures do not involve a financing for a not-for-profit, tax-exempt corporate structure. As a result, the most common form of debt financing available to tax-exempt hospitals, tax-exempt revenue bonds, is unavailable for the joint venture project. If the ability to finance a project on a tax-exempt basis is an overriding consideration, this suggests that the joint venture structure will have to resemble a contractual model between the exempt hospital and the contracted physicians.

Tax-exempt financing is a more attractive financing vehicle today than it has been in many years. This results from the steep yield curve for tax-exempt debt, the relatively sharp difference in interest rates on tax-exempt and taxable debt for short maturity (zero to five years) financings, and the innovations that have been occurring in the short-term tax-exempt market in recent years (see Figure 12–2). One third of hospital tax-exempt financings in the last quarter of 1984 and the first nine months of 1985 were short-term issues involving commercial paper, variable rate demand notes, and put bonds (see Figure 12–3). Most issues had tender (put) features ranging from a day to a year, with a letter of credit from a major commercial bank supporting the indebtedness in case it was tendered back to the issuer and not successfully remarketed. Significantly, most of the short-term issues had nominal maturities of 30 years though the letters of credit had initial maturities of 5 to 7 years. Hence, the hospital borrower could hope to keep an issue outstanding for its full maturity at short-term rates (5 to 6 percent currently) instead of conventional long-term fixed rates (9 to 10 percent currently) so long as the letter of credit was renewable. The steepness of the yield curve for tax-exempt securities (much higher interest rates for longer maturities) continues to encourage hospitals to take advantage of the low-cost, short-term financings and bypass the "security" of locking in a longer-term rate (see Figure 12–4).

The changes anticipated in the capital cost reimbursement system under Medicare provide strong incentives for hospitals to finance new projects "off balance sheet" (through joint ventures involving subsidiaries and separate corporations) and to make use of the lowest-cost financing methods available.

FIGURE 12–2   Government Yield Curve Tax-Exempt Yield Curve ("a" rated municipal bonds)

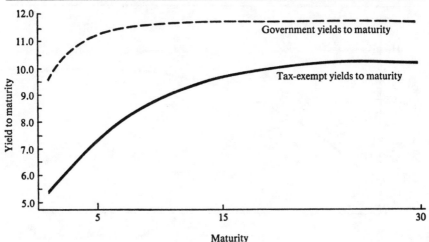

FIGURE 12–3 Monthly Volume: Fixed and Variable Rate Issues

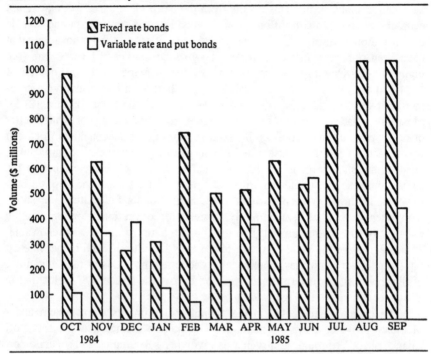

SOURCE: *Health Care Financing*, Prescott, Ball & Turben, Inc., New York, 1985.

FIGURE 12–4 Tax Exempt Yield Curve ("a" rated municipal bonds)

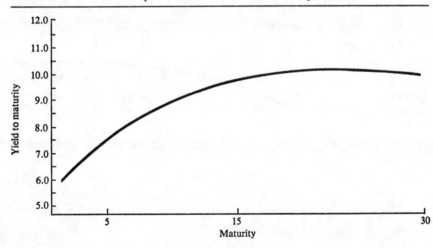

Pooled Equipment Financings

One innovation many hospitals have taken advantage of recently is the use of pooled equipment financings (sometimes referred to as "blind" pools or HELP, for Hospital Equipment Loan Programs). These financings, for single hospitals or groups of hospitals, provide funding for a hospital's equipment expenditures over a three-year period, reimbursement for equipment purchases made prior to the financing, an attractive short-term tax-exempt financing rate, and the ability to "arbitrage" funds not yet invested in new equipment in taxable short-term securities. The arbitrage potential has reduced the effective interest rate on these issues to very low rates (1 to 3 percent). Blind pools have provided another incentive for hospitals to finance new acquisitions through the existing hospital structure and establish joint venture activities contractually. Alternatively, the hospital's ability to save substantially on its capital costs through variable rate demand notes for major capital financings and blind pools for routine equipment purchases can free up the cash for joint venture investments with physicians outside the hospital corporate structure.

Industrial Development Bonds

A hospital-physician joint venture that takes the form of a taxable model can still make use of tax-exempt debt through the use of industrial development bonds (IDBs). IDBs, while limited in total volume annually by state (as a result of the 1984 Tax Reform Act), are available to taxable borrowers through two "small issue" exemptions. The first exemption is that the issue size not exceed $1 million. Alternatively, an IDB for a larger amount can be sold, so long as total capital expenditures of the borrower three years prior to the date of issue and three years after (including the project financed by the issue) do not exceed $10 million. If the issue size limitation is violated, the IDBs become taxable to the holder. The Tax Reform Act of 1986 severely curtails the use of IDBs, and this source of financing may not be around much longer. Most IDBs have been traditional long-term issues. Nonetheless, tax-exempt long-term (20- to 30-year maturity) IDBs still provide a less expensive financing source than taxable debt offerings of similar maturities.

Future of Tax Exempt Debt

The Tax Reform Act of 1986 will severely limit the use of tax-exempt financing for private not-for-profit hospitals beginning in 1987. The 1986 Act is expected to shift the attention of hospitals to taxable debt financings and equity financings. Both of these methods of hospital capital formation are also available for joint venturing activities with physicians.

Taxable Debt

Taxable debt sources for joint venture financings include short-term bank financing, asset-based financing, mortgages, leases, and convertible debt instruments. Short-term bank financings (lines of credit and letters of credit) are almost always unsecured. As a result, they require a stronger credit rating and history than financing secured by equipment or property. Revolving credit lines generally must be paid down (cleaned up) at least once a year for a short period of time. Asset-based financings involve short-term credits secured by a pledge of accounts receivable. Unsecured bank financings and asset-based financings are both generally floating rate obligations tied to the prime rate. Sometimes the rate can be fixed for short periods of time.

Mortgage-backed financings are debt instruments secured by real or personal property (land, buildings, equipment). This kind of financing is very common in association with limited partnerships where the equity capital is raised by partners' contributions. Mortgages have maturities that tie to the useful life of the item financed, though in some cases (buildings) they are shorter. The amortization period for a mortgage financing can be based on a schedule longer than the final maturity, necessitating a balloon payment and typically a second-stage financing. Mortgage financings typically involve "points" up front in addition to interest rates currently in the 10 to 12 percent and higher range. However, lenders will sometimes be willing to reduce interest rates substantially in exchange for a percentage of the gross revenues on a project. Such a combined debt/equity arrangement is increasingly common in start-up joint ventures.

Lease Financing

Leases are financings secured by the leased item (equipment or structure). Leases can be financing leases (where ownership is eventually transferred to the lessee for a nominal price) or operating leases, which are really "rentals" (ownership can be transferred at the end of the lease period at market prices). Sometimes a joint venture will undertake a sale and leaseback arrangement thereby obtaining capital through the sale of an already owned property.

The effective interest rate on leasing deals is typically higher than bank financings, despite the fact that lessors can take advantage of tax benefits in leasing deals (investment tax credits, accelerated depreciation) and can structure interest rates on leasing packages that are lower than bank rates. Furthermore, the Tax Reform Act of 1986, by eliminating the investment tax credit and lengthening depreciable lives will make lease financing rates more expensive and therefore less attractive.

Bond Financing

Long-term taxable bond financings have been used in the healthcare field by proprietary hospital management companies and some not-for-profit religiously affiliated hospital systems. Generally a borrower must be considered very creditworthy to secure this kind of financing, and start-up joint venture corporations may not be strong enough to compete in this market. "Junk bonds," which are high interest rate obligations of less creditworthy companies (often used to finance leveraged buyouts and corporate takeovers), have not yet been used for joint venture financings.

Convertible Debt

Convertible debt obligations, borrowings that involve an equity conversion feature at some time in the future, are a favored technique of venture capital investors. This kind of obligation typically involves a standard fixed interest rate prior to any partial or total conversion of the debt into equity.

Equity Financings

Most of the recently established hospital-physician joint ventures have used limited partnerships to raise equity capital. Other equity sources (venture capital financings, public stock offerings, self-financing by single owners or partners) are increasing in use, however.

Public Offerings

A public stock offering is probably the most visible financing vehicle because of the dramatic success stories associated with healthcare companies that have gone public. Between January 1983 and December 1984, healthcare companies were able to attract significant financing from a market very hungry for this kind of investment. Many of the companies financed with extremely high price earning multiples have fallen off to more modest premium multiples because their growth rates have slowed and new competitors have entered health maintenance organization, urgent care, day surgery, and other new markets.

Nonetheless, companies, including joint ventures, that can successfully raise money through an initial public stock offering (IPO) will find many favorable aspects to this method of financing. These include the unrestricted use of stock sale proceeds, dramatic increases in debt capacity (to reflect the market value of the stock), availability of a currency other than cash or bank loans for acquisitions, the ability to provide incentives to management and physicians through stock options, and an active secondary market for those investors desiring liquidity. The negative aspects associated with this type of financing include the difficulty in getting an issue sold without some successful operating history, heavy front-end costs (underwriters' fees, attorneys, and registration costs can exceed 10 percent of the proceeds), and public scrutiny over the day-to-day management of the operation.

In many cases, an IPO will be an ideal second-stage financing after venture capital or owner-supplied financing gets a project off the ground. It is important

FIGURE 12–5 1980–1984 Initial Public Offerings (partial list)

Company	Company Description
American Surgery Centers	Owns and operates surgery centers
CP Rehab Corporation	Cardiac rehabilitation facilities
Healthamerica Corporation	Health maintenance organizations
Surgery Centers Corp.	Outpatient surgery centers
U.S. Healthcare Systems	Health maintenance organization
Personal Diagnostics	Self-care diagnostic kits
Rehab Hospital Services Corp.	Rehabilitation hospitals
Urgent Care Centers of America	Freestanding medical care facilities
Medical 21	Outpatient surgery centers
Advanced Imaging Corporation	Medical digital imaging facilities
Foster Medical Corporation	Medical supplies and equipment
Healthcare & Retirement Corp.	Owns/operates nursing/retirement facilities
Healthdyne, Inc.	High technology homecare/hospital products
Nutri/Systems, Inc.	Weight loss centers
Basic American Medical	Acute care hospitals
Home Health Care of America	Home hyperalimentation, chemotherapy, antibiotic therapy
Continental Health Affiliates, Inc.	Feeding equipment & nutrients for hospital and home care
Republic Health Corporation	Acute care hospitals
Horizon Health Corporation	Psychiatric, drug, and alcohol services
Manor Care	Nursing homes
Shared Medical Systems	Computerized record-keeping systems for hospitals
Care Enterprises	Nursing facilities
National Health Corporation	Long and short-term convalescent centers, physical and speech therapy
Surgicare Corporation	Freestanding surgical centers
Community Psychiatric Centers	Psychiatric hospitals
Greatwest Hospitals	Hospitals and a health maintenance organization
Comprehensive care	Alcohol rehabilitation centers
HBO & Co.	Computerized record-keeping systems for hospitals
Compucare, Inc.	Information processing services and software to health care institutions
Amherst Associates Inc.	Health care consulting and computer services
Maxicare Health Plans Inc.	Health maintenance organizations
Summit Health Ltd.	Hospitals and nursing facilities
Preferred Health Care Corp.	Mental health care services
Family Health Systems, Inc.	Site selection, administrative, and marketing services to dental and emergency medical centers
Healthgroup International	Health maintenance organization
Imatron, Inc.	High speed computed cinetomography scanners
Medical Management Corporation	Freestanding medical clinics and clinic management services
American Physicians Service Group, Inc.	Management services to insurance companies and physicians' groups
Doctors Officenters Corporation	Freestanding emergency centers
American Emergicenter, Inc.	Freestanding emergency centers
Peak Health Care, Inc.	Health maintenance organization
Healthcare Services Group, Inc.	Nursing home support services
Safeguard Health Enterprises	Dental health maintenance organization
The Mediplex Group, Inc.	Alcohol & substance abuse facilities

SOURCES: Anne B. Fisher, "A 'Cutback' Play in House Stocks," *Fortune* 108, no. 5 (September 5, 1983), pp. 137–38; *The Med-Tech Advisor*, May 16, 1983.

to note that well over one half of the healthcare IPOs from 1980 through 1984 were for ambulatory care facilities or alternative delivery vehicles, many of them regional or even local in character. A partial listing of these IPOs appears in Figure 12–5. Hence, hospital-physician joint ventures, especially those that develop into franchises or multiple-unit enterprises, may have access to this market.

Venture Capital

Until recently, venture capital was very hard to come by and expensive (owners would have to give up substantial pieces of their business to obtain this financing). The record-breaking increases in stock market values since 1982 have spurred the development of venture capital groups, many of them representing the first real venture capital activity in certain parts of the country. It is not uncommon now for venture capital firms to compete for worthy projects with funds in venture capital partnerships sometimes remaining unexpended for one to two years after the money is raised.

Venture capital is a very attractive financing option for start-up joint venture projects. Typically, cash is exchanged for a significant ownership share (20 percent or more) and a voice in management (board participation, preparation of ongoing management reports to the venture capitalist). The venture capitalist will sometimes have preferential rights in offering his stock in an initial public offering. While venture capitalists will look at start-ups, if a very rapid growth potential does not exist, the venture capitalist will likely pass. It is common for venture capitalists to only invest in projects promising a return of three to five times the investment in five years or less. A major advantage of this kind of financing is that front-end fees are minimal and the deals can be put together quickly. A factor that the joint venture owners may initially consider as negative (the venture capitalist's involvement in running the business) should really be looked at positively (the venture capitalist is investing his management expertise in growing small businesses).

Preferred Stock

Preferred stock is a form of hybrid financing whereby the investor is paid a fixed dividend (generally a lower rate than for a long-term taxable debt obligation), but in the event of liquidation is paid off prior to common stockholders (though behind other secured creditors). Unlike conventional debt, preferred stock does not have a fixed maturity but offers a tax advantaged return to a corporate investor (80 percent of dividends received are deductible). This latter feature provides a broader potential market for preferred stock.

Venture Capital Companies

A few hospital-physician joint venture arrangements are becoming venture capital companies themselves. This typically requires a large number of physician investors attached to a single hospital and a substantial capital contribution by the hospital. The corporation becomes a holding company for a variety of investment opportunities that can be structured as general or limited partnerships, individual venture capital investments, or contractual relationships. The venture capital company, because of the size of its physician investor group and capital strength, should be able to successfully leverage its equity base with a lender to further increase its investment stake. This type of corporation is also sometimes called a MeSH (medical staff hospital model) or PHO (physician-hospital organization). A venture capital company is also a suitable arrangement for a franchise business (for example, urgent care centers or ambulatory surgery centers). Venture capital companies are discussed in detail in Chapter 13.

Self-Financing and Limited Partnerships

Self-financing occurs because the joint venture participants have all the front-end equity they need (and hence want to avoid the ownership dilution and loss of control that occurs with venture capital) or because the joint venture cannot find any external financing or does not need any. Limited partnerships are a form of self-financing. Where self-financing occurs in a corporate model, stock options, contingent compensation, and bonuses can be awarded to management and physicians. The limited partnership is a very suitable financing mechanism for most joint venture activities. Physicians are familiar with this technique and for reasons discussed previously will probably find a healthcare joint venture investment more attractive than most of those they have reviewed or participated in. Limited partnership deals can be privately placed (35 or fewer investors) or publicly syndicated. They are most attractive to individuals or institutions with substantial tax obligations since the taxable gains and losses are passed directly to the partners. It is important that a limited partnership joint venture be attractive economically for other than tax reasons, however, since the tax advantages usually are only timing considerations that eventually will be reversed.

Most limited partnership investments in the healthcare field have required investments of between $5,000 and $15,000 for individual interests. Hospitals are generally less interested in a pro rata share of the income generated by the venture (and not at all interested in the tax benefits) than in the increased volume of business generated for the new activity and related service (ancillaries or inpatient referrals) or in the ability to maintain management control over the new service and strengthen the ties of staff physicians to the institution.

SELECTION PROCESS

Selecting among financing alternatives is a complex task. Joint venture participants need to agree on the degree of management control and ownership desired and accurately assess an external financing agent's perception of the riskiness of the venture and the track record of the venture's participants. Finally, the amount of financing required, timing considerations, and the financing available and required for the front-end costs of a debt or equity deal are factors that will enter the equation. Not all joint venture participants have the luxury of selecting among alternatives. Frequently a package of owner-financed equity shares and mortgage debt are the only saleable combination for a start-up project.

DEVELOPMENT OF A BUSINESS PLAN

Joint venture financings require a great degree of trust among the hospital and physician partners and investors. A project that reaches the stage where active solicitation of limited partners or other financing sources occurs must have a solid business plan investors can evaluate. This plan will contain excerpts from a preliminary feasibility study, if one has been prepared, but will involve a lot more than this. Specifically, the plan needs a clear concise executive summary that describes the essence of the investment opportunity or the debt financing sought. This should be followed by a statement of the purpose of the joint venture (the nature of the business and the financial and utilization targets) and a detailed description of the business, including a market analysis with information on current and likely future competitors. Most critical is a discussion of management and their expertise in this area or related areas. Finally, some financial pro formas are included along with accompanying comments about risk factors (changes in tax or other laws). The success of a project and the positive features of a business plan cannot be dependent on the project obtaining financing from a particular source.

THE FUTURE OF HOSPITAL-PHYSICIAN JOINT VENTURE FINANCING

Hospital-physician joint venture projects are one aspect of an emerging joint venture process involving individual hospitals, groups of hospitals, suppliers, hospital management companies, insurance companies, alternative delivery systems, entrepreneurs, and physicians. The financing vehicles established to date for hospital-physician joint ventures will change as greater sophistication is achieved on the part of investors and a track record is established for both the successes and the inevitable shakeout of business failures that will occur. The originators of joint venture projects that offer substantial value to investors can be confident of finding funding for the project regardless of tax law changes or changing market conditions. As indicated earlier in this chapter, these projects should be consistent with a hospital's strategic objectives and enable the institution or the participants to acquire needed management expertise or marketing resources, support its competitive position, or make use of nonhospital financing sources.

13

The Venture Capital Company

Douglas M. Mancino, J.D.

INTRODUCTION

The venture capital company is a unique form of hospital-physician joint venture designed to address a number of needs and concerns of hospitals and physicians.

Most joint ventures are designed to raise funds for direct participation in a *single* project or business. The venture capital company, however, has as its primary purpose the raising of funds for investment in *several* projects or businesses of interest to both hospitals and physicians. Indeed, the projects or business frequently may be defined only in general terms at the time the funds are raised.

Unlike true venture capitalists, the venture capital company is likely to limit its activities to a particular geographic area and to particular types of projects, specifically capital-intensive projects in healthcare. Nevertheless, the venture capital company is intended to serve a function similar to that of venture capitalists in that it brings risk capital to fund such projects and businesses in order to provide reasonable returns on investments to its owners.

Numerous other types of hospital-physician joint ventures may seem at first to be similar to the venture capital company. One such organization is the Medical Staff Hospital Joint Venture, commonly known as MeSH. Unlike a MeSH, however, the venture capital company is intended to focus its efforts on new business development opportunities rather than on alternative delivery systems and insurance types of contractual arrangements.

ADVANTAGES

The interest of hospitals and their medical staffs in the development of venture capital companies is a relatively recent phenomenon driven by a number of perceived advantages. From a hospital's perspective, the venture capital company provides a relatively uncomplicated means of soliciting the participation of all its medical staff members in a true, economic risk-sharing joint venture. Typically, the minimum investment required of individual physicians is relatively small, particularly when compared to other types of hospital-physician joint ventures. Further, the venture capital company helps address the concern that many hospitals have about excluding some physicians from joint venture opportunities.

From the physicians' perspective, the venture capital company represents a relatively uncomplicated method of pooling substantial resources to engage in a variety of business development opportunities. Unlike hospitals, few physicians individually have adequate resources to fund the start-up costs associated with business development activities, not to mention the capital requirements needed to implement a business development activity. The venture capital company for physicians represents a means of assembling the critical mass of capital from the hospital and physicians, not only to fund the business development phase of the project, but also to fund its implementation and operations. Further, from a physician's perspective, the venture capital company also provides a means of spreading financial risks among a large number of investors and a broad range of types of investments. As a consequence, the downside risk of failure of a particular project may be offset by the upside potential for profit from several other business opportunities. In this manner, an investment in the venture capital company may be less risky than a similarly sized investment in a single business venture.

The venture capital company also creates an opportunity to develop two tiers of investment opportunities for hospitals and physicians. The first type of investment opportunity is intended to appeal to a broad cross section of the medical staff. The venture capital company can pursue activities that offer reasonable returns on investment from the provision of services and goods of interest to a wide variety of the medical staff. The venture capital company also can pursue second-tier investment opportunities that are specifically tailored to appeal to narrower segments of the medical staff and would be offered by selling stock in corporate subsidiaries of the venture capital company or selling partnership interests in partnerships in which the venture capital company is the general partner.

For example, a first-tier type of business development opportunity may be the development of a billing and collection service, a durable medical equipment supply business, or a group purchasing business. These types of business opportunities normally would be of interest to a broad cross section of the medical staff membership, as well as to potential customers who are not owners of the venture capital company. The second-tier type of investment would be ambulatory surgery centers, diagnostic centers, cardiac catheterization laboratories, and similar types of projects that, while capable of producing substantial revenues, will depend for their success on a smaller amount or more focused type of physician involvement and support, such as the support of surgeons for an ambulatory surgery center. Using two tiers of investment opportunities may assist a hospital in creating a broad economic base and may provide an incentive to physicians to resist efforts of outside organizations that would set up freestanding clinics or other enterprises in the hospital's service area.

Among its other advantages, the venture capital company also provides some measure of assurance to the persons operating its businesses that they can count on funding levels for such businesses and that such levels of financial support will be adequate without the need of capital calls, dependence on the success of subsequent offerings, and similar types of risks that future projects may go unfunded or be insufficiently funded.

Additionally, the venture capital company provides a formalized decision-making structure for business development by hospitals and physicians. Through its board of directors and management, hospitals and physicians are forced to deal with business issues of importance to both camps in a collaborative non-adversarial setting. While the venture capital company is not immune to pressures that otherwise exist in hospital-medical staff relationships, the common financial interest and commitment of hospitals and physicians can help reduce the risk that external pressure unrelated to business development will override business judgments and the realities of acting promptly in a competitive marketplace.

DISADVANTAGES

Notwithstanding the substantial benefits that may be achievable through the use of the venture capital company, the venture capital company has several disadvantages and poses risks to future hospital-physician relationships.

As an initial matter, it is unlikely that the venture capital company will be able to distance itself from hospital-medical staff conflicts and problems to such a degree as to make it truly independent. Thus, there may be great difficulty in approaching business development objectively, as would be the case of a true venture capitalist. This lack of objectivity is likely to arise not only in connection with the selection of the business development opportunity, but also in dealing with problems that arise during its operations. It is probable that the management of the venture capital company will be faced with the need to act decisively, and in some cases ruthlessly, because of business exigencies. Because any hospital-physician joint venture has inherent political overtones, this could become a very serious problem.

Related to this problem will be the urge of the venture capital company to seek out all profitable lines of business, even if this requires cannibalization of some of the hospital's profitable businesses rather than focusing only on developing new businesses or on businesses of competitors. In addition, a true venture capitalist will attempt to lure away the best managers from the hospital.

Another potential disadvantage is the lack of resources that may hamper the development of the venture capital company's business development activities during its early stage of development. The types of businesses undertaken by the venture capital company may not support the development of marketing, finance, and other types of support staff functions.

Both hospitals and physicians need to come to grips with the realities of a shareholder-venture capital company relationship. Investors who buy shares of stock in a publicly traded corporation are making capital investments and expect to get their money back, plus a return on their investments, with little or no direct involvement. In fact, stockholders of publicly traded companies normally try to maximize their wealth by freely moving in and out of the corporation without loyalty, simply in order to generate profits from securities trading. By contrast, the shareholders of the venture capital company will be the true owners of the corporation and its underlying assets. The board of directors, of necessity, will need to be more responsive to the needs of the shareholders and as a consequence will be more subject to individual shareholder pressure.

Finally, the venture capital company is unlikely ever to become an entity that is totally independent of the hospital, its physicians, and the day-to-day problems and conflicts between and among them. Because of the inability to distance the venture capital company from the hospital, both the hospital and the physicians may continue to have a "protected" feeling that is not warranted. Hospital managers typically feel a need to provide, and medical staff members typically demand of them, assurances that business development opportunities will be successful and, if not, that the physicians will be made whole by the hospital. This type of attitude in the venture capital company context is misplaced and cannot be maintained if the venture capital company is to succeed.

ORGANIZATION AND MANAGEMENT

The venture capital company concept assumes that a new entity, typically a corporation, will be formed. One or more classes of stock can be authorized and issued by the corporation.

Medical staff members typically will make investments in the venture capital company individually or through their qualified retirement plans. In some instances, the stock may also be acquired by a separate entity formed by the medical staff membership.

The hospital participating in the establishment of the venture capital company either will purchase the stock directly or will purchase the stock through its parent corporation or another affiliate.

The allocation of hospital and physician ownership of stock can be critical to the degree of support that both constituencies will give to the venture capital company and its programs. In the few venture capital companies that have been established to date, stock ownership has been divided equally between the hospital and the medical staff membership. The feeling generally has been that equal ownership of the venture capital company is essential to the creation of a sense of fairness that the hospital, which typically has the deepest pocket, is not dominating the activities of the venture capital company. This feeling is premised, of course, on the assumption that the medical staff membership is monolithic and will always act in unison when confronted with a decision where the interests of the hospital shareholder and the physician shareholders differ. It goes without saying that medical staffs are not monolithic entities, but rather are typically composed of a diverse range of personalities and thus the 50 percent medical staff ownership may not, in reality, be as crucial as it may seem.

In addition, venture capital companies can utilize different classes of stock with different voting rights, different types of securities such as debt instruments, and different board arrangements such as staggered terms to deal with the intricacies of resolving hospital-physician conflict over management prerogatives.

Generally, the shareholders of the venture capital company will elect a board of directors that will be responsible for general supervision of the businesses and activities of the venture capital company. Most hospitals believe it necessary to have, and most physicians demand, equal representation of the hospital and physicians on the board of directors. The exact form of board structure and composition will have to be tailored to the political and business context in which the venture capital company is being established.

The board of directors is responsible for the selection of the officers of the venture capital company who will ultimately be responsible for day-to-day operations. The impulse in forming venture capital companies is initially to select management using the same criteria that were used to select the board of directors, that is, to have a blend of hospital and physician presence in the management structure. This may be a satisfactory approach in the short term, but it is doubtful that the long-term interests of the venture capital company and its shareholders will be served by this approach.

Ultimately, the venture capital company will need to have a management team and decision-making structure that are experienced and effective in developing and carrying out business opportunities. In this regard, two issues will need to be addressed from a management perspective. The first is where the hospital's business development personnel should reside. Should business development personnel remain in the hospital or its parent corporation and perhaps share time with the venture capital company, or should the venture capital company develop its own business development team? Further, if the venture capital company develops its own management team, should the hospital reduce or eliminate its business development team? These are difficult questions for which no simple solution is available. However, the hospital contemplating the sponsorship of a venture capital company needs to think about these issues and develop resolutions that are compatible with its own long-term needs as well as the needs of the physician shareholders. This is one area where the potential for conflicts of interest is likely to be greatest.

The second issue critical to the ultimate success of the venture capital company is management compensation. In the hospital setting, incentive compensation programs for management personnel are the exception rather than the rule, although that is changing. In addition, equity-based incentives, such as qualified and nonqualified stock options, phantom stock plans, and so forth are found only in the investor-owned setting and are virtually nonexistent in the not-for-profit sector. By contrast, in the true venture capital setting, compensation of management is predominantly contingent in nature and is designed to provide incentives for management to generate the maximum amount of wealth for its shareholders. If successful, the compensation of venture capital company managers may become quite substantial, and the shareholders may have difficulty with this fact.

It is virtually impossible today to describe the optimal form of management compensation that will be right for a hospital/medical staff–owned venture capital company. This is, however, an extremely important issue that needs to be addressed and continually reevaluated as the venture capital company develops.

CONCLUSION

The venture capital company is a new idea. The few venture capital companies that have been established to date have not yet been truly tested as to their long-term viability or even as to their short-term successes.

It is clear, however, that hospitals and their medical staffs must form more formal economic bonds between them if both are to survive and prosper in the future. The venture capital company is intended to be a proactive organization that seeks out business opportunities beneficial both to physicians and hospitals. It is intended to be the converse of the typical hospital-physician joint venture that is usually undertaken on a project-by-project basis, often in reaction to what other competitors are doing.

The venture capital company may also serve as the building block for hospital-physician involvement in hospital systems, alternative delivery systems, and insurance activities. We have already seen venture capital companies formed to serve, among other things, as investors in health maintenance organizations and preferred provider organizations. This may simply be the forerunner of more extensive, broad-range financial collaboration and involvement by hospitals and physicians in delivery as well as financing projects and businesses.

As with any other type of hospital-physician joint venture, the venture capital company must be examined carefully to see whether it fits within the overall strategy of a hospital and its medical staff. Hospitals and physicians forming venture capital companies need to plan carefully for their successes and be prepared for possible failures. The promise of the venture capital company will ultimately be realized from its facility in bringing together physicians in a proactive rather than reactive environment that is one step removed from the political issues normally confronting hospitals and physicians, sometimes impairing their ability to work together.

14

Enlisting Physician Participation

Enzo V. DiGiacomo, M.D.

INTRODUCTION

As the concepts of fast food, 24-hour banking, and shopping mall convenience clinics have taken their place in today's highly mobile society, the family physician has become an anachronism, and convenience has taken the place of familiarity and tradition. The hospital as an institutional entity has taken priority over the physician as the primary identity for healthcare service. The government and other third-party payors are also attempting to minimize and decrease expenses for employers who are subsidizing massive healthcare bills. Payments to both hospitals and physicians are being reduced as a result, leaving the physician to struggle with a power base that has greater identity and community support and more purchasing power than private practice. A joint venture with such a power base can therefore appear very attractive to many physicians.

THREE LEVELS OF MEDICAL STAFF

A medical staff is divided into three levels, each based on age, circumstances, goals, and economic and psychologic factors. The first group, elder physicians (EPs), consists of those physicians age 60 and over, near or on the verge of retirement. Most EPs have no mortgage or car payments and are looking for retirement funds in which to place their money. Though they may have the cash flow, EPs have a great concern for security and may be reluctant to invest. The career goals of EPs may be merely to maintain stature on staff and, though the EPs are usually a minority in number, they are sometimes the most vociferous and contentious members of the medical staff since they hold the power base in staff positions.

The middle physicians (MPs), between the ages of 45 and 55, sit on the fence between the EPs and the young group. Most MPs put all their money into educating their children and maintain career balance by keeping one foot on the side of the elders and the other with the young group. Their career goals are focused on trying to be the biggest or the best.

The young physicians (YPs) are the residents or those in practice fewer than five years. Their greatest concern is usually cash flow: paying off medical school loans, the new car, and the mortgage. The YPs' goals are to become accepted as members of the medical staff.

In marketing the joint venture, each level must be addressed separately, keeping in mind the different needs, economic factors, and psychological elements inherent in each group. This analysis forms the base on which the initiator of the joint venture may begin formulating a marketing strategy. The most important statement the initiator of the joint venture must consider is: "The benefit to you, the physician, is _____." Through close consideration of each group's needs, the initiator may then determine the specific benefits that will appeal to the target group of physicians.

GENERAL BENEFITS

In general the physician will be attracted to the personal and professional economics of a joint venture.

Benefits may also be derived through joint ventures outside of healthcare including corporations that participate in joint ventures with hospitals, insurance companies, or other economic ventures. For example, one group of 300 physicians incorporated and joined in a joint venture with a gasoline station. Their study of gasoline usage among members determined that expenses could be cut in half through joint ownership.

Physicians have also been interested in clinical joint ventures with freestanding emergency centers, surgery centers, pharmacies, and home care. From a clinical standpoint, one benefit to the physician is the convenience of participating in a medical office building adjacent to the hospital. An added economic convenience is that the physician can join as a limited partner or through condominium ownership. The physician also gains purchasing power through association with the hospital's own purchasing power base. Now the hospital is able to help the physician, and if a large group of physicians enters into the joint venture, their added power will help the hospital. This presents an additional benefit: The physicians and the hospital can work together. Both bring economic return in a viable situation of which the physician plays a part—the healthcare business. The physician is actually investing in a real estate venture, but maintains control through professional occupancy as opposed to reliance on investing in a nonmedical office building or a residential rental property. Also, since the physician must have an office somewhere, locating it near the hospital is economically and logistically sound.

MAKING IT HAPPEN

The marketing strategy must be planned with a dual purpose: to address the generic needs of the physicians and to address specifically the needs of each of the three groups. The primary consideration is determination of an identified need for a joint venture, which may be perceived differently by the physicians, the hospital, and community members. Following identification of the need, common ground must be found that will bind everyone together, for instance, quality of care or economics. With these factors in hand, a strategy can be developed to approach the EPs, MPs, and YPs, either generally, individually, or as groups.

THE FIRST MEETING

When each of the three groups is approached, the words to be remembered are: "The benefit to you is _____." If no benefit can be identified, marketing the joint venture will be nearly impossible. Consider tangible and intangible benefits such as economics, convenience, and ego. Explore the potential benefits to each of the three groups, and keep in mind their circumstances, economics, and career goals. Define needs and benefits specifically for each group and then plan the first meeting. Since up to this point the initiator has not yet met with any of the participants, the first meeting can be either the downfall or the launching point of the joint venture.

In order to win the support of the group, individuals with joint venture experience must be identified. These physicians should be approached on neutral ground, not in a meeting where the topic may be perceived as a surprise or, worse, where a group of people may express negative reactions. Also, those people who are certain to oppose the project should be approached individually. This will provide opposing views for which preparation can be made prior to the first meeting. This may help to defuse negative attitudes or questions before they are expressed. Find out who is for the project, who is against it, and why. The project may be continued at this time or dropped because there is more opposition than support.

The first meeting is a simple presentation of the ideas of the joint venture: the definition of need and benefits, proposed timetable, and committee structure. Up to this point, planning has been the key; the first meeting ushers in the importance of the new marketing focus: communication. The hospital must be the facilitator of communication between the physicians, all participants, the community, and the hospital. The physicians should not be counted on to do the work; count on them to generate ideas and provide vocal support. Listen and respond to their ideas and desire to be heard. Leaving them out will result in an unsuccessful joint venture.

"I know you believe you understand what you think I said, but I am not sure you realize that what you heard is not what I meant."

Communication is not talking or listening; it is talking, listening, and perceiving that what is actually *meant* is understood by the listener. Communication is not accomplished solely by the spoken or written word. Facial expressions, the ability to perceive beyond what a person says, and nervous gestures all contribute to the communication between two people. Questions or statements are often taken at face value, but often there is another meaning behind the question. For example, if an employee complains or explains a problem to a manager, the smart manager lets the employee finish, then asks: "What's really bothering you?" The real reason is the second one.

During the joint venture communications, meetings, development of business plans, and organization, two additional elements must be considered. The first is ego; the second is the ability to give in. In a joint venture, one party is dominant in one facet; the second party is dominant in another facet. Compromise is necessary, but that may be difficult in a confrontation with the hospital administrator, the president of the medical staff, and each member of the medical staff. An understanding of the workings of the egos involved is necessary in order to achieve any degree of communication.

The hospital administrator has evolved from the concept of a physician running the hospital as a part-time job to the level of management and leadership comparable to the CEOs at General Motors or IBM. The individual members of the medical staff have greater or lesser egos, depending on their personalities. For example, a neurosurgeon who undergoes internship, four years of general surgical training, and two or three years or more of neurosurgical training may have a much different personality than a pediatrician. It becomes the responsibility of the joint venture facilitator to understand the ego structure of the medical staff in order to facilitate communication. In understanding a physician's personality and specialty it is easier to perceive the total complexity of the physician as both a professional and a human being with stresses just like the rest of the world.

The greatest challenge often lies in bringing together the hospital administrator and the president of the medical staff. These two very powerful individuals sometimes have opposite points of view. Know with whom they are dealing, identify the benefits to each, and always keep in mind the underlying personalities of all parties involved.

OPPOSITION

Knowing the participants, understanding their groups, identifying needs and benefits, and bringing together the CEO and head of the medical staff are vital strategies for beginning a joint venture, but if the disadvantages of a joint venture are not recognized, the strategy may be too weak to succeed. Physicians may voice many objections, depending on their needs, profile, goals, and potential benefits.

"I have no need to change my office," or "I have no need to go into a surgery center; I don't do surgery."

There may be no need for certain physicians to agree to a joint venture: they may be independently wealthy; their own ethics may not warrant their participation; there may be no benefit. Despite careful planning and strategy, not every physician will wish to participate in the joint venture. For example, a group of orthopedic surgeons owns its own building seven blocks from the hospital; the group has a 20-year mortgage. If the group is presented with a joint venture including a doctors' office building next to the hospital, it may be ideal for the group, but it would be economically unfeasible.

Certain specialties may be able to take advantage of an office building attached or adjacent to the hospital, especially all surgical subspecialties, all subspecialties in the internal medicine groups (e.g., neurology, gastroenterology), specialties that take advantage of the hospital's special procedure rooms, operating rooms, or special equipment that is too costly for a physician to have in his office.

Despite the apparent advantages of joint ventures, sometimes it is better to remain independent. If all of the general practitioners from the surrounding community were attached to the hospital, another internist could set himself up between the hospital and the community on a direct line and, as a convenience, patients would visit the physician instead of traveling to the hospital.

"I like being a sole practitioner; I don't want to work with anyone else."

Some physicians have a particular philosophy about the practice of medicine. Each should be allowed to practice according to personal beliefs. It is always advantageous, however, to understand these different approaches which, of themselves, can constitute an objection to a joint venture.

"Why would I want to go into business with the hospital?"

Most commonly voiced by EPs, this question results from the antagonistic relationship between medical staffs and hospitals over the last two decades. The EPs say "I don't want any part of the administration." The MPs are then concerned about their relationship with the EPs. "What will the EPs think of me if I do this? I will not be in their good graces." The pecking order often dictates the behavior and attitudes of the MPs. They are in line for EPs' practices after retirement, so they often wish to agree with the EPs. Also, MPs sometimes get referrals from EPs so they are reluctant to disagree with the EPs since opposition will cut off referrals.

"Where am I going to get the money? How can I participate?"

YPs' objections center around a lack of cash flow and a hesitancy about which direction to take, the latter a result of EP influence. The role model for residents and interns has changed from the solo practitioner of the past to the current group practitioner. YPs may wish to have less work at night and on weekends, yet they have big bills to pay. The joint venture looks appealing, but the YP asks the above question. In addition, a group of EPs, totally against the program, can influence YPs. The psychological conflict confuses YPs, so that they do not know which way to go.

If the YPs' objections can be addressed (based on the EP antiadministration stance), there are solutions to the economic needs of YPs. For example, the joint venture could involve construction of an office building with a limited partnership. The physician then can use cash out of pocket or borrow money from the bank, or perhaps the hospital can provide the physician with a loan at the current interest rate (or less) for 10 years with a balloon payment to pay off the principal (or renegotiate the loan after 10 years).

CONCLUSION

This example of creative financing points up the objective of the joint venture: the relationship between the hospital and the physicians (EPs, MPs, and YPs). The joint venture creates a bond of economics, loyalty, and friendship.

15

Operational Problems in Joint Venture Management

Gary Meller, M.D., M.B.A.

INTRODUCTION

The ultimate success of a joint venture comes as a result of careful attention to the structure and financing of the venture and well-managed operations. Those joint ventures that fail, however, typically do so because of problems that arise in the ongoing management of the business for which the joint venture was formed.

Success rates for joint ventures vary considerably depending on the nature of the underlying business. Joint ventures for investment or real estate management appear to have the highest likelihood of success. On the other hand, joint ventures that produce products or deliver services have very high failure rates. Some estimates of the failure rate in the product or service sector are as high as 90 percent. [1]

There is often a tendency, even among experienced managers, to look at management problems and find the individual who is at fault. It is much easier to assign individual responsibility or blame than to take a determined look at the structural or situational reasons for failure.

This chapter presents a structural model for analyzing potential management problems that often arise in joint ventures. Addressed in this chapter are problems related to ownership, control, allocation of resources, timing, and corporate culture.

ISSUES OF OWNERSHIP

Ownership of the joint venture may be structured in a variety of ways to meet goals that are addressed elsewhere in this book. The ultimate expression of ownership can directly affect the managers who must implement the activities of the business. In its simplest form, joint ownership can create confusion as to who is really in charge of the business. While some ambiguity can be tolerated, particularly in large or matrix-type organizations, a small company can be effectively hamstrung if ownership, rather than expertise, becomes the predominant consideration in settling operational issues.

This problem is often exaggerated in hospital-physician joint ventures because the two parties must get along outside of the joint venture, regardless of its outcome.

Reporting Requirements

Reporting to a governing board or senior management is a time-consuming and necessary function of management. For senior management to make decisions, they must have timely information concerning the state of affairs of the business. In a joint venture, the owners may have specific questions or information needs that require regular reports. While the entrepreneurial company or physician partners may be interested in current cash flow, staff salaries, or response to advertising programs, the hospital partner may be significantly more interested in the number of referrals to its emergency room or the utilization of ancillary hospital services. Physician entrepreneurs may be particularly constrained as a result of time pressure placed on them by an ongoing medical practice.

Information always has a cost associated with its collection and reporting. That cost may be expressed in either money or time. If the joint venture management is engrossed in the preparation of continual ad hoc reports, they may be unable to address problems in a timely manner. Entrepreneurial managers may express impatience with these reporting requirements.

Influence and Votes

Issues of ownership are not limited to direct equity shares. The on-site manager may be subjected to additional influences that can undermine his autonomy or effectiveness. Frequent requests from subordinates in the hospital can interfere with the manager's time schedule. Particularly if relationships between the owners degenerate, the on-site manager may be running back and forth trying to satisfy both parties. A clear sign of this problem arises when the governing board of the joint venture is forced to vote on the daily activities of the on-site manager. If this occurs, the whole subject of joint venturing should be reexamined. When constructive communication ceases, the joint venture should be restructured and one or more parties will usually be eliminated.

Another indication is turnover or burnout of successive managers. If management of the daily operations of the business has burned out two successive individuals, then either the position must be restructured to create a viable one or the owners should negotiate an alteration of responsibility. In medical joint ventures, the physician partner may be very difficult to replace.

Reward and Responsibility

While most hospitals operate with professional managers, until very recently these managers were compensated solely on the basis of fixed salary and benefits. Now there has been an increase in the number of institutions in which specific financial incentives have been created to reward successful hospital managers. In the joint venture setting, management incentives are often both useful and essential to rewarding key managers. Particularly when the joint venture operates in an environment with for-profit competition, a program to reward managers based on performance may be essential to keeping good managers. Physician managers not only respond well to incentives, but also may require them. This may result from their common experience of piecework compensation.

The management incentive system should be based on those measurable key success factors that are directly within the control of the manager. The bonuses should be given at time intervals that are relevant to the manager's performance. A general rule is that senior management should be rewarded annually, second level managers every six months, and staff monthly, if appropriate goals and targets can be established.

The incentive system and the basis for measurement should be clearly defined and communicated to the individuals involved. In general, management incentive systems should be created for a single year and redesigned annually as the goals and responsibilities of management change.

Jealousy and Interference

The joint venture, especially in its early stages, will be immensely attractive because of the glamour and excitement it can create. This can be very stimulating for the managers involved, but it can also create conflict, jealousy, and envy on the part of others in the organization.

If the joint venture has been established as a independent operation, it will undoubtedly fall in an area that some existing hospital management regard as their own territory. This may be in the area of shared services, outpatient services, marketing, or community relations. The hospital's managers in these areas may interfere constructively or destructively in the operations of the joint venture. Similarly, if the physician partner is a group practice, all partners in the group may not be similarly enthusiastic about the joint venture.

The extreme example of this would be the manager or physician who would like to see the joint venture fail in order to retain or regain his power. The senior management of the hospital may have specifically created the joint venture to compensate for the weakness of a department manager. The group practice may be seeking to diminish the power of a physician or faction or to augment the influence of younger members. This will rarely go unnoticed. This individual may seek to punish or even create problems for the joint venture by spreading rumors, delaying check payment or authorization, or imposing burdens on the joint venture manager. Problems of this sort are occasionally revealed during the formation stage of the joint venture. If an individual is a persistent pessimist at this stage, he or she will rarely convert to full support. The governing board must then decide how to overcome this resistance as the joint venture enters its operational stage.

Unresolved Conflict from Negotiations

Issues that the owners have been unable to resolve during negotiations, such as depository accounts, fiscal years, banking relationships, and officers of the company, will always impair the actual operations of the joint venture. While management may work out accommodations for these problems, they are usually the first issues that resurface at difficult moments. Accusatory interactions will create further conflicts and will often escalate into a full breakdown. The joint venture manager should be informed of these unresolved areas of conflict and should be instructed to prepare recommendations on the resolution of these issues within an appropriate time frame. The governing board of the joint venture should then specifically adopt recommendations to resolve these issues and forestall subsequent conflict. Further conflict after at this point is very damaging to operations.

ISSUES OF CONTROL

Issues of control often derive from issues of ownership. Control is used here to identify the day-to-day responsibilities of management.

Ownership Versus Control

As discussed above, it is essential to the successful operation of a joint venture that control of operations not be determined solely by ownership interest or equity position. Not only is this cumbersome, unwieldy, and impractical, but it also is nonviable because it ignores the specific skills or experience that each party brings to the joint venture.

Confusion in Goals

For managers of joint ventures to perform effectively, they must be aware of the goals of the organization. These goals may be either short or long term and may affect financial or nonfinancial results. In any case, managers must know precisely what targets to shoot for in order to effectively schedule their time and resources. When confusion as to appropriate goals arises in joint ventures, managers will be unable to perform.

The most obvious goal confusion arises when the two joint venture partners have different objectives for the business. The physician entrepreneurs may desire rapid growth, high visibility, and early net income. On the other hand, the hospital may desire high patient referrals, low political impact, and protection of its investment. While none of these goals is necessarily exclusive of any other, there are certainly implicit conflicts in the day-to-day activities necessary to achieve them.

This confusion can be augmented if the personal goals of the managers involved are considered. The managers' motivation may be either public or personal. Managers seeking personal power or public recognition for their actions may be drawn to the joint venture as a means to achieve these. Careful and repeated interviews should bring out these motivations prior to hiring an individual. If problems arise, then a tradeoff must be made between the manager's effectiveness in the organization and ability to satisfy personal goals. This trade-off can be managed if the issues are made known to the governing board of the joint venture. Physician managers may have additional needs for status or recognition because of the perceived "personal risk" involved in their undertaking. These needs should be recognized and met where possible.

Unempowered Managers

Managers respond to many motivations. In general, a careful balance between power and responsibility is essential for effective management. When managers' hands are tied by lack of authority to effect changes or by continual review and reversal by higher authority, they will shortly become ineffective. Managers' subordinates will soon recognize the limits of their authority and will seek alternate mechanisms to solve their problems.

If the joint venture partners find that several employees are consistently going around the manager in order to get timely solutions to their problems, it may be a sign that the manager is being second-guessed on too many decisions.

A certain amount of direct observation and supervision is necessary, particularly in the training period of a new manager. However, if this goes on too long, the managers will become resentful and their subordinates will lose respect.

Managing Up and Down

The manager of the joint venture is the captain of the ship. All captains answer to admirals as well as to their crew. Managers who ignore either group will fail. Managers who consistently seek to ingratiate themselves with superiors will be as ineffective as the ones who constantly defend subordinates.

The most effective way to address this problem is to hold confidential evaluations of the managers on a timely basis. Both superiors and subordinates should be given an opportunity to review the managers in private in order to obtain accurate information. If this information is subsequently communicated to the managers in a constructive manner, it will exert a corrective effect on their behavior. The review should probably be conducted by a committee of two representing the governing board and made up of both parties to the joint venture.

The Runaway Success

Extreme early success of the joint venture can be as damaging as failure. Management may be tempted to slack off, the joint venturers may be too quick to pull out profits and not allow reinvestment, or other managers may intrude in order to share in the glory. Success can be a pleasurable problem to have, but it also can interfere with long-term results.

The joint venture partners may need to review the goals of the business in order to accommodate early success. Speeding up the timetable for future expansion or investing in increased capacity may solve some of these problems.

ISSUES RELATED TO ALLOCATION OF RESOURCES

The Starving Subsidiary

Entrepreneurial companies are notoriously understaffed. They rarely can afford a full complement of functional managers. Each member of the staff must "wear many hats" during the start-up period. In contrast, most hospitals are fully staffed. This situation can result in a syndrome of starvation amidst plenty. The joint venture should try to make use of the hospital's expertise in management or operational areas without creating conflicting loyalties. The shared services may be in such areas as finance, accounting, personnel, and purchasing. Caution must be exercised with regard to the problems discussed above. Physician partners may need to be educated as to the roles and expertise of these functional specialists.

Make versus Buy Decisions

The make versus buy decision applies to several areas of the joint venture. As discussed above, the joint venture may "buy" managerial resources during its early phase. Similarly, the hospital may be willing and able to lend purchasing strength or marketing personnel to the business. Each of these decisions entails an estimation of the true cost to the joint venture.

The decision to use hospital resources may benefit the hospital more than the joint venture. If the purchasing department is unable to deliver supplies in the appropriate quantity or within a short time frame, the joint venture may experience stockouts or oversupply storage problems. The supply department may be unable to stock appropriate items or may not obtain the lowest pricing on certain items because of established supplier relationships.

If the hospital marketing department supplies advertising services, it may be unwilling to adopt the aggressive strategies often required to launch a new venture. While the expense savings in the short run may seem attractive, the time savings over the long term may make this choice impractical.

The management of the joint venture must approach each of these decisions with a complete make versus buy analysis, including the cost of buying from outside suppliers. This analysis can be short and straightforward. The indirect result of such a decision-making program will strengthen the management team of the joint venture and will enable them to budget their resources more effectively.

A Huge Part of a Tiny Firm

The key resource in any service-based company is its managers. The joint venture managers will recognize their importance to the joint venture and may need additional recognition or reward in order to maintain their motivation. In joint ventures where market share goals are important, the managers and staff often feel that they are in a front line combat situation. Extended combat always entails casualties. Burnout is common in entrepreneurial ventures because of the high degree of commitment required and the limited resources that are available. Psychological rewards and recognition of accomplishments are useful tools in maintaining the motivation of these individuals. Arranging for special educational opportunities, increased vacation time, or the financial incentives discussed above can all assist in keeping the motivation level high.

ISSUES OF TIMING

How Long To Give It

Capital investment decisions are often made on a "best guess" basis. Despite all available information and the experience of both parties, this guess may be wrong. Overestimates of capital requirements or time to profitability usually create few problems. Underestimates can be disastrous. It is prudent to consider the worst case scenario when making the capital investment in a joint venture, particularly if the venture attempts to establish a new market with a new product and a new management team.

Monthly reviews of operating results are essential. Comparisons with expected results and ongoing projections of future cash requirements are critical. In this light, it is wise to equip any new venture with a personal computer so that the managers can produce internal reports that will provide this data. Financial statements and annual reports are barely adequate for making decisions, particularly when a crisis develops.

In the joint venture agreement, there is usually a clause for dissolution of the joint venture. Even more appropriate for consideration is a clause governing the conduct of the parties in the event of a capital deficiency or sudden negative turn of events. Such a clause will be welcome if the occasion arises. If both parties understand the impact of such a crisis on equity, control, and operation responsibility, recriminations and bad feelings may be minimized. In the situation where the parties have business or professional relationships outside the joint venture, this problem is especially difficult.

It is important here to differentiate this situation from the venture capital strategy of intentional underfunding in order to seek greater future equity. For a venture capitalist, the desired result is profit and capital gains. For a joint venture, the noneconomic results may be equally important to both parties.

The time frame established for pulling the plug on an unsuccessful venture should permit an adequate opportunity to achieve both the financial and nonfinancial goals of the joint venture. When market penetration or market share goals are involved, the time frame must allow for changes in consumer behavior, which may take several years.

Market Responsiveness

The greatest uncertainty in healthcare joint ventures arises from market response to new products or services. The market under consideration includes the patient market as well as other groups, such as physicians and competitors. The least likely result is for rapid acceptance of the service into a willing market. Pressure from public groups, third-party payors, and competitors must also be considered in developing a timetable for market penetration.

The joint venture is often considered to be a means of deflecting perceived responsibility for developing a controversial service away from the hospital. That means that full responsibility will fall on the joint venture partner. Management time or resources must be allocated to this problem. The physician partner must be willing to bear this burden amidst his colleagues and associates.

Extreme opposition to market acceptance is rare, but it can occur. This usually dissappears within six months to one year as market attitudes change. The solution to this problem is dependent not only on marketing communications, but also on politics and operational management.

Marketing communications should be designed to create acceptance and use of the service and should not cause problems. This extends to the public relations area. The joint venture partners should be circumspect in their public announcements in the early stages of the venture. Political conflicts should be either addressed quietly with political pressure or defused by co-opting the opposition whenever possible. Operations managers must conduct themselves with care and focus on the quality of the service in order to avoid giving the opposition any ammunition.

Planning Horizons

Planning and reporting are activities that are usually very formalized in the hospital setting. In the entrepreneurial joint venture they may be very informal, if not nonexistent. The hospital board may expect frequent status reports and financial reviews from the joint venture, while the understaffed on-site managers are struggling to grow the business. A compromise must be reached. Each party has legitimate concerns.

Usually a quarterly review of results with a variance analysis from the financial plan is sufficient. If particular problems arise, then more frequent meetings to address those specific problems can be scheduled.

Looking Ahead

It is sometimes difficult to focus on the long term when in the short term we are being strangled. A conscientious effort to look at the long term will sometimes carry a company through very difficult times. Review of the areas where progress is being made will assist this effort. A meeting that focuses exclusively on the negative will detract from the willingness of both partners to proceed and from a manager's motivation. It is very rare to find a manager who flourishes under constant adversity. Proper planning, timely management reports, and a motivated management group will help avoid situations where crisis management techniques are required.

ISSUES RELATED TO CORPORATE CULTURE

Corporate culture includes all of the attributes of a company not specifically related to functional areas of management, such as "lifestyle." It is very difficult to define but it is easily recognized. Corporate culture can be a key success factor in many companies, both entrepreneurial and conventional. Corporate culture can include the ideology of the company or the embodiment of the corporate mission in specific activities and behaviors. The following areas address some of the reasons why conflict that arises over disparate corporate culture can affect operating results in a new venture. Traditional elements in the culture of physicians and hospital administration incorporate an antagonism between the two groups that must be overcome or altered.

"They Are Not Like Us"

The most common perception on both sides is the unqualified awareness that there is a difference in style between the hospital management and the joint venture management. While this may be limited to perception of clothing styles or personal or business manners, it can often extend to more basic areas such as salary structure or proper respect for authority. Particularly when these conflicts arise between a bureaucratic organization and an entrepreneurial one, the side effects can be damaging.

Resolving this issue can be essential to the success of the joint venture. The very attractiveness of the joint venture may be its willingness to operate with less certainty and greater insecurity. For psychological reasons, this method of doing business may require perceptible differences in style. Employees of the joint venture may be attracted to the camaraderie, emphasis on results, profitability incentives, or flexibility that is offered.

"They Don't Like Us"

The possibility exists that differences in corporate culture that create conflicts result from simple intolerance of difference or change. Unfortunately, this is not rare in bureaucratic organizations. Sometimes, no amount of discussion or coercion can correct this corporate xenophobia. The solution may lie in distancing the parties for a sufficient period of time to allow the feelings to be worked out. If the joint venture's offices are within the hospital, this may require relocation. Efforts to educate both sides in the goals, organizational roles, motivations, and concerns of the others may help foster understanding and eventual acceptance.

"We Don't Answer to Them"

The management team of the joint venture may feel that the problems they are having may not be understood by the governing board or the owners. When this perception exists over a long period of time, the managers may adopt a self-protective isolation from the governing board that further impairs communication. Symptoms of this problem are the inability of the governing board to obtain information about operations, unwillingness of managers to prepare for meetings, or unreturned phone calls and other frustrated attempts at communications.

As with most of the issues discussed in this chapter, there are at least two problems here. One is the perceived unwillingness or inability of the governing board to address issues that may be of great concern to management, and the other is the reaction to this by the managers. Frequent choruses of "you just don't understand" are the most obvious indication of this problem.

If this situation arises, replacement of the managers will usually create only short-term solutions. The best response is for the two sides to get together for an extended session of clarification, often on a weekend away from the office, in order to analyze and reestablish communication.

"What Happened to Your Tie"

The converse of the serious issues discussed above occurs when divisiveness is brought about by more trivial but equally charged differences in style. These may vary from colorful ties, company parties with alcohol present, and the presence of pets in the office, to phone calls not returned and refusal to come together three times a week for meetings. These are all examples of stylistic issues that are usually not essential to the operation of the business but that can create lingering bad feelings that do affect the truly important issues.

The easiest and earliest solution to this type of problem is to have an open conversation among the individuals involved and attempt to secure an agreement as to the relative importance of these behaviors.

JOINT VENTURES IN OTHER INDUSTRIES

International Joint Ventures

Historically, joint ventures have been a traditional mode of entry into a foreign market. The reasons for this are instructive. In a foreign country many of the ways of doing business are quite different from those at home. In order to acquire local marketing skills, a distribution network, and local labor managers, a manufacturing company may form a foreign subsidiary or joint venture. The problems that the company seeks to overcome are basically related to the "foreignness" of its new operating environment. The more the basic rules change, the more a company will seek to find a partner with local experience and operating skills.

Joint ventures have been used increasingly as large companies have become multinational. Joint ventures are particularly frequent between Eastern and Western companies. In many ways joint ventures have overcome the criticisms of colonial expansion by incorporating local ownership and management. Companies with many experiences in foreign joint ventures now favor the rapid development of several layers of local management talent as one way of offsetting some of the risks of entering the market in a new country.

Real Estate Joint Ventures

Real estate joint ventures are perhaps the most common form of joint venture in the United States. They also appear to have the highest success rate. Perhaps this results from two factors that are specific to real estate as an investment: the relatively low risk associated with real estate as an asset and the lack of confusion about the boundaries of the investment. As we have seen, uncertainty and insecurity are especially disruptive in the operation of a healthcare joint venture. While a real estate deal may fail, the basic asset is usually a salable item.

Financial Joint Ventures

Financial joint ventures are usually concerned with specific investment opportunities. While they are not directly relevant to our topic, they do raise a very important point. Although a significant capital investment may be required for the hospital-physician joint venture, it is a mistake to regard this investment as strictly a financial transaction. While the analytic criteria, such as present value, rate of return, and alternative use of funds, should be applied to the decision process, the business underlying the investment should also be of primary concern.

The exception to this rule occurs when the hospital is going to make an investment in an existing company. In this case the major issues relate to the decision to maintain or alter the management interest of the present owners. If the current owners will receive money for their interest and are expected to continue to operate the company, then the issues discussed above must all be addressed.

Manufacturing Joint Ventures

Manufacturing joint ventures are usually begun in order to take advantage of significant knowledge or cost advantages among the partners. According to a recent study, 50 percent of these joint ventures have failed.[2] The reasons for failure usually involve many of the issues discussed earlier. Disappearance of the market for the product of the joint venture also appears to be a consistent reason for failure.

The Nonprofit Sector

Recently a number of joint ventures, particularly for research and development of high-technology products, have been established between corporations, universities, state health departments, and other nonprofit entities. These joint ventures often are created to take advantage of licenses and patents that are held by the nonprofit party. While these ventures are extremely risky, the benefits to both parties can be considerable. Usually the nonprofit party receives funding for additional research as well as potential profits. The industry partner receives the benefit of existing or future patents without having to support the entire research and development staff. The quality of the researchers may be enhanced because of the security and intellectual stimulation offered by the university setting to scientists.

HISTORICAL RESULTS

Unfortunately, the historical results of joint ventures in other industries have been very poor.[3] Although accurate data from large samples of companies are not available, several studies indicate a failure rate that often approaches 90 percent.[4] The rate of success appears to be the highest for the more traditional forms of joint ventures, real estate and international. The failure rate is highest for joint ventures that attempt to enter new markets with new products. Companies with experience in forming and managing joint ventures appear to be more successful than those who are trying it for the first time. Most hospital-physician joint ventures to date, other than medical office buildings, have been oriented to expanding market share or entering new markets. This would seem to indicate that a high failure rate is more likely than frequent success. As discussed above, the causes of failure most often relate to the interaction of the joint venture partners and the management team.

For the hospital that is committed to establishing joint ventures as a means of expanding and growing, a successful strategy may require the creation of a new business development group specifically empowered to learn the business of managing joint ventures. Many large corporations have taken this route with considerable success. A further caution would be to engage in joint ventures with a high probability of success and with an experienced partner in order to minimize the downside risk in the first attempts.

THE "NEW" JOINT VENTURE

Joint ventures between hospitals and physicians are a new and evolving form of joint venture management. Properly formed, these joint ventures offer the best of both worlds. The hospital partner can contribute resources, capital, and established markets to the company. The physician partners can contribute energy, enthusiasm, and flexible management responses to changing market conditions. Together the partners must secure adequate resources to be able to develop the business over the long term. A joint venture should be able to survive at least three to five years in order to develop a new service. Healthcare services in particular require a longer period for market acceptance because of cautious behavior on the part of patients. Certain operational problems are increased as a result of the joint management of a business venture. Early attention to these areas of potential conflict may increase the likelihood of success.

Notes

[1] Mack Hanan, "Corporate Growth through Venture Management," *Harvard Business Review*, January–February 1969, pp. 43–61; Edward Roberts, "New Ventures for Corporate Growth," *Harvard Business Review*, July–August 1980, pp. 134–42; Sally Jacobs, "The Perfect Partnerships (and Why Most Aren't)," *New England Business*, April 15, 1984, pp. 28–34; "Joint Ventures: For Better or Worse," *Industry Week*, February 20, 1984, pp. 39–45.

[2] Roberts, "New Ventures"; Jacobs, "Perfect Partnerships."

[3] Hanan, "Corporate Growth"; Roberts, "New Ventures"; Jacobs, "Perfect Partnerships"; "Joint Ventures: For Better or Worse."

[4] Hanan, "Corporate Growth"; Roberts "New Ventures"; Jacobs, "Perfect Partnerships"; "Joint Ventures: For Better or Worse."

REFERENCES

SHERYL ARNDT. "Hospital/Insurance Ventures May Pose Threat." *National Underwriter*, June 1, 1985, pp. 26–27.

MACK HANAN. "Corporate Growth Through Venture Management." *Harvard Business Review*, January–February 1969, pp. 43–61.

SALLY JACOBS. "The Perfect Partnerships (and Why Most Aren't)." *New England Business*, April 15, 1984, pp. 28–34.

LASERRE, PHILLIPE, et al. "Selecting a Foreign Partner for Technology Transfers." *Interfaces*, November–December, 1984, pp. 70–79.

GARY MELLER. "Joint Ventures in Ambulatory Care." in *Freestanding Emergency Centers*, ed. Friend and Shriver. Rockville, Md.: Aspen Systems Corporation. 1984.

EDWARD ROBERTS. "New Ventures for Corporate Growth." *Harvard Business Review*, July–August 1980, pp. 134–42.

"Collaborative Ventures, A Strategy For the Eighties." *CPA Journal*, February 1985, pp. 74–77.

"Joint Ventures: For Better or Worse." *Industry Week*, February 20, 1984, pp. 39–45.

"Public Policy Issues Involved in Joint Ventures in American Industry." *Mergers and Acquisitions* 4 (1979), pp. 18–29.

"Structure Joint Ventures Carefully to Avoid Future Problems." *Mergers and Acquisitions* 1, (1980), pp. 4–14.

V

PERSPECTIVES ON JOINT VENTURES

16

A Physician's Perspective on Joint Ventures

Michael L. McCullough, M.D.

INTRODUCTION

Interest in hospital-physician joint ventures is skyrocketing. The movement has been called the most significant organizational development in the healthcare industry since the advent of corporate restructuring of not-for-profit hospitals.

The reasons really are not hard to find, if we notice how we are moving away from an environment shaped by politics and regulation to one shaped by economics and competition. Whether it is called allocation or rationing of resources, the bottom line is the same—in the future there will be fewer dollars to pay for the care of individuals than there are today, and the dollars spent for care will be scrutinized carefully to assure that the purchaser is receiving value.

This development requires some very careful analysis by hospitals and physicians regarding the future of the practice of medicine in this country. Clearly, survival of hospitals and physicians in the future will be predicated on the formation of genuine working relationships between hospitals and organized groups of physicians who function as partners in an environment in which the financing and delivery aspects of hospital and medical services are merged.

In May 1983, we physicians at Baylor University Medical Center, a 1,500-bed, not-for-profit teaching hospital located in Dallas, Texas, began to look seriously at these issues and to examine the ways in which we could respond. How would we preserve patient access to physicians and physician referral patterns in an environment that demands accountability for both cost and quality? How could we continue our commitment to medical education and to indigent care and still survive economically? These are difficult questions to answer, particularly in an environment of distrust, poor understanding, and apathy. The typical physician response at that time was, "I don't know and I don't care." We do know. The real issue is do we care? If we care, what do we do?

After considerable discussion, debate, and confrontation, the physicians concluded that one required course of action was to develop a prepaid health plan in which the physicians would become the principal providers of medical services. In implementing this strategy, we identified four issues that had to be dealt with very carefully:

1. Formation of an individual practice association (IPA).
2. Choice of a "partner."
3. Structure and content of a shareholder's agreement.
4. Implementation of the joint venture.

CREATING A PHYSICIAN ORGANIZATION

The first step that we undertook was to establish a physician corporation that would, among other things, eventually contract to provide the medical services to a prepaid health plan as an individual practice association (IPA).

I am personally convinced that physicians cannot approach and deal effectively with the present competitive environment through existing medical staff structures. A joint venture that involves a medical staff collectively or individually as shareholders is destined to face very difficult problems because of the collegial nature of the medical staff and the fact that it is directly linked to hospital staff privileges. Existing medical staffs need not be replaced nor are they obsolete. The IPA is simply a tool that is less limited, less collegial, and more adapted to the present contractual environment.

The basic concept of the IPA was quite simple: the IPA would define the financial conditions of participation and practice patterns and then would contract with individual physicians for medical services. If a physician did not like these constraints, then the physician could stay in and change it or the physician could leave the IPA. This is undoubtedly a difficult and yet most important step in the whole process. How do you get a group of skilled and highly motivated physicians to take the time and agree with one another on how and with whom they will share these decisions? The answer is barely.

The first attempt we made to establish an organized physician corporation was not successful. First we formed a committee of 17 physicians. This steering committee met with great resistance throughout the medical staff of Baylor which consisted of over 1,000 physicians, more than 580 of whom were on the active medical staff. Much of this resistance was caused by the tremendous fear and uncertainty about the fast pace with which things were happening in the Dallas area as well as nationally. Next, we had a recruitment period for membership and permitted anybody on the active medical staff to join by investing $1,000. We had 380 physicians join but could get no consensus among those physicians on various organizational proposals.

After almost two months of struggling, we finally formed an advisory committee composed of the membership in our fledgling organization. That committee then came up with a list of names that were voted on by the membership to serve as the first board of directors of the physician corporation. After the board of directors was elected, we held several meetings, adopted bylaws, and retained a consultant to assist in developing a strategy for dealing among ourselves and with the hospital. This physician corporation was named *Baylor Physician Associates, P.A.*

Once the organization of the physician corporation was complete, we then moved on to the business of structuring the organization to function as an IPA that would contract with one or more prepaid healthcare plans.

It is imperative that groups of physicians that wish to compete and wish to succeed form IPAs that are legally structured to credential colleagues, provide effective utilization review, and go at risk financially and professionally to make it work. Anything short of this is a commitment destined to fail in the marketplace.

Credentialing and Utilization Review

The selection of physicians with whom we share practice and risk and how we define our practice styles must be totally controlled by the IPA. It is of interest to reflect back on this as our number one goal. I found this generally to be the case in nearly every physician group I have helped organize.

We developed uniform credentialing that is ongoing and includes review of subjective and objective information relating to quality, cost effectiveness, and appropriateness of care. It is important to note that this credentialing is only for a contract to see patients for Baylor Physician Associates, P.A. and is not related to the hospital's credentialing process for its medical staff members. We obtained all available data from insurance companies and others regarding practice styles and utilization of services. Among the factors that we examined were length of stay, the ratio of ancillary service costs to the total cost of getting the patient out of the hospital, pre-op days, weekend days, undiagnosed illnesses, readmissions for the same diagnosis in a 12-month period, morbidity and mortality, caesarian section rates, and other objective measures of quality of care. We also conducted a subjective review concerning quality, efficiency, and flexibility of the physicians. Combining this internally and externally generated information, decisions were made as to which physicians would be eligible to become and remain providers in the IPA. As of January 1986, 515 physicians in the Dallas/Fort Worth metroplex were credentialed and seeing patients in Baylor Physician Associates, P.A.

Related to credentialing is the development of a detailed utilization review plan that has built-in second opinion on every admission as well as concurrent and retrospective review, quality assurance, and medical record review for inpatients and outpatients. The utilization review plan has built in the parameters of "practice style" to which the IPA providers have collectively agreed. The utilization review plan not only serves to assure cost accountability and quality but also to generate data for the ongoing credentialing process.

It is significant to note that one of the driving forces behind the formation of the IPA was the fact that it provided a means through which the physicians could control credentialing and utilization review decisions, rather than abdicating or delegating this responsibility to hospitals or insurers.

Selecting an Investment Vehicle

One of the first objectives identified by the physicians was the desire to obtain a substantial ownership interest in any joint venture because we recognized that control and governance were related directly to equity investment. We also recognized that the need to raise sufficient capital to purchase our equity position would require a vehicle other than Baylor Physician Associates, P.A. Accordingly, we formed Med Southwest, Inc. in January 1985 and sold $5 million of stock in an offering made available only to physician members and/or contract holders of the IPA who wished to invest. At the time of the offering, credentialing had been completed so that physicians neither could "buy a contract," nor were forced to invest. The offering, which was registered with the Securities and Exchange Commission, was oversubscribed in 15 working days.

CHOOSING A PARTNER

One might ask initially, why have a partner? The issues of capital, name identity in the marketplace, and certain antitrust issues were major reasons for seeking a partner. We discussed at length our goals and plans with every potential partner in Dallas, including major insurance companies, venture capitalists, national hospital chains, national HMO chains, management and consulting firms, and even the Big 8 accounting firms who have joined a list of experts in the delivery of healthcare in this country. After extensive discussions and deliberation, it became clear to us that the only partner that would allow us to achieve our goals was the one who shared our goals—the hospital.

Baylor University Medical Center had what the other potential partners had—capital and name recognition in the marketplace. More importantly, however, the medical center leadership supported our development, was willing to share policymaking decisions, and was willing to share both risk and equity with the physicians.

SHAREHOLDERS AGREEMENT

A shareholders agreement is simply a legal document that spells out the relationship between two equal shareholders—Med Southwest, Inc. and Baylor Health

Care System. The equity position for either risk or gain is equal to the funding of the project (i.e., 60 percent equity equals 60 percent funding). Governance of the joint venture is consistent regardless of equity position. A board of nine is elected, four from each shareholder with the ninth being the chief executive officer. A two-thirds vote is required for substantive issues such as contracts and budgets. There is a freedom to compete clause allowing either shareholder to do other things and buy back-dissolution-arbitration agreement that is spelled out.

IMPLEMENTATION OF THE JOINT VENTURE

We chose to concentrate our efforts in the marketplace initially on activities designed to give us a significant market share in the Dallas/Fort Worth prepaid health plan market. A market survey was initiated at the medical center's expense and was completed by a consulting firm which was jointly selected by the medical center and the physician group. The survey was designed to identify the needs and preferences of potential purchasers of healthcare services, specifically focusing on prepaid healthcare plans. After the market survey was completed, we proceeded to develop an alternative delivery system, which included a preferred provider organization and a prepaid health plan that would respond to those needs (see Figure 16-1).

In sequence, we created three organizations:

- Southwest Preferred Health Network, Inc. (a preferred provider organization), which is owned and funded on a 50–50 basis. We have marketed this product since January 1985 and presently have more than 45,000 enrollees.
- Southwest Health Plan, Inc. (a federally qualified IPA model health maintenance organization), owned and funded 60 percent by Med Southwest, Inc. and 40 percent by the Baylor Health Care System. Licensed since September 1985, Southwest Health Plan, Inc. has more than 10,000 enrollees.
- Health Systems Texas, Inc. (a management company), owned and funded 55 percent by Med Southwest, Inc. and 45 percent by the medical center. Health Systems Texas, Inc. was designed initially to bring an element of economy to the health plan. Although the chief executive officer and marketing efforts of Southwest Health Plan, Inc. must, by law, be separate from the other entities, the remaining personnel, data processing and management information systems, and clerical support for both Southwest Health Plan, Inc. and Southwest Preferred Health Network, Inc. are common.

It was very important to the physician-shareholders of Med Southwest, Inc. that physicians be actively involved in the day-to-day operations and management of Health Systems Texas, Inc. in addition to merely contracting to provide medical services to Southwest Health Plan, Inc. We recognized that

FIGURE 16–1

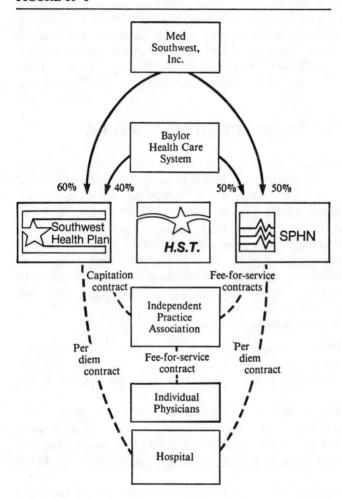

the generation of premium income by Southwest Health Plan, Inc. required an allocation of that money into three budgeted areas: management, hospital, and physician services. By minimizing management expenses, we could increase the allocation of each premium dollar to the hospital and medical providers who actually deliver the services to plan enrollees. Therefore, we manage our plan at cost.

CONCLUSION

In my opinion, physicians must maintain professionalism and ensure that quality medical services are delivered. But at the same time, I submit that without risk-reward incentives, improvements in healthcare delivery and financing will not happen.

Likewise, having all the financial incentives in place without the participation by quality professionals and management will not work either. This will undoubtedly generate controversy and criticism among my colleagues, yet physicians have a very clear choice. Either they can respond to the changing environment as a profession or they will be left as a public utility.

> It is not the critic who counts, not the man who points out how the strong man stumbled, or where the doer of deeds could have done them better. The credit belongs to the man who is actually in the arena.

> > Whose face is marred by dust and sweat and blood
> > Who strives valiantly
> > Who errs and comes short again and again
> > Who knows the great enthusiasms and great devotions
> > Who spends himself in a worthy cause
> > Who, at the best, knows in the end the triumph of
> > high achievement
> > And who, at the worst if he fails, at least fails
> > while daring greatly.

> > > > *Theodore Roosevelt, 1910*

The direction of hospital-physician joint ventures in the financing and delivery of hospital and medical services is beginning to become clear. Physicians and hospitals have to understand that the ability to generate and manage premium dollars in the marketplace is where the action is going to be in the future. A managed premium product is going to be much more important than a health maintenance organization in the future.

Much more needs to be done by hospitals and physicians to gain and maintain control over the financing of services. We are in the process of developing an indemnity insurance option and are continually exploring other means of gaining and maintaining the initiative by doing business with the hospital and strengthening our combined, long-term, professional, competitive, and financial positions.

17

The Chief Executive Officer's Perspective on Joint Ventures*

Douglas D. Hawthorne, M.S.

INTRODUCTION

The successful development and implementation of hospital-physician joint ventures necessarily involves the completion of a variety of steps as outlined in Chapter 5. However, these steps are carried out in the context of an existing organization, and it is the chief executive officer's (CEO) responsibility to assure that the joint venture under consideration is consistent with the goals and business objectives of his health care organization. Moreover, the CEO must assure that the resources, both capital and human, are sufficient to sustain and carry out the venture as planned and that the organizational dynamics are not inhospitable to joint venture arrangements. The long-term success of any particular joint venture, no matter how elegantly structured, well-financed, or potentially profitable in its own right, is tied inextricably to the ability of the partners to execute and implement the joint venture, because he or she represents the hospital that is a large and complex organization. The CEO generally is the most publicly visible of the partners, and has a special responsibility to shepherd the joint venture through its developmental and implementation stages.

No senior executive other than the CEO should be expected to create board support for joint venture approaches to developing and implementing healthcare programs. In addition, the CEO must communicate his commitment to joint venture approaches with physicians to the senior management of the organization so that the senior managers will not obstruct their development. Finally, successful development of joint ventures requires both financial capital and hu-

*The author wishes to acknowledge the assistance of David Ashworth, vice president–strategic planning and marketing, in the preparation of this chapter.

man capital investments. It falls to the CEO to assure that joint venture initiatives will not overtax the existing managers by unrealistically expecting them to manage existing programs as well as launch new ones.

CONSISTENCY WITH STRATEGIC PLAN

The primary question to be answered prior to entering into any particular joint venture is, "Is the venture a good deal for our business?" To arrive at the answer, a number of associated questions must be asked. These include:

- What is the mission of the organization?
- Who are the ultimate decision makers of the organization (e.g., shareholders or a not-for-profit board of directors)?
- Does the joint venture fit in the organization's long-term strategic plan and diversification strategies?
- What is the ultimate goal of the joint venture: To maximize return on investment? Strengthen relationships? Tie in a consuming market? Form an offensive or defensive strategy?

It is necessary to have a firm understanding of the goals, mission, and established operating methods of the organization in order to structure the framework of any joint venture. Couching the joint venture in such a fashion is a requisite step prior to a more thorough analysis of the opportunity at hand.

STRUCTURING THE VENTURE

There is no universal recommendation on structuring joint ventures. However, this is not to say that any structure is suitable for a particular organization. The CEO's perspective in reviewing a particular structure is shaped to a large extent by understanding the objectives of the organization, understanding the objectives of the venture partner(s), and understanding the objectives of the joint venture business plan. To expand on the above points, it is necessary to realize that there will be significant overlap with respect to the objectives of the organization and the venture partners, as well as the operating objectives as expressed in a written business plan.

With respect to the objectives of the organization, a joint venture represents an opportunity to address a number of underlying forces favoring joint ventures:

- Changes in the regulatory and payment environment.
- Improving access to capital.
- Strengthening relationships through partnerships.
- Risk sharing.

- Hedging against competition and/or strengthening the competitive position of the organization.
- Diversifying the base business.

Similarly, a joint venture represents an appropriate model for potential venture partners to:

- Gain greater involvement in management decisions.
- Tap into existing and/or new revenue streams.
- Strengthen relationships with the hospital.
- Strengthen competitiveness.

IMPORTANCE OF A BUSINESS PLAN

The business plan must directly address the objectives described above and do so in a fashion which fits a variety of legal, political, tax, insurance, and other considerations. For example, antitrust issues concerning noncompete clauses and price-fixing must be addressed; management issues with respect to authority, control, representation, and a clear understanding of responsibilities must be negotiated and agreed upon. Tax and insurance issues, Securities and Exchange Commission rules and regulations, as well as quality assurance, dispute resolution, and participant eligibility requirements are also subjects partially addressed by understanding the objectives of the parties involved in the joint venture. For example, the selection of partners and the designation of eligible investors can divide a medical staff as can issues such as control, the timing and amount of capital contribution, and pro forma assumptions, if not clearly understood and agreed upon. Written goals and objectives of the joint venture should be agreed upon in advance by the parties developing the proposal and should then be used to resolve key decisions in an effort to minimize disputes and avoid impasses.

The CEO should have an established mechanism to efficiently evaluate joint venture proposals. The CEO must control the temptation to participate in "good deals" which are outside of the strategic plan, mission, goals, and objectives of the organization. Minimum evaluation criteria to screen joint venture opportunities should include: return on investment/ratio analyses, market share analysis, degree of control, contribution of capital, impact on the medical staff, cost to the consumer, acceptable risks, quality assurance, and the protection of the rest of the other assets of the organization.

ESTABLISHING A TRACK RECORD WITH THE FIRST VENTURE

Success of a joint venture is always important, perhaps more so when it is the hospital's first attempt. Credibility is critical and all parties must feel ownership of and responsibility for the projections in the business plan. The CEO should designate a joint venture development team with clearly understood parameters of responsibility and authority. By doing so, management has committed its top resources to the success of the program. Furthermore, management must be prepared to broaden its experience through consultants and/or full-time employees for the planning, implementation, and operation of the joint venture. Parenthetically, it is desirable to select legal and accounting counsel in a fashion to avoid the conflicts (and expense) associated with an "us versus them" scenario. Communication also plays a vital role, as the CEO must be sensitive to problems which arise when accurate and timely information is not readily available to appropriate persons (e.g., board, medical staff, hospital staff).

LONG-TERM IMPLICATIONS

Successful joint ventures *and* joint venture partners more often than not develop long-term win-win relationships. In the future, potential investors in joint ventures will move away from participating in joint ventures strictly for tax shelter purposes. With recently enacted tax changes, a potential investor will be looking for an attractive return on investment consistent with the level of risk; thus, pro forma analyses based on thorough market assessments will be critical. Credibility, confidence, and a true sense of "partnership" are, therefore, key success factors.

CONCLUSION

At all times the CEO must be cognizant that joint ventures are systematically changing the relationships of hospitals and physicians. The measure of the success of the CEO is not only the immediate short-term performance of a particular joint venture, but also the long-term improvement in the hospital's competitive position.

18

A Trustee's Perspective on Joint Ventures

Arthur D. Aston

During my 29 years of service as a member of the board of trustees of Valley Presbyterian Hospital in Van Nuys, California, I have been witness to numerous changes in the organization, delivery, and financing of hospital and medical services. During that time, I have seen our institution grow from a fledgling 63-bed, not-for-profit hospital to a 363-bed hospital with a full range of inpatient and outpatient services. We have also shifted our emphasis from primarily that of an inpatient, acute care institution to one that provides a broad array of sophisticated outpatient and outreach services in addition to acute inpatient services of the highest quality.

I have also witnessed the San Fernando Valley, in which Valley Presbyterian Hospital is located, grow from a sparsely populated, distant suburb of the city of Los Angeles to a densely populated, dynamic urban environment with community needs that have increased in both depth and breadth with each change in its demographic structure.

Physician-hospital-trustee relationships at Valley Presbyterian Hospital have always been complex and in the past have sometimes been more adversarial than collegial. During our early years the hospital administration, with the best of intentions, generally acted first and then consulted the medical staff in a paternalistic manner, which often raised the ire of physicians. Physicians also acted independently, driven in large measure by the highly competitive medical marketplace in the San Fernando Valley.

During the past five years, however, the administration and board of trustees have been working together to improve medical staff relationships, through enhanced communication, increased involvement of physicians in hospital activities, and two successful hospital-physician joint ventures involving a medical office building and a freestanding ambulatory surgery center. Each of these ventures is discussed below.

THE MEDICAL OFFICE BUILDING JOINT VENTURE

Valley Presbyterian Hospital's first hospital-physician joint venture involved the construction of a new medical office building on land owned by the hospital immediately adjacent to the hospital facilities.

We have always felt a strong need to develop more medical office building space on or adjacent to our hospital campus because we have recognized the important contribution to our programmatic and financial success from having physicians located conveniently to the hospital. When the medical office building project was first explored, we went through a process of evaluating if we should build and own the project ourselves, involve a developer, or encourage some form of physician ownership.

We decided that physician ownership was the preferred way to go for a number of reasons. First, we wanted to provide a solid investment opportunity for physicians which would help attract to an on-campus location those physicians who we felt were key to the future success of the hospital. Second, we wanted to structure the joint venture in such a fashion as to minimize the amount of capital that the hospital would need to place at risk, particularly since we already owned the land on which the building would be located.

Having decided that physician ownership was a primary objective of the project, we then explored a number of different ways of structuring the joint venture. We looked at the condominium form of ownership, but we rejected that approach because of marketing, resale, and other problems that were particular to the type of building we contemplated. We then concluded that the most effective means of establishing the joint venture would be a partnership in which the physicians would be partners and from which the physicians would also lease space. Consequently, with the assistance of various consultants, including legal counsel and financial advisers, we structured an offering of general partnership interests, units of which were then made available to physicians whom we sought to attract to our campus.

The project was not without its difficulties. My experience in the banking and savings and loan businesses, both of which heavily involved real estate finance, prepared me for some of the typical problems that I knew we would encounter. For example, such projects are more salable when construction is well underway than before ground is broken, which proved to be the case with this project. Another problem we had was that while prospective physician investors were quite willing to commit themselves verbally, many were unwilling to write their checks until the very last minute. Again, this problem is not necessarily unique to hospital-physician projects, but it is one that we had to anticipate in our planning and implementation.

Despite these pitfalls, the partnership ultimately was completely sold out, and we now have as partners many physicians who we feel are making very substantial contributions to the success that Valley Presbyterian Hospital currently enjoys. These key physicians are on campus and are particularly committed to the hospital due to their ownership interests. These physicians are not only utilizing to a much greater degree the inpatient, outpatient, and ancillary services of the hospital, but they are also referring more patients to other physicians in both the new medical office building and its surrounding area. In addition, the location of one group of physicians in the medical office building has prompted them to explore with another physician group of the same specialty the possibility of the latter group's relocation of its practice to the medical office building. In other words, the physicians have also benefited from their prime location on the hospital campus.

Finally, we feel that because the physicians have an ownership interest, they will be more committed to the future success of Valley Presbyterian Hospital, will be more willing to weather the normal ups and downs associated with any business, and will be less likely to be lured away by one or more of our competitors.

If there were lessons to be learned from this project, I believe that two would be most significant. First, if we had to do it all over again, we would have made the medical office building much larger to attract and involve even more physicians. Although this would have entailed more risk for us and perhaps even more significant delays, I believe that the greater capacity would have been worth it. Second, when we proceed with similar types of projects in the future, we intend to have the hospital's parent corporation, Health Dynamics, Inc., become a general partner and retain a more significant equity interest in future projects than we did in the first medical office building. This would increase our control and would enable us to participate in the profits.

THE AMBULATORY SURGERY CENTER JOINT VENTURE

Our second hospital-physician joint venture involved the establishment of a freestanding ambulatory surgery center in a professional office building approximately 500 feet from the hospital.

Several years ago, we as an institution recognized that there was a major shift occurring from inpatient to outpatient utilization of our services, particularly in the area of surgery. We also recognized that using our inpatient surgery suites for outpatient surgery was not a very effective way to use those rooms. We were encountering scheduling problems, physicians and patients were finding it increasingly inconvenient to use our outpatient surgery department for routine cases, and we needed to open up inpatient surgery scheduling in order to attract surgeons who would use the inpatient surgery suites to a greater extent.

We also found ourselves in an increasingly competitive environment. One of the investor-owned ambulatory surgery companies was aggressively courting several of our surgeons with its own joint venture proposal. Another large surgical group was exploring the possibility of establishing its own surgery center because many of the group's surgeries were done in an outpatient setting.

Therefore, we recognized that we not only had to build a freestanding ambulatory surgery center but also had to involve the physicians in some kind of joint ownership.

With these objectives in mind, we asked our legal counsel to propose several forms of joint hospital-physician ownership that could facilitate achieving our objectives while avoiding the need to obtain a certificate of need for the new surgery center.

The structure we ultimately chose involved several elements. The first and principal element was the formation of a professional corporation as the entity that would operate the surgery center. Twenty-one physicians elected to participate in the venture by purchasing stock in the professional corporation through a private placement offering. No certificate of need was required because California law provides an exemption for surgery centers operated in space owned or leased and operated by one or more physicians in the form of a physician's office, as opposed to in a hospital or separately licensed surgical clinic.

The second element involved the renovation and expansion of space for the surgery center in an office building we already owned. The hospital assumed the obligation for these expenditures and then leased the completed facility to the physicians. In drafting the lease, we had to draw a careful balance between the financial and nonfinancial interests of the hospital and the physician group. Consequently, we provided for a contingent rental arrangement and used devices such as short lease term and incentive targets to assure that the performance of the surgery center would be maintained at a level satisfactory to us.

The final element of this joint venture was a management contract. Again, during the development phase several physicians questioned the desirability of having the hospital involved in the continuing management of the surgery center during the first year of its operations. However, I believe that the physicians now recognize the considerable value of professional management that the hospital administration has added to the success of the surgery center joint venture.

I believe that Valley Presbyterian Hospital has accomplished much through the use of this joint venture. First, because of its success (the surgery center operations reached the break-even point earlier than had been projected) this joint venture has set the stage for future joint ventures. In addition, from the viewpoint of the hospital's medical staff physicians, this project has given the board and administration increased credibility by demonstrating their willingness to engage in a patient care project as a true economic risk-sharing joint venture with members of its medical staff. Further, due to hospital management's involvement in surgery center operations, communications between the physicians and the hospital have continued to improve and, as previously noted, the physicians are more appreciative and understanding of the role and responsibilities of hospital management and more sensitive to the many operating issues that we face on a daily basis at the hospital. Finally, I believe that physicians now recognize that they could not have undertaken this project successfully on their own.

We did have some problems with this project. First, because of various physician concerns as well as a financing problem, we had to restructure the project twice before it finally proceeded. Second, the project involved selecting some physicians and not others to benefit from it. We were able to ameliorate the concerns of nonparticipating physicians, however, by communicating to them our commitment to explore future arrangements with them.

A final and particularly significant issue that we had to face was that creating a freestanding ambulatory surgery would cause a large number of hospital surgeries, from which we previously benefited exclusively, to move over to the new surgery center where we would have to share the benefits with the physician investors. On balance, however, I do not believe that this negative effect has been detrimental. While many outpatient surgeries are now performed at the surgery center and our participation in the revenues of the surgery center is clearly less than if those surgeries had been performed at the hospital, we have seen increased use of our inpatient surgery suites. A couple of our medical groups who participate in the outpatient surgery center have recruited physicians who are primarily users of our inpatient surgery suites. Moreover, I believe that had we not acted forthrightly in initiating this venture, an untold number of our physicians would have shifted their practices to our competitors. Therefore, we believe that at the very least we have broken even and, most importantly, that the venture has progressed to a far greater degree than it could have if we had proceeded without physician participation.

ALTERNATIVE DELIVERY SYSTEMS

We are now actively exploring participation in a multihospital joint venture to establish and operate a health maintenance organization. I believe that the credibility that we gained by having successful medical office building and surgery center joint ventures has paved the way for this as well as other joint ventures. In fact, while it is often very difficult to attract physicians as investors in hospital-sponsored joint ventures, we are now finding greater receptivity on their part to put more money at risk in such ventures.

Indeed, the medical office building and surgery center joint ventures set the stage not only for the health maintenance organization joint venture but also for current discussions regarding clinical laboratories, diagnostic centers, and physical therapy programs.

CHANGING MEDICAL STAFF–HOSPITAL RELATIONS

Looking back over the past five years, I have perceived a dramatic change in the degree of openness and trust in our hospital–medical staff relations. I attribute much of this change to increased communications generally, but I also believe that the two successful joint ventures we have undertaken to date have made a substantial contribution as well.

The evolution from improved communications to an increased willingness to engage in joint risk-taking is, I believe, a natural one. Physicians are no different from other people in that they are less likely to invest in a project if they have an inherent mistrust of the project's managers. Therefore, I believe that if we are going to carry out our healthcare mission successfully and involve physicians in that mission on an economic risk-sharing basis, the first step is to ensure that effective lines of communication exist and that each side understands the needs and objectives of the other.

During this process, I have also perceived the need to look closely at the role that hospital trustees have played in the management of the hospital. In 1982, our hospital reorganized and formed a parent corporation, Health Dynamics, Inc., which is now governed by a board of seven trustees. Those trustees who have been most active in hospital affairs became members of the board of trustees of the parent corporation as well as the hospital. Concurrent with this change, we streamlined our hospital board by reducing its size from 60 to 17 trustees and, because all of our trustees are highly valued for their commitment to the hospital, we appointed the remaining 43 trustees to the board of our new foundation. Thus, other than by natural attrition, we did not lose a single trustee's involvement while making these changes.

We now charge the parent corporation with responsibility for setting overall strategy, identifying what our corporate focus should be, and serving as the strategic decision maker for joint ventures and other types of opportunities.

GENERAL OBSERVATIONS

The past five years have been increasingly challenging for Valley Presbyterian Hospital, its trustees, its management, and its medical staff. Increased competition, dramatic changes in the financing of healthcare delivery, and other environmental factors have caused us to streamline our operations, improve communications, and, in general, be significantly more responsive to our environment.

Five years ago, healthcare joint ventures were unheard of and, had they been attempted, they probably would have been unsuccessful because the foundation for successful joint ventures—good hospital-physician communications—was absent. Today, by contrast, we have completed two successful joint ventures in a four-year period and are actively working on several others. We are sure that we will become involved in more joint ventures, though we are not certain what form they will take. We are sure, however, that there will be greater economic interdependence between the hospital and its medical staff; without such interdependence, neither will be able to survive and prosper to the end of this century and beyond.

Thus, it is incumbent upon hospital trustees to develop a keen sense for the marketplace and, in particular, for the needs of the hospital and its medical staff to work together. With this understanding will inevitably come an acceptance of the fact that hospital-physician joint ventures are one of the most important means of ensuring that Valley Presbyterian Hospital will remain among the leading providers of high-quality healthcare services in southern California.

VI

CASE STUDIES

19

Ambulatory Surgery Centers

Wesley B. Thompson, M.B.A.

INTRODUCTION

The concept of outpatient or ambulatory surgery is attracting a great deal of attention in today's healthcare environment. However, the development of treating surgical patients as outpatients has its roots in England and Scotland during the early 1900s. During a 1909 meeting of the British Medical Association, Dr. J. H. Nichol reported on 7,320 outpatient surgical cases he had performed at the Royal Glasgow Hospital for Children.[1] Successful outpatient surgery programs were developed at the University of California, Los Angeles, and George Washington University in the 1960s, with the first recognized freestanding surgical center opening in Providence, Rhode Island, in 1968.[2]

The growth of ambulatory surgery, in freestanding as well as hospital-based facilities, has been due primarily to the following factors: (1) significant improvements in surgical and anesthetic technology; (2) increases in hospital costs; (3) patients desiring greater control over their environment (e.g., recovering at home); and (4) surgeons desiring alternatives to the complex hospital inpatient environment. At the end of 1985 there were approximately 350 freestanding surgical centers in operation or development in the United States, and that number is expected to exceed 800 by 1990.[3] The major attractions of the freestanding surgical center over the hospital-based outpatient unit include: (1) costs savings of about 10–15 percent for similar procedures;[4] (2) greater efficiency and convenience for the surgeon; (3) a less institutionalized environment for the patient; and (4) investment and joint venture opportunities for physicians.

The concept of performing surgery in the freestanding center has been accepted and supported by the majority of insurance companies as is demonstrated by Medicare's 1982 decision to pay a facility fee to ambulatory surgical centers (ASCs) for selected cases. Blue Cross and other third-party payors have also been very supportive of reimbursing ASCs in most parts of the country. In a recent survey of the Fortune 500 companies regarding strategies they were desirous of pursuing to lower their healthcare costs, ambulatory surgery was ranked as the top priority.[5] The growth in outpatient surgery has been significant over the past decade is expected to continue for the next 5 to 10 years. Experts used to predict that 30 to 40 percent of all surgery could be performed on an outpatient basis. They are now predicting that the number may eventually be between 50 to 60 percent.[6]

INTERMOUNTAIN HEALTH CARE, INC. AND IHC PROFESSIONAL SERVICES, INC.

IHC is a nonprofit, multihospital system founded in 1975. In the past 12 years since its incorporation, IHC has grown into a strong, diverse network of 23 member hospitals, 260 affiliated hospitals, 4 ambulatory surgical centers, 7 InstaCare urgent care centers, 5 Work-Med occupational health clinics, 23 primary care clinics serving suburban and rural areas, a home health and rehabilitation agency, a medical equipment supply service, a healthcare benefits company, a system of centers for women's health, freestanding dialysis centers, psychiatric hospitals, chemical dependency units, physician practice manage-

FIGURE 19–1 IHC Professional Services, Inc. Organizational Chart

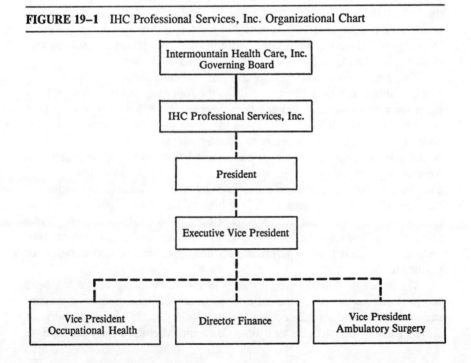

ment services, and many other programs. IHC had revenues in 1985 of more than $400 million.

IHC Professional Services, Inc. (PSI) is a wholly owned, not-for-profit subsidiary of Intermountain Health Care, Inc. (IHC) and was formed to be the diversification arm of IHC in development and management of alternative modes of healthcare delivery (see Figure 19–1). Since the formation of PSI in 1982, two lines of business have been developed, ambulatory surgery and occupational health.

ROSELAND SURGICAL CENTER JOINT VENTURE

The Roseland Surgical Center (RSC) is a joint venture between PSI and a group of physicians in Roseland, New Jersey. RSC was originally formed and began operation in October 1982 after a very difficult battle to win state certificate of need approval for the freestanding ambulatory surgery center (the Center). The Center was developed by five physicians who were directors of the Center and whose specialties are anesthesia, general surgery, ophthalmology, and obstetrics/gynecology.

THE CENTER

The Center is a fully equipped, five-operating-room, freestanding ambulatory surgery facility. It occupies 10,180 square feet of space and is located on the ground level of a three-story medical office building in Roseland, New Jersey. RSC is licensed by the state of New Jersey and is a certified Medicare facility. Fourteen full-time equivalent employees work at the Center, and an anesthesiologist serves as the full-time medical director. Having an anesthesiologist as the medical director is vital in a surgical center as he controls the efficiency of the surgical workplace. An exclusive arrangement is provided to the anesthesiologists. In 1985 the Center operated on an annual operating budget of $1,459,855.

More than 200 surgeons have applied for and received privileges to operate at the Center. Those specialties which have been responsible for the greatest volumes to date include general surgery, ophthalmology, podiatry, and orthopedics. All other surgical specialties are represented on the staff. The management of the Center is active in the recruitment of surgeons who will perform their outpatient surgical cases at the center. The marketing effort takes the approach of personal visits with surgeons, telephone calls, and discussions with the surgeons' office staff. Most surgeons have found that performing outpatient cases at the Center has made their practice more efficient because they generally are able to perform more cases in the same time frame than they could at a hospital. Patient acceptance and satisfaction have also been excellent.

The Center's primary competition comes from nearby hospitals, one of which has recently built its own freestanding surgery center. In 1984, just under 2,000 surgical cases were performed at the Center, and 2,700 surgeries were done in 1985. All physicians practicing at the Center have privileges at nearby hospitals, and changing their patterns of performing surgery is a challenging task.

Utilization of the center is monitored by review of monthly reports that indicate cases performed by each surgeon. Actual utilization by specialty through the first half of 1985 indicates the following patterns:

Specialty	Number of Cases	Percent of Total
Podiatry	365	29.6
Ophthalmology	296	24.0
Orthopedics	163	13.2
General Surgery	132	10.7
Gynecology	71	5.8
Ear, nose, throat	62	5.0
Urology	55	4.5
Dental	52	4.2
Plastic	38	3.1

KEY CAPITAL REQUIREMENTS

As the Center was constructed, several different partnerships were formed to handle the capital needs of the project:

Real Estate A limited partnership, RSC Associates, was formed to develop the office building that houses the Center. RSC signed a 20-year lease with RSC Associates.

Equipment The five physician partners created a general partnership that purchased all of the required medical equipment and furnishings and leased them to RSC. The total capital cost for these items was approximately $600,000.

Leasehold Improvements RSC constructed $775,000 of leasehold improvements and financed these through a loan from a local New Jersey bank.

Working Capital RSC was responsible for all start-up and ongoing working capital needs. Subsequently the general partner, Ambi-surg, provided all of the needed capital through loans and personal capital contributions.

PSI'S ACQUISITION OF ITS INTEREST IN RSC

PSI's primary motivation in becoming a partner in RSC came about through a relationship between PSI and Bernard Kershner, president of Medical Management and Development Corporation (MMDC) in Hartford, Connecticut. MMDC had discussions with PSI for two years regarding potential joint activities in the surgery center market in the Northeast. MMDC had also been instrumental in obtaining the certificate of need and subsequent development of the Roseland project. MMDC, RSC, and PSI began discussions for a potential joint venture in late 1982. RSC's partners also were considering offers from other surgery center firms throughout the United States.

After months of negotiations with the various parties, an agreement was reached on August 30, 1983, for PSI to acquire 60 percent of RSC. Major legal and financial components of the acquisition included:

- Sale of stock and liquidation of existing entities.
- Purchase of assets from limited partners.
- Formation of a new partnership.
- Formation of the joint venture.
- Assumption of liabilities.
- Loan refinancing.
- Adjusted working capital payment.
- Buyout.
- Management issues.
- Certain joint venture agreement.
- Provisions.
- Conditions.
- Documents.
- Closing.

PSI, through a newly formed partnership, acquired 60 percent of the Roseland Surgical Center with the physician partners retaining ownership of 40 percent. The new partnership began operation on February 1, 1984.

RELATIONSHIP OF THE CENTER TO PSI'S STRATEGIC PLAN

A major objective of PSI's entry into the ambulatory surgery market was to learn the business of operating ASCs as soon as possible. Operating an ASC requires a management mentality different from that required to manage a hospital. ASCs must be run as small business units, and the traditional hospital approach in making decisions does not work for such a small operation. While PSI had a surgery center under development in Salt Lake City, the opportunity to learn from the up-and-running Roseland center in an area away from Salt Lake City was desirous. Thus, the acquisition of an existing ASC was actively pursued.

Through discussions with MMDC, the Roseland center was identified as desiring a partner with management strength and capital resources. Although New Jersey is outside of IHC's traditional service area, the opportunity to learn from an existing operation, to be involved in a joint venture with physicians, and to obtain a good investment opportunity justified the project for PSI.

WHY A JOINT VENTURE?

PSI was motivated to become involved in a joint venture with physicians in a surgery center because physicians (primarily surgeons) control the referral of patients to the location at which the surgery will be performed (hospital, surgery center, etc.). PSI will also be exploring the inclusion of primary care physicians in future ventures. If physicians have an investment in an ASC and are at financial risk for the operation, they will have an economic incentive to use the ASC for as many of their cases as are possible and medically proper. The effects of such economic incentives have been substantiated through PSI's experiences in Roseland.

Another motivation for PSI to become a partner with physicians was a recognition of the physicians' desire to have a significant degree of control and input into the management of the ASC. An important aspect of such joint ventures is to cautiously structure the operation of the ASC so that the incentive for profitability does not lead to unnecessary and/or improper surgeries being performed. This can be controlled through effective quality control and peer review programs. The medical director plays a very important role in this process as do various quality review committees and studies.

PSI's judgment is that physicians must have enough financial incentive and risk in order for them to change their behavior and bring cases from the hospital. PSI's partners in RSC own 8 percent each and they are general partners. Thus, they have been motivated by their substantial ownership interest to enhance the success of RSC. In other settings where physician partners have an insignificant ownership interest, such as 1 or 2 percent, investment and risk have not always created the desire to put full support behind the project.

Quality care has been a vital and integral part of the Center. The quality assurance management approach has looked at all aspects of potential concern, including: physician credentialing, tissue reviews, in-service training for the staff, regular equipment servicing, telephone calls to all patients on the day after surgery, and many other aspects. The postoperative infection rate at the Center has been very low, as has been the admission rate to the hospital for postoperative complications. Quality of care serves as a key success measure for PSI's involvement in the Center.

THE LEGAL STRUCTURE AND FINANCING OF RSC

Since the involvement of PSI in RSC involved the acquisition of 60 percent of the existing business, the legal aspects were significantly more complex than they would have been had the venture involved the development and creation of a new center. This chapter will not discuss the alteration of the original structure, but will focus on the new partnership created in February 1984.

As previously noted, a joint venture agreement between PSI and Roseland Surgical Associates (RSA) was implemented on February 1, 1984. The venture was organized as a general partnership under the New Jersey Uniform Partnership Act and will be in force until December 31, 2008, unless earlier dissolved. Each partner contributed its proportionate share of assets (PSI, 60 percent; RSA, 40 percent) to the new venture and assumed its proportionate share of liabilities. Additional capital requirements (for working capital or additional equipment) can be met through capital contributions, partner loans, or loans from lending institutions. Existing loans of RSC were renegotiated, and the banks asked for and received PSI guarantees on the loans.

The venture partners have full and complete discretion in the management and control of the business. Voting power of the partners is proportionate to their respective ownership interests. An executive committee of six members was established to direct the day-to-day operations of the Center. The committee consists of two persons designated by RSA, two persons designated by PSI, and two positions to be filled by a vote of the venture partners.

The day-to-day management of the Center has been delegated to MMDC by contract. MMDC is paid a fixed management fee with a performance incentive if RSC obtains specific agreed upon objectives. Additional staff support comes from the offices of MMDC in Hartford. The duties of the manager include: personnel management, equipment and supply requisition, medical records, financial and accounting reports, budgets, marketing, professional committees and associations, and compliance with all laws. MMDC reports to the executive committee and, in turn, to the partners. All major decisions are approved by the executive committee and subsequently by the partners.

Since PSI is a not-for-profit, tax-exempt organization described in Section 501(c)(3) of the Internal Revenue Code, it required that certain clauses be included in the partnership documents to ensure the consistency of RSC's operations with PSI's exempt purposes, including: (1) providing services without regard for the ability of the patient to pay; (2) establishing the use of RSC for educational and training purposes; and (3) operating RSC in keeping with the tax-exempt purposes of PSI. RSC has performed consistently with these important provisions. The lease for the facility was continued, and the lease with Mediquip for the medical equipment was also continued, although the financial terms of the equipment lease were altered.

FINANCIAL RETURNS

The first year of the operation of RSC did not meet the financial objectives of the partners. Higher than anticipated working capital loans from all partners were needed. The main reasons for the poorer than anticipated performance were low patient volumes, ineffective cost control, and reimbursement problems with Blue Cross of New Jersey. Through intense management, marketing, and negotiations efforts, RSC's operating performance was greatly improved in early 1985.

IMPACT ON PHYSICIANS–PSI RELATIONSHIPS

A major market force affecting RSC is physician ownership. It is generally felt that the ownership position of PSI has neither positively nor negatively affected the using physicians' perceptions of RSC other than enrichment of the management. However, some nonowner physicians have indicated that they would use the Center if it were not owned by physicians perceived as competitors.

A few key surgeons are now interested in purchasing equity interests in the Center. Competition from all surrounding hospitals has increased by their attempt to improve their existing outpatient operations and by one hospital that has constructed a freestanding surgery center of its own. The existing relationships with the physician partners are excellent and there exists a high level of trust.

SUCCESSES, DISAPPOINTMENTS, AND FUTURE IMPLICATIONS OF THE JOINT VENTURE

The Roseland Surgery Center Joint Venture was the first joint venture with physicians for IHC and PSI. While the first year of operational performance was very disappointing due to problems in marketing, cost control, and reimbursement, current performance is very satisfactory. The relationship with the physician partners has been a very positive one for PSI. The venture combines an appropriate blend of management and clinical expertise, and both partners have developed a great degree of respect for each other's capabilities.

The nature of the healthcare marketplace is changing so rapidly that PSI believes that similar ventures with physicians in the future will be critical. The major environmental trends leading to more hospital-physician joint ventures are: (1) changes in the regulatory environment (e.g., elimination of certificate of need); (2) declining physician incomes; (3) changing medical technology; (4) proactive consumers; and (5) changing reimbursement patterns. These forces, along with proactive hospitals, will lead to more hospital-physician joint ventures for surgery centers and, potentially, other medical services in the future.

LESSONS LEARNED

The greatest lesson PSI learned regarding joint ventures with physicians is that the expectations of both parties must be clearly specified and agreed upon before initiating the venture. Such expectations include projected financial performance, decision making, balance of power and authority, personnel hiring, and working capital commitments. These expectations should be clearly defined, negotiated, and agreed upon at the beginning of the venture.

In order for a venture to succeed there must also be a high level of trust between both or all parties. While legal agreements spelling out the mechanisms for solving disputes are necessary, they serve a minimal purpose if the parties are not dealing with each other with trust and honesty. PSI has seen great benefits come from a closer relationship between physicians and management. The skepticism that exists between the two parties in the traditional hospital-physician relationship dissipates when a partnership or joint venture exists. The physician brings clinical strength and judgment into the board meetings, and the management team brings financial and management-related ideas. The synergy comes when all parties view the decisions to be made from the viewpoint of board members representing their respective disciplines.

Other lessons learned include:

• Create and agree upon the specific goals/objectives together.
• Identify as many issues as possible prior to signing final agreements.
• Retain legal counsel who is experienced in tax law, partnership law, and corporate law.
• Act quickly but responsibly in approaching the business deal. Inertia breeds problems.
• Use your best personal judgment and wisdom in finalizing the arrangement.
• Bring in legal counsel after the partners have agreed, in principle, on the business deal and let the attorneys structure the deal appropriately.

EPILOGUE

The RSC experience to date has been invaluable for IHC and PSI. We have learned that joint ventures are very difficult to create and manage, but that the closer relationship between hospitals and physicians is vital if we are both to succeed in the difficult future facing the world of healthcare. PSI will be involved in many joint ventures with physicians in the future. We have learned through our RSC experience that the easiest way to structure such relationships is to create and develop the project from the beginning with the physicians, instead of entering into an existing operation.

Much energy was expended in amending the existing legal structure of RSC in order for PSI to obtain equity, and this process would have been much easier had the organization been created for our project from the beginning. PSI is very pleased with the RSC joint venture experience and plans on developing similar programs in the future.

Notes

[1] J. H. Nichol, Paper Presented at the British Medical Association Meeting, *British Medical Journal* 2 (1901), p. 753.

[2] "Outpatient Surgery," *Hospital Administration Currents* 16 (April 1972), pp. 1–4.

[3] *Biomedical Business International*, McKinsey Consulting Group.

[4] IHC Market Research Study (1985).

[5] S. Gardner, "Big Business Embraces Alternative Delivery," Hospitals 59 (March 16, 1985), pp. 81–82.

[6] IHC Market Research Study (1985).

20

Diagnostic Imaging Centers

Ronald B. Barkley, M.S., J.D.

INTRODUCTION

Historically, diagnostic imaging equipment, or more commonly, radiology equipment, was found predominantly in the hospital radiology department. Although the hospital still represents by some estimates as much as 90 percent of today's imaging equipment market, the less expensive imaging modalities, such as radiographic or ultrasound units, have become commonplace in the private physician office.

This diversion of the more economical imaging modalities to the private setting seems to have resulted from several factors. First, the purchase price of select modalities has become affordable for the private practitioner. Second, the technology and mechanics of the equipment have been simplified; operating and maintaining the equipment have become easier, and throughput, or machine capacity, has been enhanced. Third, clinically it has become common for nonradiologist physicians, particularly some subspecialists such as cardiologists, orthopedists, neurologists, and obstetricians, to interpret images of anatomy particular to their subspecialization, often without assistance from radiologist specialists. Finally, there are increased opportunities to generate additional office income from imaging procedures while providing one-stop convenience to the patient. The risk posture of the private physician investing in office imaging equipment has become minimal because of the relatively low purchase price, the ability of the physician directly to manage procedures ordered for patients, and the new-found income to be generated from medical interpretation.

Until recently, the more expensive high-technology imaging equipment remained at the hospital. This list included computed tomography (CT), digital radiography, fluoroscopy, nuclear cameras, and linear accelerators, to name a few. Such equipment was simply too costly or too complex to use efficiently in the private office setting. The hospital generally was the one who assumed a high-risk posture by investing in high-technology imaging equipment. The purchase price alone created a high-risk-oriented investment. In addition, hospitals often had difficulty in accurately predicting procedure volume, particularly for newly introduced modalities, let alone influencing or controlling referral patterns. The hospital always seemed to be the one to bear the risk of obsolescence.

The hospital-based radiologist, who traditionally had been somewhat protected from competition, began to experience challenges to his financial security. High-technology imaging equipment and its operations became more computer-oriented and technician-intensive, and relatively less radiologist-intensive. In addition, certain of the imaging modalities that might have belonged at one time within the radiology department were diverted for direct use in other specialized departments. These included cardiac catheterization laboratories and echocardiography in the cardiology department, ultrasound in obstetrics and, most recently, magnetic resonance imaging (MRI) under various combinations of medical directorship. This additional diversion of professional procedures created even more challenge to the security of the hospital-based radiologist.

The imaging center joint venture has come to be a popular approach to the complex dynamics of this changing environment. The joint venture brings numerous benefits to all parties involved:

Hospital The investment in the imaging joint venture can be beneficial to hospitals seeking alternative revenue sources in response to the prospective payment "squeeze." If situated in a freestanding setting on or off the hospital campus, the venture can help the hospital in shifting to an outpatient orientation. The capital risk of equipment acquisition is spread and shared with the physicians who use the equipment. Finally, the successful joint venture has proved to be a mechanism for solidifying physician-hospital relationships and even increasing market share.

Patients Diagnostic and therapeutic services in the freestanding setting are often attractive to patients because of the informal, nonthreatening environment as compared to the institutional hospital setting. Volume efficiency and reduced overhead costs can result in a lowering of patient charges for services rendered.

Physicians An imaging equipment investment can be attractive to both primary care and specialist physicians. A physician is able to invest in a business with which he is familiar and which he can help support directly. Additionally, the practicing physician can expect to recoup income lost as a result of intensified competition for patients and reductions in insurance payments for his own services.

Radiologists Radiologists, particularly those who are hospital-based, have the opportunity through the joint venture to reestablish relationships with the outpatient imaging market and solidify referral patterns.

Among others, National Diagnostic Services, Inc. (NDS), Woodland Hills, California, has become identified with the business of organizing, syndicating, and operating hospital-physician joint ventures in the diagnostic imaging field. Through August 1985, NDS had successfully completed 14 imaging center joint ventures in the western United States. These range from mobile imaging applications, hospital-placed CT scanners, and hospital-placed cardiac catheterization laboratories to freestanding comprehensive imaging centers.

The joint ventures take the form of limited partnerships which provide for various tax flow-throughs for the individual investors. NDS serves either as the sole general partner or as a cogeneral partner in its 14 existing imaging center limited partnerships. The limited partners are physicians, hospitals, and other related healthcare providers within the respective medical services area. NDS has been solely responsible for planning, budgeting, and organizing its numerous ventures, and through its wholly owned broker/dealer subsidiary, National Diagnostic Securities, NDS has been responsible for syndicating and selling the limited partnership investment units.

Two case studies of imaging center joint ventures follow. The first study is that of a venture among NDS; Memorial Hospitals Association, Modesto, California; and local physicians. The venture acquired and now operates a General Electric Model 9800 CT Scanner and is responsible for providing CT services at Memorial Hospital Medical Center, Modesto.

The second study is that of a joint venture located in Fresno, California, and involving Saint Agnes Hospital and Medical Center. This venture commenced operations with a hospital-placed CT scanner and is expanding to include an MRI system in a freestanding setting.

For purposes of these case studies, an "active hospital staff physician" is defined as one who conducted all or the majority of his hospital-related activities at the sponsor hospital's facility (Memorial Hospital or Saint Agnes Hospital) prior to involvement in the joint venture. An "outside physician" is defined as one who conducted his hospital-related activities at the sponsor hospital's facility infrequently, if at all, prior to involvement in the joint venture.

MODESTO 9800 CT LIMITED PARTNERSHIP

Memorial Hospitals Association is headquartered in Modesto, California, and consists of Memorial Hospital Medical Center, a 168-bed, general acute care hospital specializing in oncology, renal, orthopedics, obstetrical, and general medical services. Memorial Hospitals Association also includes Memorial Hospital, Ceres, a 74-bed, general acute care facility, and a 48-bed, distinct part skilled nursing facility. Memorial Hospitals Association manages the 22-bed West Side Community Hospital under a full service management contract. Other programs include a 20-bed chemical dependency program, an inpatient chronic pain evaluation program, and the Medi-Flight Air Ambulance Helicopter Service.

The physician-investors in the Modesto 9800 CT project are comprised of 15 active hospital staff and 12 formerly outside physicians. The Modesto 9800

TABLE 20-1 Modesto 9800 CT Investor Mix

Category	Active Hospital Staff	Outside Physicians	Total
Neurologist/neurosurgeon	1	2	3
Orthopedists	0	6	6
Other specialists	14	4	18
Total	15(55%)	12(45%)	27

CT partnership demonstrates the potential for a successful joint venture to capture referrals from outside the immediate medical staff. The physician-investor mix includes multiple investment units acquired by multiple-physician groups (see Table 20-1).

The partnership's CT scanner was installed in the Department of Radiology, Memorial Hospital Medical Center. A service agreement is in effect between the hospital and the partnership. The partnership charges a "wholesale" service fee to the hospital for equipment use and equipment services. The hospital is the provider and bills its "retail" charges to patients or their insurers. The project's capital requirements are set forth in Table 20-2.

One element of Memorial Hospital's strategic plan is to acquire major equipment or establish significant clinical programs in conjunction with the medical staff and other area physicians wherever possible to help assure a program's success. The joint venture approach is now being considered as a vehicle for other projects sponsored by Memorial Hospitals Association, such as ambulatory surgery, a regional cancer center, and a freestanding, off-campus diagnostic imaging center.

Memorial Hospitals Association could have readily afforded to acquire the CT scanner with its own funds, but it wanted to validate the demand for the

TABLE 20-2

Sources of capital:	
Physician cash contributions	
(34 × $10,000)	$ 340,000
Hospital cash contributions	100,000
General partner contribution	100
Equipment financing	1,026,700
Total	$1,466,800
Uses of capital:	
Equipment down payment	$ 240,000
Equipment lease	1,026,700
Organization/syndication costs	100,000
Working capital	100,100
	$1,466,800

new equipment and not put solely its own funds at risk. Validating the volume of procedures during the selling process helped to confirm the demand. Through the joint venture, Memorial was able to reduce the amount of funds it otherwise would have had to expend to acquire the CT scanner. In addition, Memorial now has physician coventurers sharing in some of the costs of ongoing operations, such as supplies and payroll.

Memorial has established several criteria for determining when a joint venture is appropriate. The equipment to be acquired or program to be launched must be one with sufficient unknowns that it is considered "risky." For instance, the acquisition cost may be high, the operating costs might be high, or the equipment or program may be very volume sensitive. The premise is that if the potential supporters of the project—the area physicians and hospitals— are willing to put their cash up or "go at risk" with Memorial, then the project has a certain commitment that reduces the risk of Memorial being the sole owner with all of the inherent risks of sole ownership, such as underutilization.

The project to be joint ventured must be one that results in Memorial achieving its targeted internal rate of return on invested capital. This target rate for Memorial is currently the prime rate plus 2 percent.

The project needs to be one that either creates new relationships or involvements with physicians or other hospitals or at least enhances existing relationships. These relationships can be either directly related to or peripheral to the joint venture itself. Memorial has termed this criteria "symbiotic dynamics."

Finally, the project should have the capability of capturing market share from a competitor or protecting existing market share from erosion due to new entrants in the market. Frequently, market share of diagnostic imaging referrals can be obtained from physician-investors who are affiliated with a competitor hospital. Often, new entrants to the market are local physicians who attempt the same project on their own in competition with the hospital.

There are several significant elements of the partnership arrangement. The sole general partner of the partnership is NDS. NDS contributed $100 to the initial partnership capitalization and acquired a 1 percent equity position in the partnership for this contribution. NDS provides management, accounting, and tax services and is paid, on an ongoing basis, 5 percent of the gross collections for partnership operations. There are 27 limited partners, owning a total of 35 partnership investment units. Memorial Hospitals Association acquired one Category B unit at the purchase price of $100,000. Twenty-six physicians or multiphysician groups acquired Category A units at a price of $10,000 per unit.

The life of the partnership is seven years, through December 31, 1991, although Memorial may exercise an option to purchase the CT scanner in 1989 and, if so exercised, the partnership would be dissolved at that time. Each of the Category A limited partners agreed to be assessed up to an additional $19,430 per Category A unit owned in the event that the general partner determined that additional funds were needed. The Category B limited partner (Memorial) agreed to be assessed up to an additional $194,300 if additional funds were required. These sums represented the balance of the purchase price of the partnership equipment. Distributable cash available from operations is distributed 99 percent to the limited partners collectively and 1 percent to the general partner. Each Category A limited partner receives 2.25 percent of distributable cash, and Memorial, the Category B limited partner, receives 22.5 percent of distributable cash. Taxable income, tax losses, and investment tax credits are allocated on a pro rata basis.

At the time of the project's inception, Memorial was using an outdated CT scanner. Much of the CT volume in Modesto was being performed at a competitor hospital. There was insufficient volume on Memorial's existing equipment to cost-justify a new General Electric 9800 without increasing patient CT charges substantially, which Memorial did not feel was warranted. The real risk in the venture was that sufficient CT volume could not be generated to create a profitable venture. The local CT market was saturated with either hospital-based scanners or mobile CT services. Due primarily to the high purchase price of the new scanner, the project had high fixed costs. However, once a certain procedure break-even volume was achieved, the profit margins were expected to be high.

The engagement of NDS as the organizer and syndicator seemed to help address medical-political issues somewhat: NDS could be used as a "fall guy" if necessary, although politically sensitive issues were not particularly prevalent in the Modesto project, perhaps due to Memorial's open-staff policy in their radiology department. The primary function of NDS was to provide a trained and experienced sales force capable of achieving full project funding.

Historical procedure volumes at Memorial were combined with certain sales expectations based on the physician surveys performed by NDS. The projected returns to a physician-investor, assuming the successful distribution of investment units, are set forth in Table 20–3.

The project has been successful with procedure volumes higher than expected primarily due to the ability of the syndication to draw CT scans from competitor hospitals. Many staff physicians from Memorial's primary hospital competitor personally invested in the program and are referring outpatients to the partnership's CT scanner, which has accounted for a higher than expected

TABLE 20–3

	Year 1	Year 2	Year 3	Year 4	Year 5
Cash distribution per Category A unit	$4,989	$ 2,892	$ 2,892	$ 2,892	$ 2,892
Cash return on $10,000 unit	49.9%	28.9%	28.9%	28.9%	28.9%
Taxable loss per Category A unit	$ (375)	$(3,201)	$(2,409)	$(2,052)	$(1,747)

shift in CT business. During the partnership's first reporting year, 1984, there were only seven months of actual operations (start-up in May 1984). Cash distributions were $3,878 (39 percent), for an annualized amount of $5,157 (52 percent), relatively close to the expected results. Cash distributions through the first 13 months of operation resulted in a cash return per unit of 81 percent, significantly higher than budgeted.

The impact on physician-hospital relationships has been improved significantly by the application of the joint venture. One of the many spin-off benefits of the Modesto 9800 CT partnership has been that some specialists who use the CT scanner have shifted some of their inpatient business to the facility. This shift was due not only to the joint venture, but also to the syndication process that helped key management at Memorial make inroads with unaffiliated physicians. For instance, the chief executive officer of Memorial Hospitals Association accompanied NDS sales personnel on many of the crucial sales calls. He was able to gain insights as to why neurosurgery and orthopedic surgery were performed primarily at the competitor hospital. The CEO was able to "sell" some of his own surgery suite block time at Memorial Hospital, while the NDS sales staff sold investment units in the CT partnership.

There has been no outward negative reaction from noninvestors. Their message to Memorial Hospital has been that they hope the next time the hospital initiates a joint venture, they are contacted first for their potential participation. According to a senior vice president, Memorial Hospitals Association will consider joint venturing almost any item of medical equipment or service where better than historical levels of profitability to the hospital can be attained while assuring long-term market share.

CENTRAL VALLEY IMAGING CENTER

The initiator of the Central Valley Imaging Center limited partnership was Saint Agnes Hospital and Medical Center, Fresno, California. Saint Agnes Hospital is one of 11 acute care hospitals operated by the Order of the Sisters of the Holy Cross, South Bend, Indiana. Imaging Corp. is the name under which Professional Office Corporation, a not-for-profit affiliate of Saint Agnes Hospital, conducts its business as the managing general partner of the Central Valley Imaging Center. Imaging Corp. is controlled by Saint Agnes Hospital through common board membership. Saint Agnes Hospital is a 320-bed, acute care hospital serving the greater Fresno area and is a significant provider within its service area of a broad range of services including general medical/surgical, obstetrics, and intensive and coronary care. It also serves as a regional referral center in the Central San Joaquin Valley area for a number of specialized services including open heart surgery, neurological surgery, opthalmologic surgery, orthopedic surgery, and oncology.

Saint Agnes became interested in pursuing a joint venture with its physicians after a nearby surgery center partnership was successfully organized by area physicians, including many of its own staff. It had been rumored that another physician-sponsored syndication was being planned by radiologists to form an imaging center venture. In addition, it was learned during the sale of investment units that another contender in organizing a second competing imaging center was one of Saint Agnes Hospital's own radiology staff members.

Saint Agnes Hospital's overall strategic plan called for involving its physicians directly as partners in the long-term financial viability of the institution. In addition, Saint Agnes Hospital desired to bolster medical staff relations by demonstrating a willingness to be financially flexible with the medical staff. It seemed appropriate to involve physicians directly in this equipment acquisition project, particularly with the introduction of the high-cost MRI modality. The imaging partnership project represented a sound investment opportunity that achieved the objective of demonstrating the hospital's flexibility and willingness to share risks and rewards of high technology.

It was certain that there was not enough business in town to support two ventures in addition to this one, particularly with the new high-priced MRI modality involved. The venture that could be organized and syndicated the most quickly would have the greatest chance of success. NDS agreed with the president of Saint Agnes Hospital to participate in the formulation of the hospital's project because Saint Agnes Hospital had a fundamental understanding of what it wanted to achieve by undertaking the venture and seemed to demonstrate the depth of commitment and "fighting spirit" needed to withstand the three to six months of syndication pressures. Project budgeting was commenced in August 1984; the offering circular was prepared and approved; the syndication was completed thereafter in January 1985, a total time period of five months.

Central Valley Imaging Center, like Modesto CT, was organized as a California limited partnership. It was formed to acquire a General Electric Model 9800 CT scanner and includes a mechanism to acquire a General Electric 1.5 Tesla superconductive MRI system. The partnership would commence operations of the CT Scanner upon the sale of the minimum amount of the offering (40 units). Upon the recommendation of its medical advisory committee, the general partners would elect to continue the sale to the maximum 125 units and with these additional funds acquire the MRI system.

NDS and Imaging Corp. are the general partners in Central Valley Imaging Center. The general partners contributed $100 to the initial partnership capitalization and acquired a 1 percent equity position in the partnership for this contribution. Imaging Corp. is the managing general partner. For their management, accounting, and tax services, the general partners are paid, on an ongoing basis, 5 percent of the gross collections of the partnership. This amount is divided between NDS and Imaging Corp. in proportion to their respective service roles. There are currently 40 limited partners owning a total of 40 partnership investment units. Imaging Corp. acquired one investment unit at the purchase price of $8,400. The partnership has a 10-year term through December 31, 1995, although Saint Agnes may exercise its purchase option for the partnership's equipment should the partnership dissolve earlier. Each of the invest-

TABLE 20–4 Capital Requirements

	Minimum Subscriptions (40 units)	Maximum Subscriptions (125 units)
Source of capital:		
Initial cash contributions ($8,400 per unit plus $100 from general partner)	$336,100	$1,050,100
Use of capital:		
CT 9800 (10% down payment)	$125,000	$ 125,100
MRI deposit	50,000	50,000
MRI developmental costs	10,000	40,000
MRI (10% down payment)	—	151,400
Imaging center renovations (CT)	—	75,000
Imaging center renovations (MRI)	—	300,000
Minor medical equipment	30,100	61,100
Furnishings	—	20,000
Syndication/organizational costs	60,000	146,000
Outside legal counsel	10,000	10,000
Working capital	51,000	71,500
Total	$336,000	$1,050,100

ing limited partners agreed to an assessment of up to an additional $28,150 per unit owned in the event that the partnership is found to be in default of its equipment financing obligations. The general partners receive no distribution of cash until the limited partners have received cash distributions equal to the limited partners' cash capital contributions (the "payout"). Thereafter, the general partners will begin receiving 20 percent of the partnership's distributable cash. The capital requirements are set forth in Table 20–4.

Physician-investors in the Central Valley Imaging Center were primarily active hospital staff with only a small representation of outside physicians. This syndication did not have a significant drawing effect from other area hospitals. The investor mix includes multiple investment units acquired by multiple-physician groups (see Table 20–5).

Subsequent to partnership formation, the CT Scanner was installed initially in the Department of Radiology at Saint Agnes Hospital. The MRI system is

TABLE 20–5

Category	Active Hospital Staff	Outside Physicians	Total
Neurologist or neurosurgeon	5	1	6
Orthopedic	2	0	2
Other	30	2	32
Total	37(92%)	3(8%)	40

to be located in a new diagnostic services facility near the Saint Agnes campus. The partnership's CT scanner may be relocated to the new facility to complement the MRI. A service agreement was put in effect between the hospital and the partnership whereby the partnership is paid the excess remaining from CT operations after deducting all items of direct operating expense from actual CT collections. Under the guidance of Saint Agnes Hospital's executive vice president and chief financial officer, the hospital negotiated a discounted fee for services provided to inpatients whose hospital care is paid for on a fixed reimbursement basis (e.g., diagnosis-related groups).

The procedure volume to be expected on the partnership's CT scanner was sufficiently validated such that acquisition of the CT did not present a particularly high-risk investment. However, the MRI component of the acquisition does present a substantial economic risk. The MRI is a new diagnostic tool, with its attendant clinical learning curve. The hospital felt that a stronger commitment than a "straw poll" from the physician support base would be necessary. The combination of the two modalities presented a reasonable compromise between the high and low risks of the two modalities separately. Anticipated returns to the investor were projected as follows. The results of the partnership's first half year of operations have been consistent with the budgeted projections (see Table 20–6).

Some members of the medical staff raised the question as to the ethical and legal nature of such an investment. The American Medical Association (AMA) in its Principles of Medical Ethics has permitted physician ownership of health facilities and should be applicable to ownership interests in the Central Valley Imaging Center. The AMA continues, however, that the physician has an affirmative ethical obligation to disclose ownership in a health facility to his patient prior to admission or utilization. In addition, the physician may not place his own financial interests above the welfare of his patient. Medicare/Medicaid regulations, as well as many state laws, address physicians' proprietary interest in organizations to which patient referrals are made. In California, where the partnership is located, ownership is not prohibited; however, patient disclosure is required where the physician has a financial interest over a threshold dollar amount.

TABLE 20–6

	1985	1986	1987	1988	1989
Cash distribution per unit (40)	$ 3,496	0	0	0	0
Cash distribution per unit (125)	0	$3,429	$3,803	$3,154	$3,493
Cash return on $8,400 unit	42%	41%	45%	38%	42%
Taxable income (loss) per unit	$(1,287)	$ 578	$2,498	$1,469	$1,821

CONCLUSION

Although the partners in both the Memorial project and the Saint Agnes project appear to be satisfied currently, the general partners do have concerns about future developments. For instance, medical imaging equipment regularly undergoes rapid technological advances and technical obsolescence is a real concern. The introduction of MRI is expected to render CT obsolete for many neurological procedures. In fact, Memorial and NDS are currently engaged in the syndication of a new MRI and special procedures partnership. The Saint Agnes project was structured originally to address the procedure trade-offs of CT and MRI. Government regulation, state and federal, related to reimbursement for services and related to issues of physician "self-referral" (referral to entities in which a physician has a proprietary interest) could affect the partnerships. Changes in the tax law affecting flow-throughs, particularly with regard to the investment tax credit, will affect the individual investor's interest in the joint venture concept. Competition who might offer a "fatter" return on a new joint venture investment could reduce referrals to an existing project.

Regarding hospital-physician joint ventures in general, it may be that they are just a short-lived trend. No one really knows how many joint ventures a community can absorb. The personal funds of physicians that are available to invest are finite. At some point a given medical community will have invested all of the available funds, leaving nothing for additional ventures. In addition, a certain number of existing ventures will fail. These business failures may have a chilling effect on the formation of new ventures.

However, the economic realities of today's healthcare environment require that the informal relationships of the past between hospitals and physicians must become more formalized. This formalization of relationships and commitments, regardless of its label, will continue. NDS, for one, is willing to chance that the hospital-physician joint venture in some form is not just a fad but is here to stay.

21

Health Maintenance Organizations

John K. Springer, M.H.A.

INTRODUCTION

Hartford Hospital was founded in 1854 by Hartford's leading citizens. Its growth and stability throughout difficult times has been due to the trust and support of a generous community, farsighted private practicing physicians, and a management philosophy that encouraged taking risks to solve problems. Hartford Hospital's distinctive characteristics have evolved in large part as a result of hospital-physician joint ventures long before that term was commonplace. The hospital and its medical staff grew rapidly, physicians with specialty and subspecialty training appeared in the 1930s, and graduate medical education began in the 1960s.

Hartford Hospital is now a 900-bed, general hospital with 550 attending physicians, 200 residents in 12 specialties, full-time chiefs of service in major departments with predominantly private practice medical staff, and a close affiliation with the University of Connecticut School of Medicine and Dentistry. Post–World War II hospital-physician joint ventures included establishing a director of medical education (the first in the nation) in 1946, a physicians' office building attached to the hospital constructed in 1950, and a major portion of the clinical teaching accomplished by volunteer clinical faculty at the undergraduate and graduate medical levels.

Hartford Hospital is one of the founding institutions of the Capital Area Health Consortium, a voluntary association of 14 hospitals in the health service area, most of which have affiliations with the University of Connecticut School of Medicine and Dentistry. Connecticut hospitals have been operating within a heavily regulated environment since 1973 when the legislature established the Commission on Hospitals and Health Care to regulate hospital revenues, expenses, and capital projects. In 1984 the hospital admitted 44,327 inpatients, including 6,481 ambulatory surgery, accumulated 160,277 patient visits in the emergency room and outpatient departments, and performed 35,350 operations, 18.3 percent of which were ambulatory surgery.

PHYSICIAN-HOSPITAL WORKSHOPS

In the fall of 1971, T. Stewart Hamilton, M.D., president and executive director of Hartford Hospital, planned a two-day workshop to be held in Williamstown, Massachusetts. Twenty members of the board of directors, medical staff, and management met to discuss and critique the hospital's corporate objectives, decision-making processes, resource allocation decisions, and a method for private practitioners to gain influence over important hospital decisions. One conclusion reached at the first workshop was that the hospital corporation would be strengthened if physicians were granted increased authority so that priority-setting, long-range planning, and major objectives could be developed jointly with the obvious advantage of improved implementation. It was also agreed that the medical staff and its clinical departmental components operated in a disorganized "town meeting" fashion, which left the board of directions strongly supporting joint decision making but concerned that collaborative decisions agreed to by the medical staff leadership would have doubtful support among their constituents.

The challenge motivated the leaders of the medical staff to restructure its bylaws to establish a representative form of governance that has served the medical staff, the hospital, and its patients well and provided an environment in which the concept of a hospital-based health maintenance organization could be nurtured despite the inevitable contrary opinions.

The workshop has been an annual occurrence in which 50 members of the hospital participate (including 160 private practitioners in 14 years). The formation of a staff model health maintenance organization three miles from Hartford Hospital was discussed at the 1978 workshop. Members of the board of directors felt that employers and union representatives would be interested in the concept and urged hospital management to become better acquainted with the HMO enterprise and to consider a corporate response to this competitive development. A consulting firm was contacted that had successfully advised employers and other clients about the HMO concept, and Hartford Hospital was advised to consider establishing an individual practice association/health maintenance organization.

The IPA/HMO concept made an ideal joint venture since it would require some hospital investment in accomplishing a research and development analysis to this variation of fee-for-service medicine. The HMO would be established to offer prepaid health benefits to employers at a guaranteed premium, while the medical services would be provided by physicians in private practice treating private patients as well as HMO patients in the same office setting. This project would have failed initially if it were not for about 15 physicians who became interested in the IPA/HMO concept as a method of preserving fee-for-service medical practice while participating in a market which was tiring of purchasing medical care by the "quart" and was shopping for quality medical care by the "carload."

Committees of physicians were established to review with the consultants physicians' fees, risk arrangements, and legal structures. The consultants were encouraged to learn that existing physicians' fees, hospital utilization and charges, as well as medical practices, conformed nicely to provide a high-quality HMO package at a competitive premium.

Meanwhile, abundant coverage of IPA/HMOs that had gone bankrupt appeared in medical literature and was liberally circulated by individual physicians who were opposing the HMO concept as low quality and socialistic. Hartford Hospital covered the cost of the consultants and the travel expenses of physicians willing to visit existing IPA/HMOs to learn from private practitioners first-hand the joys and sorrows of practicing in an IPA/HMO model. As anticipated, the majority of critics aimed their comments at hospital management, and the success of an IPA/HMO therefore rested on those physicians who were evaluating the concept. Fortunately, as the opposition of the critics intensified, the enthusiasm of the physicians analyzing the IPA/HMO concept increased significantly.

As the IPA/HMO concept was discussed broadly, primary care physicians were largely in support, while the surgical and medical subspecialists aligned themselves in opposition. This surfaced in the committee discussing physicians' fees when primary physicians pressed for additional equity in compensation for the cognitive versus procedural skills, as well as reaching a decision whether a primary care "gatekeeper" should be assigned to each patient whose referral to a subspecialist would be required in order for the subspecialist to be paid.

The group practice health maintenance organization team was increasing its enrollment, and our primary care physicians were the first to notice that patients had joined the competitive HMO by requesting that their records be transferred. The controversy grew with the opponents arguing, "Why should an MD accept 80 percent of the usual and customary fee with the 20 percent hold-back to be paid only if the plan succeeds?" The supporters recounted, "Isn't 80 percent of a fee better than no fee at all?"

Over the objections of the medical staff leadership the issue was forced to a vote by a majority at a meeting of the entire hospital medical staff, and when the ballots were counted, the supporters carried the vote by the margin of 208 to 206. This joint venture succeeded as a result of some very wise compromises which have served the IPA/HMO very well since it became operational on April 1, 1982.

GATEKEEPERS

It was decided that since the Hartford Hospital medical staff was highly specialized and utilization was under reasonable control, a primary care gatekeeper would not be required. Since this increased the risk that the annual allowance of inpatient days per 1,000 enrollees might exceed the 450 allowance and threatened the expenses of the plan, Hartford Hospital agreed to share in the risk by accepting a reduced payment for every hospital day in excess of 450 days per 1,000 enrollees.

FEES

There were only a few subspecialists who requested fees higher than the committee felt to be reasonable, and compromises were reached without major controversy.

STRUCTURE AND GOVERNANCE

By definition the board of the IPA would be comprised of physicians and dentists. There was some opportunity for flexibility in appointing the original board of directors of the HMO. Since the success of the HMO in the planning phase depended on the diligence of individual physicians, hospital management appointed one dentist and six physicians (one of whom was the president of the board of directors). The balance of the board was comprised of corporate leaders and two hospital representatives. The IPA/HMO was named "ConnectiCare," and the original consultant arranged for it to be managed by a firm skilled in management of IPA/HMOs. The management contractors agreed to absorb the initial start-up deficits in exchange for a five-year management contract.

The only capital requirements were $300,000 to bring ConnectiCare through the development phase to the point of becoming operational. The hospital paid the initial $300,000 with the understanding that $150,000 would be reimbursed by the physicians as they joined the IPA for $500 per physician.

The popularity and success of ConnectiCare augmented the hospital's strategic plan since it provided a means of keeping Hartford Hospital and its medical staff competitive and bringing additional patients to our combined organizations. Since ConnectiCare has succeeded, the HMO board has authorized the establishment of other IPAs in three other hospitals in the Hartford Hospital service area, using ConnectiCare as the HMO hub.

That ConnectiCare was the first IPA/HMO established in the region was advantageous since the group practice HMO established in 1978 was bought by Kaiser Permanente in 1981 and a second IPA/HMO has been established by the Hartford County Medical Association.

ConnectiCare has been a very successful joint venture because the IPA has paid the 20 percent fee hold-back to its members each year, its enrollment growth has increased from 600 at the end of 1982 to a projected 24,000 in 1985, the ConnectiCare benefit package is as comprehensive as the other two HMOs, and its premiums are slightly less than those of its competitors.

This was a complicated project but an excellent joint venture experience. Despite the early turbulence it has served to strengthen the bond between the hospital and its medical staff. As our consultants predicted, the amount of total premium paid to doctors is 60 percent rather than the customary insurance plans which direct an average 40 percent of the premium to physicians.

The Federal Office of Health Maintenance Organizations qualified ConnectiCare on November 1, 1982. The conservative nature of the physicians in private practice initially urged that ConnectiCare avoid accepting federal loans and avoid federal qualification by the Office of Health Maintenance Organizations. The management contract obviated the need for federal money, but employers insisted that ConnectiCare be certified by the Office of Health Maintenance Organizations as authentication that its structure and benefits met prescribed standards.

When ConnectiCare was incorporated, Connecticut statutes required that HMOs be nonstock and nonprofit. Statutes have since been updated and the ConnectiCare board must decide on its future ownership structure.

The original marketing projections for the first two years of operation were missed by about 40 percent, but the growth rate, with an improved marketing department, has met projections and kept the growth in ConnectiCare in good balance with the ability of management to service new enrollees and new employers. ConnectiCare has the lowest reported disenrollment rate on record, indicating very high customer satisfaction, and an operating gain of $700,000 was reported in the audited financial statements for 1984.

The Hartford Hospital IPA has members from all subspecialties, and about 75 percent of eligible physicians have joined. Some have joined more than one IPA, and young physicians just joining the medical staff have found HMOs to be a source of patient referrals. This experiment has been a success due to hard work on the part of private practicing physicians committed to investigating alternative delivery systems, to hospital management willing to take some risks, and to excellent consultative advice. The experience enhances the trust that must exist between a hospital and the medical staff if they are to compete successfully in the new environment which requires more accountability for cost and quality from both.

Hartford Hospital is a shareholder in Voluntary Hospitals of America, and the ConnectiCare experience should enhance our ability to provide comprehensive hospital and medical coverage within a managed premium concept. Next year, ConnectiCare will be a $25 million business and has the potential for becoming a statewide IPA/HMO. Some entrepreneurs have sought to purchase ConnectiCare, but its continuation as a viable example of a successful joint venture is far more important to the future of Hartford Hospital than the cash that could be realized from its sale.

CONCLUSION

Joint ventures offer an opportunity for a hospital to risk some capital and share the rewards and penalties of business ventures. Hospital managers must become increasingly concerned about operational opportunities to increase the gross revenue of physicians and to decrease their expenses of practice. ConnectiCare has been an example of a joint business venture that satisfies employers' demands for lower, predictable health insurance premiums, added some patients to Hartford Hospital's inpatient flow, and improved the competitive position of physicians in private practice. Patients appear to prefer ConnectiCare because they maintain their private physician and have no forms to complete. Hartford Hospital physicians continue to have a major influence over the direction and business policies of ConnectiCare and have impressed the corporate leaders on the ConnectiCare board by their willingness to concentrate on very high-quality medical benefits for patients within the limits of an HMO insurance premium.

VII

COMMENTARY AND CONCLUSIONS

22

A Look at the Future of Joint Ventures

Douglas M. Mancino, J.D.
Linda A. Burns, M.H.A.

This book has reviewed the state of current thinking concerning the reasons for, the available structures for, and the process of developing and operating hospital-physician joint ventures. In addition, case studies have illustrated in practical terms many of the problems and opportunities available through the development of joint ventures, programmatically as well as financially. They have also served as usable tools for identifying a number of the human issues that need to be dealt with in terms of sharing of control, marketing to medical professionals, and operating small businesses associated with large bureaucratic organizations.

The first question that must be addressed is whether joint ventures are merely a fad or are the manifestation of an evolutionary change in the delivery and payment for healthcare services. We believe that the latter is the case and that physicians and hospitals will continue to become more economically inter-dependent and develop more methods by which they can combine their skills and resources to deliver health and medical services. Whether or not the developing relationships between hospitals and physicians are denominated as joint ventures is not important; what is important is that the interests of hospitals and physicians will be served more effectively if both parties become more economically interdependent, recognize the need for greater sharing of control and management responsibility for new business ventures, and continue to develop means whereby both can participate in the risks and rewards of successful or unsuccessful business ventures in healthcare.

One of the keys to the success of joint ventures, in addition to the mutual commitments of time, capital, and professional expertise, will be a recognition of the need for different types of managerial talent, including managers who can be affiliated with the traditional bureaucratic hospital environment and, at the same time, can accomplish entrepreneurial projects while making maximum use of the resources of the hospital.

In addition, managers at all levels of the organization, as well as boards of directors, must become more knowledgeable about joint venture investment opportunities and develop additional skills in order to evaluate and manage joint ventures. Every level of an existing hospital organization, as well as the physicians and the managers of the new venture, are likely to require skills different from those they typically are utilizing today. In order to cope successfully with screening, developing, and implementing joint venture opportunities, hospital managers, physicians, and managers of new ventures are likely to become purposive business opportunists.

There are many factors that will be determinative of the success or failure of joint ventures. Many of these factors will involve the type of planning that has been undertaken, the type of legal structure that is utilized, and the type of financial resources that are committed to the joint venture. However, we believe that one of the most important factors will be the actual ability of the joint venture, once it has been established, to develop and package its products and services effectively to meet its competition and maintain or increase its market share and profitability. This important task falls to the manager of the joint venture.

We also believe that there will be failures of joint ventures that must be acknowledged and dealt with. These failures may result from the wrong business concept, inadequate structure, an under-capitalized business, inadequate execution and management of the business, and other reasons. Probably, many of these joint venture failures will receive widespread attention, and pressure will be placed on others to learn from these early failures. With the increased level of competition and the growing number of joint ventures, hospitals and physicians are going to be less likely to share the details of their business plans and activities, and it will thus become more difficult to ascertain with certainty the reasons for failures of joint ventures. This raises the possibility that some people will denigrate the concept of joint ventures as a strategy as opposed to focusing on the specific reasons for the business failure. This emphasizes the fact that joint ventures are not going to be a strategy for every institution or for every physician or group of physicians. It also underscores the importance of using the joint venture approach toward business development as a specific tool to deal with the specific needs of a hospital and physicians in their particular marketplace. A joint venture should be analogized to the use of laser surgery, which is designed to target a very precise area and to accomplish a specific objective. While the technology is inherently powerful, the technology must be used effectively and mistakes must be avoided.

From the perspectives of the boards of directors of hospitals and physician groups undertaking joint ventures, we believe that new roles and responsibilities will evolve over the next decade. From a management and governance standpoint, hospital boards of directors will need to develop the kind of corporate culture that encourages risk-taking, rewards successes, and does not unfairly penalize failures. Moreover, hospital boards of directors will have to deal with the increased scrutiny that will be placed over their activities by shareholders and other investors in businesses, which is likely to create a new level of accountability.

The trend toward the use of joint ventures will result in a continued differentiation of hospitals by their clinical product lines and services, the legal and financial structures utilized to deliver those services, and the nature of their returns on their investments in such services. In the near future, we believe that joint ventures will maintain a distinctly local focus, being developed and operated to meet the particular needs of hospitals and physicians in their market area. However, as diversification within the healthcare field continues, it is quite possible that regional or national networks of joint ventures will develop and that companies will be established to consolidate these resources and to expand participation in these joint ventures beyond hospitals and physicians. It is not inconceivable that major employers, major suppliers, and the public at large will begin to develop interest in many hospital-physician joint ventures and that reasons for the involvement of such persons may become more apparent in the years to come.

We also anticipate that with the growth of the number of joint ventures there also will be increased competition for the managers who can successfully operate them. This human resource need will encompass physician medical directors as well as managers and is likely to stimulate growing creativity in the development of compensation, equity participation, and other short- and long-term compensation incentives to enable a joint venture to retain such persons and to provide the appropriate incentives for them to manage the joint ventures effectively and successfully.

We also anticipate that there will be well-publicized abuses that will further stimulate public policy debate over the efficacy and ethics of hospital-physician joint ventures. If joint ventures as a strategy are to emerge from this debate without severe constrictions, it will be incumbent upon all constituencies to be adequately represented and to present their views in an objective and effective manner to the policymakers. To date, there is a dearth of thoughtful commentary in the professional, medical, and hospital journals dealing with these difficult questions. We believe that much debate and discussion needs to take place before an accurate consensus can be developed that adequately resolves the conflicts between professional and business ethics raised by joint ventures.

Hospitals will have to confront the issue of control over joint ventures themselves as well as the implications that the sharing of control will have for other hospital activities. In addition, physicians, many of whom have functioned as sole practitioners or in small medical groups, will have to overcome the problems inherent in dealing within a larger organization in which their influence and control will be diluted. Nevertheless, we believe that hospitals and physicians will benefit from this sharing of control and that joint ventures will serve as a medium through which more effective healthcare decisionmaking can be channeled.

In our collective experiences, another need that has become apparent is for the medical education process to deal with and to recognize the need for training and exposure of medical students to practice management issues, including joint ventures. Given the growing competition in medicine in general and between and among specialties, it will be increasingly important for physicians to have a greater level of understanding of the economic, financial, and legal issues pertaining to joint ventures. Moreover, continuing medical education programs will need to update their curriculums to include programs and courses on joint ventures to deal with these issues for practitioners.

In conclusion, we believe that joint ventures between hospitals and physicians are not merely a passing fancy, but are a viable strategic option for dealing with professional, economic, and community responsibilities. We intend to continue documenting, reporting, and analyzing opinion and experience in joint ventures over the coming years.

Index

Abbott Laboratories, Inc. v. Portland Retail
Druggists Association, 153
Academic values, check on profit-seeking
motives, 54
Accelerated cost recovery system: *see also* Tax
issues
definition, 110
mentioned, 109
Access
CON requirements, 70
medically indigent, 54
Accreditation Association for Ambulatory
Health Care, 88
Adams, Cary M., 9
Alternative Depreciation System
definition, 114
inurement, 121–22
joint ventures and tax-exempt status, 120–
21
private benefit, 122–23
service contract rules, 117–18
special rules applicable to partnerships and
for-profit subsidiaries, 119–20
tax-exempt entity defined, 114–15
tax-exempt use property, 115
real property, 116–17
tangible property other than nonresidential
real property, 115–16
treatment of tax-exempt use of real property,
117
use of corporate subsidiaries, 123
Ambulatory care, shift from inpatient care, 12
Ambulatory surgery, 9, 45
case of a joint venture, 233–41
franchising, 67

Ambulatory surgery—*Cont.*
licensing, 83
Medicare, 83–84
operating margin, 26
start-up costs, 25
trustee's perspective on joint venture, 226–
28
volume of surgical procedures, 11
American College of Physicians, 53
American Medical Association, 9
Judicial Council, 54, 79
political influence, 52
Antitrust issues, 143–55
antitrust issues affecting joint venture
operations, 147–54
collateral restraints, 152
nonprice predation, 151–52
per se violations, 147–48
horizontal and vertical agreements
relating to price, 148–49
horizontal market allocations, 149
group boycotts and concerted refusals
to deal, 149–50
tying arrangements, 150–51
price discrimination laws, 153–54
vertical market allocations, 152
spillover collision, 152–53
overview of federal antitrust laws, 143–46
Federal Trade Commission Act Section 5,
145
penalties, 145–46
Robinson-Patman Act, 145
Antitrust issues—*Cont.*
Sherman Act Section 1, 144
Sherman Act Section 2, 145

Antitrust issues—*Cont.*
    Sherman Act Section 7, 145
    potential challenges to joint venture
        information, 146–47
    state antitrust laws, 154
Arizona v. Maricopa County Medical Society,
    148–49
Aston, Arthur D., 224

Barkley, Ronald, 243
Baylor Physician Associates, P.A., 215
Baylor University Medical Center, 213
Blue Cross and Blue Shield, payment for
    ambulatory surgery, 84
Board: *see* Trustee's Perspective
Bureau of Health Professions, 9
Burns, Linda A., 1, 7, 15, 21, 29, 263
Business plan
    CEO's perspective, 222
    components, 38
    pertaining to financing joint venture, 183
    step in joint venture development, 34, 38

Capital
    sources and ethical issues, 50
    see also Financing joint ventures
Case studies of joint ventures
    ambulatory surgery, 233–41
    diagnostic imaging centers, 243–53
    health maintenance organizations, 254–59
Certificate of need, legal issues related to joint
    ventures, 70–71
Chief executive officer's perspective, 220–23
    consistency with strategic plan, 221
    establishing a track record, 222–23
    importance of a business plan, 222
    long-term issues, 223
    structuring the venture, 222–23
Clayton Act, 145; *see also* Antitrust issues
Close corporation; *see* Corporation
Competition
    restrictions, 95–96
        noncompetition agreements, 96
        nonsolicitation and nonservicing
            agreements, 96
        use of confidential information, 96
Conflict of interest
    American Medical Association report, 79
    disclosure, 53–54

Consumer, input as it relates to ethics, 54; *see
    also* Marketing
Convenience clinics, 19
Corporate culture; *see* Operational problems
Corporate practice of medicine
    division of fees, 87
    history, 86
    legal issues defined, 85–87
Corporation
    S corporations
        tax advantages of regular corporation v. S
            corporation, 108–9
        tax advantages of S corporation v. part-
            nership, 109
        tax planning issues, 105–6
    selection of a legal structure, 63–64
    tax planning issues, 104–5
CT scanner; *see also* Diagnostic imaging
    mentioned, 152
    start-up costs, 25

Diagnostic imaging
    case study, 243–53
    costs, 16
    freestanding centers, 11
    magnetic resonance imaging, 16
    mentioned, 9, 25
DiGiacoma, Enzo, 190
Dissolution of a joint venture, methods, 93
Diversification, opportunities identified, 23
Durable medical equipment
    fraud and abuse Medicare provisions, 134–
        35
    price discrimination laws, 153

Ecclesiastes, 55
Economic incentives; *see* Incentives
Education; *see* Academic values
Emergency care center, start-up costs, 25
Ethical issues, 43–56
    access to health services by poor, 50–51
    American Medical Association, 79–80
    conflicts of interest, 53–54
    delineation of issues, 43–44
    kickbacks, 53
    lying to patients, 48, 52
    moral codes of physicians compared with
        other professionals, 46–47
    outside review, 54
    quality of care, 51

Ethical issues—*Cont.*
  research issues, 51
  teaching issues, 51, 54

Federal Trade Commission
  franchise regulation, 68
  mentioned, 59
Federal Trade Commission Act, antitrust
  issues, 145
Fee-for-service
  ethical considerations, 45
  mentioned, 53
Financing joint ventures, 170–83
  development of a business plan, 183
  financial planning process, 170–72
  future of hospital-physician joint venture
    financing, 183
  screening financial alternatives, 172–74
    amount of capital, 173
    control, 173
    evaluation of process, 174
    size of investment, 173
    term of financing, 173
    timing and costs, 174
  selection process, 182–83
  surveying alternative sources of funds, 174
    bond financing, 178–79
    convertible debt, 179
    debt financing, 174–76
    equity financings, 180
    future of tax exempt debt, 177
    industrial revenue bonds, 177
    leasing financing, 178
    pooled equipment financings, 177
    preferred stock, 182
    public offerings, 180–81
    self-financing and limited partnerships,
      182
    taxable debt, 178
    venture capital, 182
    venture capital companies, 182
Fost, Norman, 43
Franchising, 17
  definition, 67–69
  Federal Trade Commission regulations, 68–
    69
  state regulation, 69–70
    business opportunities, 70
      disclosure, 70
      registration, 70
      unfair practices, 70
Fraud and abuse, 129–41

Fraud and abuse—*Cont.*
  Medicare and Medicaid, 130–37
  State anti-kickback and related laws, 137–
    39
Freestanding centers, imaging centers, 11

General partnerships; *see* Partnerships
Graduate Medical Education National Advisory
  Committee, 9
Gregory, Douglas D., 161

Hartford Hospital, 254
Hawthorne, Douglas D., 220
Health Care Financing Administration, 71, 134
Health maintenance organizations, 13, 82
  beneficial effects, 49
  case study, 254–59
  contracts as related to selection of legal en-
    tity of venture, 66
  ethical issues, 44
  growth, 10
  relationship to mental health benefits, 52
Heraclitus, 43
Hill-Burton, 66
Home health agencies
  franchising, 67
  licensing, 83
  start-up costs, 25
Hospital-physician relationships, 13
  economic interdependence, 13
Howey test, 73
Humana Inc., 50
Hyde v. Jefferson Parish Hospital District No.
  2, 151

IHC Professional Services, Inc., 234
Implementation issues; *see* Operational
  problems *and* Physicians
Incentives, 12
  affecting utilization, 18
  as they affect physician-patient relationship,
    52–53
  contrast between not-for-profit and for-profit
    hospitals, 45–46
  existing service vs. new service, 27
  fee-for-service, 53
  related to prospective payment system, 49
  structure of rewards to physicians, 47
Income tax; *see* Unrelated business

Initial public offerings, 180
Institute of Medicine, 53
Intermountain Health Care, Inc., 234
Internal Revenue Service, 29
Inurement, 121–22

Joint Commission on Accreditation of
  Hospitals, 88
Joint venture
  capital intensity, 25
    start-up costs, 25
  consistency with strategic plan, 34–35
  defined, 1–2
  degree of control, 24–25
  determination of organizational and
    ownership structure, 33, 36–37
  determine financial projections, 33, 37
  development of business plan, 34, 38
  development process, 29–40
    organizing for development, 29–32
  evaluation, 34, 39
  existing service vs. new service, 27
  financings, 170–83; see also Financing joint
    ventures
    financial planning process, 170–72
    future of hospital-physician joint venture
      financing, 183
    screening financial alternatives, 172–74
    selection process, 182–83
    surveying alternative sources of funds,
      174–82
  fraud and abuse; see Medicaid and Medicare
  future issues, 263–66
  health-related vs. nonhealth-related ventures,
    24
  identifying and classifying, 21–28
  implementation, 34, 39; see also Case
    studies and Operational problems
  joint ventures in other industries, 206–7
  listing of joint ventures, 22
  management issues; see Operational
    problems
  motivations for developing, 15–20
    acquisition of expertise, 17
    expediency, 19
    increase utilization and referrals, 18
    increasing market share, 19
    retain market share, 18–19
    sources of capital, 15
  opportunities for joint venture, 23
  participation, 26–27
  preparation of space program, staffing, and
    equipment requirements, 36

Joint venture—*Cont.*
  prepare legal documents, 38–39
  presentation to physicians, 34, 39
  screening new ventures, 32–33
    committee role, 32–33
    risk as a criterion, 32
  screening variables, 24
  step-by-step process, 33–34
    determining scope of services, 34–36

Kickback, 53–54
  state anti-kickback and related laws, 137–39
    conflicts between state and federal laws,
      138–39
    diversity of state law provisions, 137–38

Laboratory, 19
  licensing, 83
  start-up costs, 25
Legal issues, 59–97
  formation stage of venture
    authority to enter into joint venture, 62–
      63
    contractual issues affecting hospitals, 65–
      66
      financial covenants, 65
      physician contracts, 66
    contractual issues affecting physicians
      control and related issues, 66–67
      franchising, 67–68
    selection of legal structure, 63–64
      contracts and leases, 63
      partnerships and corporations, 63–64
  need for written agreements, 60
    composition of written agreements, 60–62
      books and records, 61–62
      business definition, 60
      capital requirements, 60–61
      distributions, 61
      management, 61
      profits and losses, 61
      termination of venture, 62
      withdrawals and transfers, 62
  operational phase of a joint venture, 82–97
    accreditation, 88–89
    buy-sell agreements, 93–94
      estate planning restrictions, 94–95
      other options, 95
      restrictions on encumbering joint
        ventures, 94
      restrictions on transfers, 94
      restrictions tied to medical practice, 94
      valuation, 95

Legal issues—*Cont.*
　corporate practice of medicine, 85–87
　dissolution stage, 92–93
　licensure requirement, 82–83
　ownership limitations and disclosure
　　requirements, 90–91
　payment for services, 83
　professional and other liability concerns,
　　89–90
　quality assurance and peer review, 84–85
　restrictions on competition, 95–96
　　noncompetition agreements, 96
　　nonsolicitation and nonservicing
　　　agreements, 96
　　use of confidential information, 96
Lehman, E. P., 44
Liability
　issues pertaining to corporations, 64
　issues pertaining to partnership, 63
Limited partnerships; *see* Partnerships

McCullough, Michael, 213
Magnetic resonance imaging, physician
　contract, 66; *see also* Diagnostic imaging
Malpractice, 51
Management
　expertise, 17
　issues addressed in written contracts, 61
　issues pertaining to general partnerships, 63
　joint venture development team, 39–40
　　members and roles, 40
　role of venture manager, 31–32
　venture screening committee role, 32
　　composition, 32
　vice president of business development, 32,
　　40
Management expertise: *see* Joint ventures and
　Operational problems
Mancino, Douglas M., 1, 7, 15, 59, 102, 143,
　184, 263
Market; *see* Market analysis, Market
　assessment, and Marketing
Market analysis, 162–69
　defining the business concept
　　focus group results, 166–67
　　internal economics, 165–66
　　market attractiveness, 164–65
　　segment/size of market, 162–64
Market assessment, sequence in joint venture
　development, 36
Marketing; *see also* Market analysis
　advertising, 45, 47
　consumer orientation, 49–50
Med Southwest, Inc., 217

Medicaid
　as a public subsidy to poor, 48
　fraud and abuse, 130–31
　　basic provisions, 130–31
　　exceptions for discounts and employees,
　　　131–32
　　interpreting the statutes, 132
　　related to joint ventures, 132–37
　payment policies for ambulatory surgery, 84
Medical office building
　cost recovery periods for tax planning, 110
　start-up costs, 25
　trustee's perspective on joint venture, 225–
　　26
Medical staff, trustee's perspective, 228–29;
　see also Physician
Medicare, 59
　ambulatory surgery, 83–84
　ambulatory surgery payment policies, 233
　cost reimbursement, 8
　diagnosis-related groups, 45
　　beneficial effects, 49
　fraud and abuse, 130–37
　　basic provisions, 130–31
　　exceptions for discounts and employees,
　　　131–32
　　interpreting the statutes, 132
　　related to joint ventures, 132–37
　incentives, 11
　public subsidies, 48
Meller, Gary, 196
Memorial Hospitals Association, 245
MeSH, 74

National Association for Ambulatory Care, 89
National Diagnostic Services, Inc., 244
Noerr Pennington doctrine, 151
Nonprofit Institutions Act, 153
Northwest Wholesalers v. Pacific Stationary
　and Printing Co., 150

Operational problems, 196–208
　issues of control
　　confusion in goals, 199–200
　　ownership versus control, 199
　　unempowered managers, 200
　issues of ownership, 196–99
　　influence and votes, 197–98
　　jealousy and interference, 198–99
　　reporting requirements, 197
　　reward and responsibility, 198
　　unresolved conflict from negotiations, 199

Operational problems—*Cont.*
  issues related to allocation of resources,
    201–2
    make versus buy decisions, 201–2
    understaffing, 201
  issues related to corporate culture, 204–6
  issues of timing, 202–4
Organizational structure
  compatibility with joint venture, 29
  functional organization structure, 30
  importance of autonomy for venture
    manager, 31
  matrix structure, 31
Outpatient, 23; *see also* Ambulatory care

Partnerships
  Alternative Depreciation System special
    rules applicable to partnerships, 119–20
    property leased to partnerships, 120
    property owned by partnerships, 119–20
  general
    application of securities laws, 75
    mentioned, 16, 60, 63
  limited, 16, 60, 64, 182
    application of securities laws, 75
  selection of a legal structure, 63–64
  tax planning issues, 103–4
  unrelated business income tax, 125–26
Physician's perspectives, 213–19
  credentialing, 215–16
  implementation issues, 217
  utilization review, 215–16
Physician supply
  implications, 13
  number of physicians, 9
Physicians
  consumer wants and needs, 50–51
  medical student borrowing, 10
  physician-patient relationship, 52
  practice patterns and ethical issues, 44–45
  practice location, 48
Preferred provider organization, 12–13, 82
  applicability of securities regulations, 73–74
Product lines, reconfiguring existing health
  services, 32
Profit-sharing; *see* Kickback
Prospective payment system; *see* Medicare
Public hospitals
  legal issues, 80–82
    geographical restrictions, 81–82
    gift of public funds, 80–81
    open meeting laws, 81
    procurement procedures, 82

Public hospitals—*Cont.*
    public records law, 81
    sovereign immunity, 80
    stock ownership prohibition, 81

Quality of care, as affected by business orientation, 51; *See also* Ethical issues

Regulatory issues, 59–97
Relman, A., 46, 52
Return on investment, screening variable, 26
Risk; *see also* Return on investment
  inclusion in business plan, 38
  purpose, 38
  risk as screening criterion, 32
Robinson-Patman Act, 145; *see also* Antitrust
  issues
Roosevelt, Theodore, 219
Roseland Surgical Center, 235

S corporation; *see* Corporation
Saint Agnes Hospital and Medical Center, 249
Screening committee for joint ventures
  composition, 32
  role, 32–33
Securities
  broker-dealer regulation, 78–79
  federal registration and exemptions, 75–76
  fraud and other liabilities, 78
  regulation, 71–78
    security defined, 72
    stock, 73
  state regulation of securities, 77–78
Securities and Exchange Commission, 38
  memberships and securities regulations, 74–
    75
registration and exemption of securities, 75–77
Securities registration, steps in joint venture
  implementation, 38
Shaw, G. B., 43
Sherman Act, 144–45; *see also* Antitrust
  issues
Skilled nursing facility, 27
Southwest Health Plan, Inc., 217
Southwest Preferred Health Network, Inc., 217
Springer, John K., 254

Talmud, 43
Tax issues, 102–26

Tax issues—*Cont.*
  choice of business entity, 103–9
    contractual model, 103
    corporations, 104–7
      S corporations, 105–6
    partnerships, 103–4; *see also* Partnership
  comparison of tax advantage, 107–9
    corporation versus partnership, 107–8
    regular corporation versus S corporation, 108–9
    S corporation versus partnership, 109
  maximization of tax benefits, 102–3
  operational tax considerations, 109–12
    "at risk" limitations, 111–12
    cost recovery deductions, 110–11
  pertaining to corporations, 64
  pertaining to partnerships, 63
Tax Reform Act of 1986, 102, 111
  description of provisions, 112–14
    formulation on use of cash method of accounting, 113–14
    passive investment loss limitation, 113
    taxable year, 114
Taxable year, 114
Taxes, relationship to services for poor, 50
Thompson, Wesley B., 233
Trustee's perspective, 24–30
  alternative delivery systems, 228
  ambulatory surgery center venture, 226–27

Trustee's perspective—*Cont.*
  changing medical staff-hospital relations, 228–29
  medical office building venture, 225–26

United Housing Foundation v. Forman, 72
United States v. Greber, 135–36
Unrelated business, 124–26
  contract joint ventures, 124–25
  corporate joint ventures, 127
  partnerships, 125–26
Urgent care center
  case example of market analysis, 164–69
  franchising, 67
  joint venture economics, 167–69
  operating margin, 26
  participants in venture, 27
U.S. Department of Health and Human Services, 9
Utilization projections; *see* Market assessment

Valley Presbyterian Hospital, 224
Veatch, Robert, 46, 48
Venture capital, 184–89
  advantages, 184–86
  disadvantages, 186–87
  organization and management, 187
  participant in joint venture, 27
  source of financing, 182–83